Promotional market
A practical guide

CW00481192

To Gaenor,
for her enormous support, as always,
on this and in everything else.

Promotional marketing law:
A practical guide

Philip Circus MA, MPhil, DCA, FIPM, Barrister

Director of Legal Affairs, Institute of Promotional Marketing

Partner, Lawmark

Bloomsbury Professional

Bloomsbury Publishing Limited, Maxwelton House, 41–43 Boltro Road, Haywards Heath, West Sussex, RH16 1BJ

© Bloomsbury Professional Ltd 2011

Crown copyright material is reproduced with the permission of the Controller of HMSO and the Queen's Printer for Scotland. Any European material in this work which has been reproduced from EUR-lex, the official European Communities legislation website, is European Communities copyright.

A CIP Catalogue record for this book is available from the British Library.

ISBN 978 1 84766 739 7

Typeset by Phoenix Photosetting, Chatham, Kent
Printed in Great Britain by Martins the Printers, Berwick-upon-Tweed, Northumberland

PREFACE

Since the last edition much has changed, including the title.

Promotional Marketing Law is a title which it was widely felt reflected the industry for which this book is relevant—a change which mirrors the change in name of the ISP to the Institute of Promotional Marketing.

Sometimes a change of name or title is more image than substance. That is not the case here. Many important developments are covered in this edition in respect of both the law and self-regulation.

On the legal front, we have the important Consumer Protection from Unfair Trading Regulations 2008, which implement the EU Unfair Commercial Practices Directive. Much previous law has been repealed and a new principles-based approach to consumer protection introduced.

Other new legislation is covered, including new regulations on consumer credit advertising and a new Bribery Act, which updates all the previous law on bribery and corruption.

On the wider European front, three important decisions from the European Court of Justice promise to change the whole European landscape for promotional marketing.

Finally, we have important developments on the self-regulatory front. A new Code of Advertising, Sales Promotion and Direct Marketing took effect on 1 September 2010 and 1 March 2011 saw a major extension of self-regulation into online advertising and marketing.

As always, I am grateful to those who have helped me to produce this new edition. There is no precedent for a sixth edition of a book on marketing law, as far as I am aware. The success of this publication owes much to the continued support of the Institute of Promotional Marketing, in particular, for which I am grateful.

Thanks also must go to the Committee of Advertising Practice for their kind permission to re-produce the latest edition of the CAP Code.

To my wife, Gaenor, goes my gratitude for coping with the preparation of the manuscript and interpreting a lot of unintelligible scribble. And my thanks go to anyone else, unnamed but not unappreciated, who have helped in the creation of this new edition.

Philip Circus
West Chiltington, West Sussex
March 2011

ABOUT THE AUTHOR

Philip Circus has been closely associated with the legal side of advertising and marketing for over 30 years—an involvement that has combined legal work in a number of major marketing trade associations with consultancy work for individual clients.

Educated at the Universities of London and Southampton and the College of Law, Philip Circus was called to the Bar by the Inner Temple in 1975. He has two Masters degrees, one in law and one in history, as well as the Diploma in Consumer Affairs of the Institute of Trading Standards—for which he won the Joe Routledge prize—and a Diploma in European Community Law from King's College, London. He also holds the Diploma of the Institute of Promotional Marketing and was made a Fellow of the Institute in 2001 for 'outstanding services to the promotional marketing industry'. He is also a Fellow of the British Promotional Merchandise Association and was awarded their Sword of Honour for services to the industry.

Philip Circus has held numerous positions relating to advertising and marketing, including Chairman of the CBI's Consumer Affairs Committee and membership of the Government's Working Parties on prices, credit and environmental labelling. He has been a member of the National Consumer Council, a Board member of the Mail Order Protection Scheme, a member of the ITC's Advertising Advisory Committee and a member of the Committee of Advertising Practice (CAP) since 1977—being Chairman of its Sales Promotion and Direct Response Panel.

He jointly founded the Advertising Law Group, which is the group of specialist legal practitioners in advertising and marketing law.

CONTENTS

CHAPTER 1

INTRODUCTION TO THE LEGAL AND SELF-REGULATORY CONTROLS ON PROMOTIONAL MARKETING

Legal controls

Question: What do we mean by 'promotional marketing'?

Answer: Definitions of the various marketing disciplines are many. Certainly, to the author's knowledge the term 'promotional marketing' is not defined in law, although there are definitions of 'advertisement'—definitions that sometimes include promotional marketing. The Institute of Promotional Marketing (IPM) defines promotional marketing in the following terms:

> 'Any marketing initiative, the purpose of which is to create a call to action that has a direct and positive impact on the behaviour of a targeted audience by offering a demonstrable, though not necessarily tangible, benefit.'

Question: What do we mean by 'promotional marketing law'?

Answer: People talk about promotional marketing law as if it is a dedicated body of law in its own right. However, this is not so. It is doubtful whether the Parliamentary Counsel, the drafters of legislation, have even heard of the term 'promotional marketing', let alone understand what it is and how it operates. Accordingly, when we talk of 'promotional marketing law' what we mean is that collection of laws which has an incidental effect on promotional marketing . Only the Trading Stamps Act 1964 was designed specifically to control a promotional marketing technique and that legislation was repealed some time ago.

Question: When we talk about 'law', what do we mean?

Answer: The law can be sub-divided into a number of categories, and these we consider in subsequent questions. One significant characteristic of the law is its comprehensiveness of application—unlike self-regulation, for example, which would normally only apply to members of an association. The main distinction within the law is between civil law and criminal law.

Civil law

Question: What is civil law?

Answer: Civil law is designed to assist individuals in enforcing what are essentially individual rights, for example, trespass, defamation and breach of contract. The point is that society as a whole is not involved, since the object of civil law is compensation for individual wrong rather than punishment.

Question: What courts are relevant to civil law matters?

Answer: Minor matters are dealt with by the county courts, and within the county courts there is provision for what are termed 'small claims'—invariably those consumer complaints, which although they raise important issues, nevertheless relate to relatively small sums of money. Cases can go to arbitration within the county court system and this does much to overcome some of the fear that people have of litigation.

More serious matters are dealt with at the High Court. Avenues of appeal lie to the Court of Appeal (Civil Division) and the Supreme Court.

Criminal law

Question: What, then, is the purpose of the criminal law?

Answer: Criminal law deals with those wrongs that are considered to be more than just a question of individual rights. Accordingly, the State in its various guises is the initiator of the action and the objective is not compensation, but rather punishment and the suppression of crime. Having said that, the criminal courts can make use of the Powers of Criminal Courts (Sentencing) Act 2000 to award compensation to those who have suffered loss as a result of crime.

Question: Who enforces the criminal law that is relevant to promotional marketing?

Answer: Most consumer protection law is enforced by trading standards officers who are local government employees. Trading standards departments enforce areas like consumer credit and the law on unfair trading practices. An element of co-ordination of policy amongst the many trading standards departments is achieved through a body called Local Government Regulation. The Gambling Commission is responsible for enforcing the law relating to lotteries and competitions, and the Police are responsible for enforcing the law relating to bribery.

Question: What courts are relevant to the enforcement of the criminal law?

Answer: Most criminal cases are dealt with in the magistrates' courts. Some are tried there because they are called 'summary offences', which can only be dealt with by magistrates. Many defendants choose to have their cases dealt with in a magistrates' court because they often have a choice of trial by magistrates or trial by jury at the Crown Court. Rarely do defendants choose the latter because of the time, expense and potentially longer sentences that can be handed down. Appeal from a decision of the magistrates can go either to the Crown Court or, on a point of law, to the Divisional Court. Further appeals are possible to the Court of Appeal (Criminal Division) and the Supreme Court.

Question: People sometimes talk about 'case law' and sometimes about 'statute law'. What's the difference?

Answer: Unlike many continental countries, the basis of English law has been the decisions of the judges over the centuries in making precedents which are then followed in later cases. These case decisions may involve the development of the common law (ie that part of the law which is based originally on the common unwritten customs of the country). Large parts of the law, both criminal and civil, are rooted in the common law. For example, although the law establishes the penalties for murder, the definition of murder is laid down by the common law and not by an Act of Parliament.

Case law may also throw light on the interpretation of statutes. By statute law, we mean the law that has emanated from Parliament through either Acts of Parliament or statutory instruments (SIs), which are made by ministers under the authority given to them by Acts of Parliament. Statute law is increasingly important, particularly because the doctrine of judicial precedent means that decisions of judges are binding unless overruled by a higher court. As society has developed and as changes have taken place, Parliament has been seen as a far quicker way of changing the law than leaving changes to the judges. However, that does not mean that individual case decisions are not important. As we look at particular areas of promotional marketing law we shall note some highly crucial court decisions.

Codes of practice

Question: What are codes of practice?

Answer: Codes of practice are very popular these days and there are a vast number of them. They vary enormously in their status, scope and effectiveness. Broadly speaking, we can divide codes of practice into two categories: statutory codes and self-regulatory codes.

Question: What are statutory codes?

Answer: There are many different types of statutory codes, but what they all have in common is that their creation has invariably been sanctioned by an Act of Parliament. Frequently, compliance with the code will be taken into consideration in deciding whether the Act's requirements have been met. The best example is the Highway Code. Although compliance with this Code is not a legal requirement, it will be taken into account in deciding whether an offence has been committed. For example, the Highway Code says that one should look in the mirror before pulling away from the kerb. Failure to do so is not a criminal offence, but if one has an accident as a result of not looking in the mirror, which results in a prosecution for careless driving, then failure to follow the Code will be taken into consideration in deciding whether an offence has taken place.

Self-regulation

Question: What are self-regulatory codes?

Answer: These are non-governmental codes, usually issued by a trade association in order to establish and maintain certain standards for members to follow. The Office of Fair Trading (OFT) has always had an obligation to encourage the creation and dissemination of Codes of Practice. The OFT runs a 'Consumer Codes Approval Scheme' under which code sponsors make a promise that their code meets the core criteria of helping consumers identify better businesses and encouraging businesses within the trade to raise their standards of customer service. At the time of writing, ten industry Codes of Practice have received approval under this scheme.

Question: Where does the Advertising Standards Authority (ASA) fit into all this?

Answer: The ASA was founded in 1962 as a separate body with an independent chairman and a majority of members independent of the business, to adjudicate on complaints within the British self-regulatory system of advertising control. The system covers both broadcast and non-broadcast advertising as well as sales promotion and direct marketing. For non-broadcast advertisements, the ASA deals with complaints concerning alleged breaches of the British Code of Advertising, Sales Promotion and Direct Marketing. The ASA is funded by an automatic 0.1% levy on all display advertising, which is collected by the Advertising Standards Board of Finance (ASBOF). The broadcast side of the ASA's work is funded by a separate levy on advertisers of 0.1% of the cost of airtime; this is collected by a separate body known as the Broadcast Advertising Standards Board of Finance (BASBOF). A special mailing standards levy is also collected by ASBOF to fund the ASA's work on list and database management.

Question: What, then, is the Committee of Advertising Practice (CAP) in relation to non-broadcast advertising?

Answer: 'CAP' is the colloquial way of referring to the Committee of Advertising Practice, which is the industry element in the system of advertising control. Made up of representatives of the various trade associations that support the self-regulatory system, its chief responsibilities are the preparation and review of the Code of Practice, and representing the views of the industry.

Question: What is the Code that CAP is responsible for drafting and keeping under review?

Answer: The British Code of Advertising, Sales Promotion and Direct Marketing, which is a consolidation into a single code of practice designed to regulate marketing communications as a whole based on the previously separate rules on advertising, sales promotion and data base management.

Television and radio

Question: Where does television advertising fit into all this?

Answer: Broadcast advertising has, since 2004, been the responsibility of the ASA whereas previously it had been the subject of a separate statutory regime. The Communications Act 2003 gave The Office of Communications (OFCOM) statutory responsibility for broadcasting standards. Using its powers under the Act, OFCOM contracted out responsibility for advertising standards to the ASA in the guise of a separate, but related, body called ASA (Broadcast).

Question: Is there a broadcasting dimension to CAP?

Answer: A separate body known as The Broadcast Committee of Advertising Practice (BCAP) took over responsibility for the pre-existing television and radio advertising codes. Its membership includes representatives from the advertising and marketing industry with an interest in broadcast advertising—advertisers, agencies and television and radio broadcasters.

Question: Where does Clearcast (CC) and the Radio Advertising Clearance Centre (RACC) fit into this?

Answer: Clearcast is responsible for pre-clearing television commercials before they are broadcast. Similarly, the RACC continues its pre-clearance function for radio commercials. Both are funded by their broadcaster stakeholders.

CHAPTER 2

THE SELF-REGULATORY CONTROLS EXAMINED

The British Code of Advertising, Sales Promotion and Direct Marketing

Question: Tell me more about the British Code of Advertising, Sales Promotion and Direct Marketing (the Code).

Answer: As to the scope of the Code as it relates to promotional marketing, one could not do better than to quote the basic Code principles:

> '8.1   Promoters are responsible for all aspects and all stages of their promotions.
>
> 8.2   Promoters must conduct their promotions equitably, promptly and efficiently and be seen to deal fairly and honourably with participants and potential participants. Promoters must avoid causing unnecessary disappointment.'

Question: How are the sales promotion rules in the Code organised?

Answer: After the definition of sales promotion and the basic rules, there are clauses covering the protection of consumers, safety and suitability, children, availability and rules on administration. Particularly important there then follows significant conditions for promotions together with a detailed section on prize promotions which is then followed by clauses on front page flashes, trade incentives and charity linked promotions.

Question: Are there any specific provisions relating to direct marketing in the Code?

Answer: There are important sections in the Code covering aspects of direct marketing. In particular, s 9 deals with distance selling—a section which complements the rules in The Consumer Protection (Distance Selling) Regulations 2000, and in s 10 there are important rules on database practice. However, the Code has to be read and understood as a whole when it comes to making any marketing communication.

Question: Is it true that the Code now applies online?

Answer: The Code previously applied to certain online marketing communications, including online advertisements and paid-for search listings and online sales promotions. However, this digital remit has been extended from 1 March 2011. From that date, the CAP Code applies to:

> 'Advertisements and other marketing communications by or from companies, organizations or sole traders on their own websites, or in other non-paid-for space online under their control, that are directly connected with the supply or transfer of goods, services, opportunities and gifts, or which consist of direct solicitations of donations as part of their own fund-raising activities.'

Question: What is meant by 'Directly connected with the supply or transfer of goods and services'?

Answer: The purpose of this phrase is to indicate that the intention of the extended remit is to cover marketing communications, the primary intent of which is to sell something. So it goes beyond a marketing communication that just includes a price or seeks overtly an immediate or short-term financial transaction.

Question: What does the phrase 'Non-paid-for space online under (The Advertiser's) control' cover?

Answer: This phrase covers, for example, advertisements and other marketing communications on advertiser-controlled pages on social networking websites.

Question: What are the sanctions for breach of the Code in the areas of extended remit?

Answer: Where appropriate, the pre-existing sanctions will apply, such as adverse publicity. However, to recognise the challenges presented by the extension of the online remit, there are three new sanctions.

- Providing details of an advertiser and the non-compliant marketing communication on a special part of the ASA website.

- Removal of paid-for search advertising—ads that link to the page hosting the non-compliant marketing communication may be removed with the agreement of the search engines.

- ASA paid-for search advertisements—the ASA could place advertisements online highlighting an advertiser's continued non-compliance.

Question: Is there not a risk of infringing on editorial freedom as a result of this extension of remit?

Answer: Yes, however, the system has always had to make sure that editorial freedom was respected and, to ensure that the new controls do not cross the line into areas which can properly be regarded as editorial, there is, at the time of writing, a proposal to establish a special forum within the system to discuss remit issues. The proposal is to create a joint body made up of representatives from the advertising side and from the press side which can give advice to the ASA on remit issues, taking full account of legitimate press sensitivities. The two CAP panels will also have an important part to play in considering issues concerning the limit to be put on the extended remit when it runs the risk of infringing on editorial freedom.

Question: How does the system deal with Video-on-demand (VOD) advertising?

Answer: From 1 September 2010, the ASA has been designated by OFCOM as the co-regulator for advertising appearing on VOD services. A new appendix has been included in the CAP Code, which will apply to aspects of advertisements on VOD services that are subject to statutory regulation under the Communications Act 2003. These changes result from the EU Audio Visual Media Services Directive.

Note: The Code is set out as **APPENDIX 1**.

Question: What are the main sanctions of the self-regulatory system?

Answer: The main sanction is publicity, which is achieved through the adjudications published by the Advertising Standards Authority (ASA). These receive a wide distribution amongst the press, television, government departments etc. In addition, the Committee of Advertising Practice (CAP) issues media alerts, which advise media proprietors of breaches of the Code, particularly where the advertiser or promoter has not co-operated with the ASA's investigation by not withdrawing or amending a marketing communication that the ASA has decided breaks the Code. This information is useful to publishers in exercising their discretion as to whether or not to reject advertisement copy—a right which media proprietors have long cherished and which was judicially recognised in the case of *Gamage (A W) Ltd v Temple Press Ltd* [1911].

In addition, the trade associations which support the self-regulatory system make it a requirement of membership that members comply with the Code and with the rulings of the ASA and advice from CAP. CAP member trade bodies also undertake to make sure that marketing campaigns presented for a possible industry award do not infringe the Code.

Question: If I do not like an adjudication from the ASA is there anything that can be done about it?

Answer: There is no formal appeals system as such, but since 1999 there has been a system of 'Independent Review'. The Independent Reviewer at the time of writing is Sir Hayden Phillips, a former Permanent Secretary of the Lord Chancellor's Department.

A review will be considered only in two situations, which are stipulated in the Code. The first is where there is additional, relevant evidence, which was unavailable for submission to the ASA. The second is where a substantial flaw can be shown in the Council's adjudication or in the process by which the adjudication was made.

A review will not be allowed where concurrent legal action is taking place or is contemplated. Where it is allowed, the Reviewer conducts the review with advice from two Assessors—one is the Chairman of the ASA and the other is the Chairman of the Advertising Standards Board of Finance (ASBOF).

The ASA Council will consider the Independent Reviewer's recommendation on a review request that he accepts as meeting the two stipulated criteria but is not obliged to accept it, although it is fair to say that the ASA would have to have good reason not to implement the Reviewer's recommendation.

Question: Can I appeal to one of the CAP panels?

Answer: There are two specialist CAP panels—the General Media Panel and the Sales Promotion and Direct Response Panel. The Sales Promotion and Direct Response Panel considers a wide range of issues affecting sales promotion and direct marketing and has played a significant role in the creation of a number of CAP notes of guidance, for example on promotions with prizes.

The ASA Executive can and does refer issues to a panel for consideration and it is possible for those who are the subject of an ASA investigation to request that the matter be referred to one of the panels for a review. This is particularly relevant where the complainant raises an issue of general importance or a difficult question in the interpretation of the Codes.

The ASA is not bound to follow the advice of a CAP panel, but since the membership of the panels consists of experts from the industry and from trade associations, their views are persuasive.

Question: What happens if someone feels unaffected by the available sanctions, and decides to ignore the ASA's rulings?

Answer: In cases of misleading advertising—a term which is defined very widely to include all aspects of promotional marketing—the Office of Fair Trading (OFT) has the power to secure court orders banning 'misleading advertisements', as well as in the case of comparative advertisements that do not meet the requirements set out in the amended regulations. The OFT is empowered to refer complainants to what are termed 'established means', which, for our purposes, will usually be either the trading standards service or the ASA. Only a tiny number of cases call for the powers of the OFT and these usually arise where the ASA either cannot act, or cannot act quickly enough.

It is also worth mentioning that the Enterprise Act 2002 gives the OFT and other enforcement bodies wider powers to obtain court orders against businesses which do not comply with their legal obligations to consumers. The OFT can apply for a court order if they are unable, after using their best endeavours, to obtain a satisfactory written assurance from the trader that they will refrain from that course of conduct. The OFT has, for example, issued High Court proceedings against the companies and individuals behind five UK prize draw promotions in order to prevent mailings and the distribution of scratch cards which the OFT considered to be misleading.

Broadcasters are licensed by the Office of Communications (OFCOM) and the terms of their licence oblige them to broadcast advertisements that comply with the relevant Broadcast Committee of Advertising Practice (BCAP) Code. If a broadcaster does not co-operate, the ASA may refer the matter to OFCOM, which has a range of sanctions at its disposal including fines and the revocation of a licence. These powers were given to OFCOM under the Communications Act 2003.

Question: Can I get advice from CAP?

Answer: Yes. As the industry part of the self-regulatory system CAP offers a comprehensive, free advisory service on all issues relating to the application of the non-broadcast Code. They can be contacted by telephone on 020 7492 2100, and by e-mail on advice@cap.org.uk.

E-commerce

Question: Are there any particular issues with viral marketing?

Answer: Virals are e-mail, text or other non-broadcast marketing messages that are designed to stimulate significant circulation by recipients and thereby to generate commercial or reputational benefit to the advertiser from the consequential publicity. There is usually a request, either explicit or implicit, for the message to be forwarded to others and sometimes a video clip is attached.

                   Such marketing activity falls within the operation of the Code. Rule 1(a) makes clear that the Code applies to 'advertisements in … e-mails, text transmissions … follow-up literature and other electronic and printed material.'

                   Accordingly, virals are not excluded from the Code by having originated on a company website or by being forwarded on by consumers. The ASA will judge each complaint on its merits.

Question: What other industry bodies have rules or guidance which are relevant to promotional marketing?

Answer: The Institute of Promotional Marketing has issued a number of documents of interest to the promotional marketing world. These include 'Notes for guidance on coupons'; 'Notes for guidance on e-coupons' and 'Guidelines for briefing fulfilment houses'. The guidance notes mentioned are set out in **APPENDICES 4 AND 5**. The DMA has a Code of Practice, which includes a detailed appendix on sales promotion (discussed in more detail below).

PhonePayPlus (PPP)

Question: I have heard about PPP. Does that have a relevance to promotional marketing?

Answer: PPP was set up in September 1986 as ICSTIS following criticism of the use of some forms of commercial exploitation of premium rate telephone lines—especially in respect of sexually orientated services. PPP is an independent watchdog, funded by the telephone companies, to supervise premium or special rate telephone information and entertainment services. It has the power to fine and the power to ban a company from use of the network for a breach of its Code of Practice.

The PPP Code, now in a new edition, has a section on sales promotion, which should be carefully considered if a promotion is to make use of a special rate 'phone facility'. In particular, the Code requires the rates for a premium rate number to be set out clearly. It is also worth bearing in mind that PPP, like CAP, offers advice on copy clearance.

Other self-regulatory initiatives

Question: Tell me more about the Mailing Preference Service (MPS).

Answer: MPS is an organisation set up in 1983 by the direct mail industry. The service enables members of the public to register their names to be suppressed on all direct marketing lists, or added for all, or any, classes of goods or services. Use of the consumer file by list owners and users is a requirement of the Code, as well as a condition of the DMA Code of Practice.

On a wider basis, the World Convention of MPS facilitates the passing of MPS files between signatories to the Convention, in order to assist companies to avoid mailing to those who do not want to receive direct mail.

Question: What about the Baby MPS?

Answer: The Baby MPS, again set up by the DMA, helps to reduce the number of unwanted baby-related mailings. The scheme is particularly designed to prevent parents being mailed with offers of baby products in the sad circumstances of the death of a baby.

Question: Where does the Telephone Preference Service (TPS) fit in?

Answer: Following the success of the MPS, the DMA was instrumental in setting up the TPS. The TPS was established in 1995 to protect consumers who do not wish to receive unsolicited telephone marketing calls. To make marketing calls when an individual has registered with the TPS that they do not wish to receive such calls from any business or organisation is unlawful under the Privacy and Electronic Communications (European Community Directive) Regulations 2003.

Question: What about Corporate TPS?

Answer: The Corporate Telephone Preference Service enables corporate subscribers to register a wish not to receive unsolicited sales and marketing telephone calls. It is a legal requirement that companies do not make such calls to numbers registered on the CTPS.

A corporate subscriber includes limited companies in the UK and limited liability partnerships as well as schools, government departments, hospitals and other public bodies.

Question: And the Fax Preference Service (FPS)?

Answer: Based on the same principle as the MPS and TPS, the FPS enables people operating a fax machine from residential premises to register as not wanting any unsolicited marketing faxes. The service was set up by the DMA, supported by British Telecom (BT) and Mercury Communications.

Question: And what about e-mail?

Answer: Again established by the DMA, the e-MPS enables individuals to register so as not to receive unsolicited marketing information. It is based in the United States and operates globally.

Question: You mentioned the DMA. What is the role of the DMA in these various self-regulatory initiatives?

Answer: The DMA is responsible for the administration of its Code of Practice and of the Preference Services and the List Warranty Register under one management division. The DMA adjudicates on any complaints or issues arising from the operation of any of the above functions. The Direct Marketing Commission's Chairman sits with the assistance of further independent members, and those members who are appointed from the industry.

Question: So what is the DMA Code?

Answer: Described by a former Director of Consumer Affairs at the Office of Fair Trading as 'a flagship Code and an example to other industries', the Code applies to the direct marketing activities of members of the DMA.

The Code sets out the standards of ethical conduct and best practice that members must adhere to as a condition of DMA membership. Any complaint under the Code of Practice is referred to the Direct Marketing Commission.

Question: Can I appeal against a decision of the Direct Marketing Commission?

Answer: Yes, appeals on natural justice grounds are possible from any decision of the Direct Marketing Commission. Appeals lie to an independent Appeals Commissioner.

Question: What is the role of the Royal Mail in relation to self-regulatory initiatives in direct marketing?

Answer: The Royal Mail is particularly significant, since in respect of direct mail it is roughly analogous to a media owner—but without a media owner's normal rights to reject copy. The Royal Mail is a common carrier and cannot refuse to carry material unless it falls within certain categories set out in section 85 of the Postal Services Act 2000. However, the Royal Mail can operate a regime that can best be described as the withholding of trading privileges. For example, under the Mailsort Contract for bulk postage, when a discount is given, this discount is tied to compliance with appropriate legislation and industry codes.

Now that the postal delivery market has enabled other companies to compete with the Royal Mail, the latter's competitors are similarly media owners and, like the Royal Mail, are expected to penalise non-compliance with relevant codes.

Mail order protection schemes

Question: We want to advertise 'off the page' in national newspapers. What must we do?

Answer: You must comply with the National Newspapers' Safe Home Ordering Protection Scheme (SHOPS). After criticism by the-then Consumer Affairs Minister, nine Fleet Street publishing houses agreed, in 1975, to set up a protection scheme for consumers responding to mail order advertisements in national newspapers under the original name 'Mail Order Protection Scheme (MOPS). It is owned jointly by the Newspaper Publishers Association and the DMA.

You will have to join SHOPS. Apart from certain exclusions, readers who lose money because of the failure of a mail order business are reimbursed from a fund to which member advertisers make annual contributions. Applications for membership are considered by a Managing Committee that requires agencies and advertisers to give undertakings and, in particular cases, supporting indemnities. You should contact the SHOPS secretariat for full particulars of the scheme and for information about the kinds of obligations and undertakings that would be required.

Question: What are the key requirements for a reader to be protected under SHOPS?

Answer: The consumer will be protected under SHOPS if:

- the advertisement is inserted in a national newspaper;

- the advertiser is in membership of the scheme;

- the advertisement describes a product giving details of price and the address from where it may be obtained;

- the advertisement directly asks for readers to order the product and requests payment in advance.

The over-riding condition that applies is that the advertiser must have been recommended for acceptance into the scheme, and to show this, approved advertisements must include the SHOPS logo prominently in their layout.

Question: What about the regional press?

Answer: The Newspaper Society, which represents the regional press, has a scheme designed to make payments where mail order traders have failed to supply goods or refund money and also become the subject of liquidation or bankruptcy proceedings. In certain circumstances, it makes provision for a voluntary payment by the Newspaper Society to the newspaper of up to 50% of any claim refunded to a reader. Use of the scheme is limited to those in membership of the Society.

Within the scope of the Scheme fall direct response display advertisements, both those appearing on run of paper pages and classified pages. Lineage advertisements are excluded.

Question: And what about magazines?

Answer: Magazine publishers who belong to the Periodical Publishers Association (PPA) operate a Protection Scheme to act as a safeguard for their readers. Magazine publishers who do not belong to PPA are not liable for readers' losses. To be included in the PPA scheme, goods must be offered directly off the page in a display or boxed, classified advertisement. Lineage classified advertisements are not covered; nor are loose inserts.

CHAPTER 3

CONTRACTUAL ISSUES AND DISTANCE SELLING

The nature of contracts

Question: What do we mean by a 'contract'?

Answer: For there to be a contract three elements must be present—an offer and acceptance; consideration; and an intention to create legal relations.

Question: What do these terms mean?

Answer: (a) *'Offer and acceptance'*: This means that there must be a clear and definite agreement between both parties, analysed in terms of a definite offer or proposition from one party and a clear unequivocal acceptance from the other.

(b) *'Consideration'*: Every contract must have the presence of consideration. In *Currie v Misa* [1875], it was held that consideration

> 'may consist either in some right, interest, profit, or benefit accruing to the one party, or some forbearance, detriment, loss or responsibility given, suffered, or undertaken by the other'.

An illustration helps: If one party agrees with another to sell them their car for £5,000 there will be consideration and a contract. If one party agrees to give the car away as a gift, there is no consideration and no contract. One important rule is that consideration does not have to be adequate or reasonable—simply that it has value.

(c) *'Intention to create legal relations'*: This simply means that the parties must intend their agreement to give rise to legal implications. An agreement between a husband and wife will usually not give rise to such an intention, whereas an agreement between business people invariably will.

Question: What is the contractual position when we run a promotion?

Answer: The offer of goods or services with incentives and the acceptance of that offer by a consumer is an enforceable contract and any breach of the terms, conditions or nature of the offer is actionable by the consumer. So too are agreements between promotional marketing agencies and their clients, between promoters and sourcing agencies, and the many other agreements necessary to run a promotion.

Question: What about the terms of the contract?

Answer: There are two main types of contractual term— express and implied. The express terms are those stated expressly in a written contract, in written terms of business and sometimes in correspondence where they are leading up to the contract and the parties intend to be bound by them.

Courts are reluctant to imply terms into a contract, but will do so when it is necessary to give effect to the presumed intention of the parties or to reflect custom and practice in the trade.

Question: Our promotional marketing agency says in its terms of business that it is a principal at law. What contractual significance does this have?

Answer: In 1931, a survey concluded that practically all advertising agencies regarded themselves as principals and not as agents for either the client or the media. Since then, a number of decided cases have brought judicial recognition of the custom and practice of the business.

Today, there is little doubt that mainstream marketing communications agencies and public relations agencies contract as principals. So what?

The significance is that, if an agency contracts as principal, it will be bound by the contracts it makes with third parties, be they media, outside creative suppliers, sourcing companies etc. So, for example, if an advertising agency goes into liquidation and owes money to a newspaper, that newspaper will have no claim in contract for the debt against the agency's client.

Fulfilment of promotions

Question: We have offered a free set of place mats with our usual range of canteens of cutlery. Due to unexpected demand we have run out of the place mats before the expiry date of the offer. Can we offer different place mats or a price reduction instead?

Answer: This depends on the terms of the offer. If you offered specific place mats up to a definite termination date, then you have a binding contract with any buyer who takes advantage of the offer and you cannot offer other goods or a price reduction in lieu of the place mats. On the other hand, if your promotional literature made it clear that other goods of equivalent value or a price reduction of that value would be given if stocks ran out, you have no problem. These alternatives must be made clear in the original promotion. This is required by the Distance Selling Regulations (see below).

You cannot change the terms of the offer at a later date after you realise that you have insufficient stocks. The British Code of Advertising, Sales Promotion and Direct Marketing (the Code) requires that a genuine attempt should be made to anticipate demand, but in circumstances in which an unexpectedly high level of demand leads to an inability to supply, contingency plans should be made to provide unsuccessful applicants with some alternative item of equivalent or greater value, either in cash or in kind; and the promoter's intention to act in this way should be made clear to consumers before they are committed to participation. 'Equivalent value' should be assessed in terms of consumers' likely perceptions of quality and price or cost.

Limitations on offers

Question: What limitations can be placed on an offer of promotional goods other than an expiry date?

Answer: Bearing in mind what we have said above, the normal
method of closing an offer is to print 'Offer closes on
21 January' etc prominently on the promotional literature and, where appropriate, on the pack. So far
as the law is concerned, the offer could be limited to
a specified number of applicants or 'subject to availability'. However, the Code states that promoters are
not relieved of the obligation to take all reasonable
steps to avoid disappointing the consumer. This rule
is modified in respect of genuine 'limited editions'
(see below).

Extension of offers

Question: If we have stocks of promotional goods left after the
expiry date can we extend the period of the offer?

Answer: Yes, provided all consumers who have applied before
the closing date have received their goods and the
new extended closing date is clearly stated on all
promotional material.

General disclaimers

Question: Can we use words such as 'No refunds can be given if
promotional goods are out of stock or are unacceptable'?

Answer: The rights of consumers to reject goods or services
that do not conform to a reasonable standard of quality are enshrined in law and cannot be taken away.
In addition, it is a criminal offence to exhibit or state
a disclaimer that seeks to limit or remove the consumer's rights.

It is not of itself unlawful to try to limit liability where
goods cannot be delivered, but such a disclaimer will

only be effective insofar as it is 'reasonable'. What is 'unreasonable' must be determined on the facts of each case, but given that the Code frowns on any activity that would lead to consumer disappointment it is likely that a court would rule that such a disclaimer is unreasonable and therefore of no effect.

Delivery

Question: What is the maximum period of delivery of incentive goods after receipt of an application from a consumer?

Answer: There is no specified period in law. Delivery must be within a reasonable period bearing in mind the nature and cost of the goods and the type of promotion involved. However, the Code requires delivery to be within 30 days of application except where the nature of the products concerned makes it impracticable (eg in relation to plants and made to measure products). The Code rule should be adhered to except where it is impracticable, in which case an indication of the different delivery period should be stated in the marketing communication.

Terms of the offer

Question: We wish to make an 'on-pack' offer for free additional goods. What information must appear on the outside of the pack and what can we put on the inside?

Answer: By law the terms of an offer should be clear, unambiguous and easy to understand. If they are not then the contract may be enforced in favour of the consumer. The Code requires that all information that might reasonably affect a consumer's decision to buy must be given before the decision to buy is made. In particular, special attention should be given to any terms or conditions that exclude some consumers from the opportunity to participate in the promotion; impose any geographical limits on eligibility; limit the number of applications permitted; limit the

number of promotional products or prizes that an
individual or household may claim or win; require
additional proofs of purchase; or impose a closing
date.

Refunds

Question: Are we under an obligation to refund the purchase
price of the principal product when the incentive
product is faulty?

Answer: Yes. There is a single contract for the supply of the
substantive and promotional products that can be
repudiated by the consumer if either should be faulty.
The Code requires that promoters should ensure that
faulty goods are replaced without delay or that the
consumer receives an immediate refund. Where payment has been made by the consumer, the alternative
of an exchange of goods cannot be insisted upon.

Misdescription of goods

Question: What are the liabilities of promoters if incentive
goods are accidentally misdescribed?

Answer: If the goods do not conform to any description of
them, the consumer has the right to reject them and
get his or her money back. If the description is false
to a material degree, an offence may have been committed.

Question: Are there any rules about the presentation of promotional information?

Answer: It is implicit in the Code that all necessary promotional information is presented in a manner that is
easy to understand and not misleading. So far as the
law is concerned, information that, although complete in itself, is confusing, would be likely to render
a contract unenforceable. More important, perhaps,
is the judgment under the old Trade Descriptions Act
1968 in *Read Bros Cycles (Leyton) Ltd v Waltham*

Forest London Borough Council [1978] where all the information necessary for consumers to understand the offer was given, but was split between advertisements and notices and was generally confusing. The court held that an offence concerning a misleading indication of price (see **Chapter 7** below) was committed.

Unfair contracts

Question: What about legislation on unfair contracts?

Answer: The Unfair Contract Terms Act 1977 imposes major controls on the use of exclusion clauses in contracts. Exclusion clauses are those terms designed to restrict or remove the liability that would otherwise ensue for breach of contract.

In addition, the Unfair Terms in Consumer Contracts Regulations 1999 provide that an unfair term in a consumer contract is not binding on the consumer. An unfair term is one that, contrary to the requirement of good faith, causes a significant imbalance in the parties' rights and obligations under the contract to the detriment of the consumer. Schedule 2 to the Regulations contains a non-exhaustive list of matters which may be regarded as unfair.

The Regulations also provide that the Office of Fair Trading (OFT) shall consider any complaint made about the fairness of any contract term drawn up for general use. The OFT may, if it considers it appropriate to do so, seek an injunction to prevent the continued use of that term or a term having like effect in contracts drawn up for general use by a party to the proceedings.

Criminal law and failure to fulfil offers

Question: Is it an offence if the offer of incentive goods or services is not fulfilled?

Answer: Generally speaking there is no offence in criminal law where incentive goods have been offered but not supplied. In the past, the enforcement authorities have unsuccessfully attempted to employ s 14(1)(b) of the old 1968 Act to prosecute cases where this has happened. That offence concerned the reckless making of a statement which is false as to the provision of a service. In *Kinchin v Ashton Park Scooters Ltd* [1984], for example, it was held that the failure to provide free gifts offered on the purchase of a motor scooter was outside the scope of the Act. Again, in *Dixons Ltd v Roberts* [1984] it was held that failure to provide a refund claimed in consequence of an advertised offer to 'refund the difference if you buy Dixon's Deal products cheaper locally at any time of purchase and call within seven days' was not an offence under the Act. Similarly, in *Newell and Taylor v Hicks* [1983] it was held that failure to provide free video recorders with every purchase of a car was not an offence. However, in *Warwickshire County Council v Dixons* [1993], it was held that a failure to honour a price promise can give rise to liability for a misleading price indication.

It should be borne in mind that all of these cases would have been actionable at civil law, even where there is no criminal liability; all, of course, are breaches of the Code.

Quality of promotional goods

Question: Are there any requirements as to the quality of promotional goods?

Answer: In all sales of goods there is an implied term about quality by virtue of the Sale and Supply of Goods Act 1994 (the 1994 Act). Under s 1 of that Act, where the seller sells goods in the course of business, there is an implied term that the goods are of satisfactory quality. 'Satisfactory quality' is defined as goods meeting the standard that a reasonable person would regard as satisfactory—taking into account the description, price and all other relevant circumstances.

The 1994 Act says that the quality of goods includes their state and condition of the goods, and gives examples of factors that, in appropriate cases, can be regarded as aspects of the quality of goods:

- fitness for all the purposes for which goods of the kind in question are commonly supplied;

- appearance and finish;

- freedom from minor defects;

- safety; and

- durability.

If these conditions of contract are not fulfilled, the buyer may reject the goods within a reasonable period after purchase and ask for his or her money back. Any offer of an exchange of goods or credit notes may be accepted at the discretion of the buyer but cannot be insisted upon.

It should always be remembered that non-conformity with description may also be a criminal offence.

The Code requires that all promotional products meet satisfactory standards of safety, durability and performance in use. When applicable, matters such as guarantees and the availability of servicing should be clearly explained.

The quality of services

Question: Where offers such as 'free fitting' or '12 months free service' are made, are there any requirements as to the quality of such services?

Answer: As in the case of goods above, the law imposes certain implied conditions in all consumer contracts. These conditions are:

- The supplier will carry out the service with reasonable care and skill. The degree of care and skill is that which a reasonably competent person in the particular trade or industry could be expected to have. In such cases, the promoter is liable for any defective work carried out by his or her own or contracted employees.

● The service must be carried out within a reasonable time. Unless the contract specifies a time when the work will be carried out there is an implied term that the work will be completed within a reasonable time. What is reasonable is a question of fact in every case but in the typical 'free fitting' promotion the period will be a matter of hours or days so that the buyer can make almost immediate use of the product.

Suitability of promotional products

Question: Are there any precautions of which promoters should be aware as to sensitive product groups for consumers?

Answer: It need hardly be said that obscenity should be avoided, but it is often not understood that it is unlawful to send to any person any book, magazine or leaflet which is unsolicited and which describes or illustrates human sexual techniques.

In more general terms, the Code states that promoters should not offer promotional products that are of a nature likely to cause offence or products that, in the context of the promotion, may reasonably be considered to be socially undesirable. Promoters are required to take special care with promotional products, the distribution of which is subject to any form of legal restriction. Particular care should also be taken in the distribution of free samples to ensure that children or other particularly vulnerable groups are not harmed.

Question: Are there any particular issues in respect of consumer guarantees as to quality?

Answer: Yes, the Sale and Supply of Goods to Consumers Regulations 2002 (as amended) requires the guarantor in a consumer transaction to ensure that the guarantee contains a statement that the consumer has statutory rights in relation to the relevant goods that are sold or supplied and that those rights are not affected by the guarantee. These rights cover the obligations by the supplier in respect of goods being defective, not fit for purpose or not corresponding with description.

Unsolicited goods and services

Question: What are the constraints on sending out unsolicited incentives?

Answer: Goods are unsolicited if they are sent out without any prior request from the recipient. There is nothing to prevent the dispatch of unsolicited incentives that are not specifically forbidden by law on grounds of taste or safety (eg explosive or flammable goods, material on sexual techniques etc). However, under the Unsolicited Goods and Services Act 1971 (the 1971 Act), as amended by the Consumer Protection (Distance Selling) Regulations 2000 and the Unsolicited Goods and Services Act 1971 (Electronic Commerce) (Amendment) Regulations 2005, no payment of any kind may be demanded and there is no right to such payment, provided the recipient retains them for collection for a period of six months or gives 30 days' notice of such availability before the end of the six-month period. Thereafter, the goods become an unconditional gift to the recipient.

Limited editions

Question: It greatly enhances the desirability of a product if it is called a 'limited edition'. What controls are there on the use of this technique?

Answer: The Code allows editions to be limited by the number produced provided the promotion material clearly states the maximum number to be produced and the terms of the offer are in all respects clearly stated. The Code gives only grudging approval to editions limited by time (ie by the number of persons applying within a stated period of time). In such cases the word 'limited' or any of its derivatives may not be used without qualification and the advertiser must advertise its willingness to inform all interested purchasers of the number of articles eventually produced worldwide.

A statement in promotional literature that applications should be received by a certain date is not of itself the offer of a limited edition, but difficulties have been experienced in the interpretation of the Code in this respect.

Identity of the promoter

Question: What are the rules about revealing the identity of promoters in promotional literature? Could we, for example, show only the name of our handling agents, omitting any reference to ourselves?

Answer: Concealment of the true identity of a promoter would be contrary to the Code, which requires that full information shall be given in relation to all promotions and that promotions shall be fair and honest. The Advertising Standards Authority has adjudicated against a number of promotions where the promoter's proper name and address have not been given.

So far as the law is concerned, the contracting party would be that party named in the promotional material. It therefore follows that any action brought by a consumer would be against the company whose name appeared in the promotional material.

Question: But what about the situation where we use a travel company—can we give their name?

Answer: There is nothing wrong in giving the name of, for example, a travel company for the purpose of dealing with detailed questions concerning flights and hotels and questions of that sort. But under the Code the promoter remains responsible for all aspects of the promotion and, whilst a company can delegate some aspects of the execution of the promotion, it cannot delegate its overall responsibility.

Distance selling regulations

Question: There are detailed regulations affecting distance selling. What is distance selling?

Answer: The Consumer Protection (Distance Selling) Regulations 2000 (as amended) apply to 'distance contracts'. These are defined as:

> 'any contract concerning goods or services
> concluded between a supplier and a consumer
> under an organised distance sales or service pro-
> vision scheme run by the supplier who, for the
> purpose of the contract makes exclusive use of
> one or more means of distance communication
> up to and including the moment at which the
> contract is concluded.

> "Means of distance communication" is defined
> as "any means, which without the simultaneous
> physical presence of the supplier and the con-
> sumer, may be used for the conclusion of a con-
> tract between those parties".'

So, clearly, mail order trading is covered; so too
would be self-liquidator and similar offers in the
world of sales promotion.

Question: Are there any exemptions from the new Regulations?

Answer: There are a number of exemptions, including vend-
ing machines, contracts with telecommunications
operators by public payphone, immoveable property rights and auctions. There are also some partial
exemptions: in particular, information and the right
of cancellation does not apply to regular deliveries
to home and work for everyday consumption(eg milk
and newspapers). Contracts for leisure, transport or
accommodation or catering on specific dates are also
excluded. There are also specific exceptions to the
right of cancellation, as we shall see later.

Question: What information has to be given and when?

Answer: Before or at the time the contract is concluded, the
consumer must be informed of the identify of the

supplier, the main characteristics of the goods, the price, arrangements for delivery and the closing date, as well as the fact that the consumer has the right of cancellation under reg 13 of the Regulations, where applicable. Also, if the supplier intends to substitute goods of equivalent quality and price in the event of supply problems, this needs to be made clear.

Question: What is the 'right to cancel'?

Answer: Under the Regulations, consumers have the right to cancel a distance contract any time from the date of the conclusion of the contract—and for up to seven clear working days after delivery. Consumers must then be reimbursed within 30 days.

Question: Are there any exceptions from the right to cancel?

Answer: Yes:

- supplies of services that have, with the consent of the customer, commenced within a seven-working-day period;

- where the price is dependent on fluctuations in the financial market which the supplier cannot control;

- goods made to the customer's specifications, or clearly personalised, or subject to a short shelf-life;

- audio and video recordings or computer software, if they are unsealed by the consumer;

- newspapers, periodicals and magazines;

- gaming, betting and lottery services.

Question: How do I express the right to withdraw?

Answer: There has been much discussion on this, but I believe the following wording is the best and most succinct way of expressing the right to cancel: 'You can cancel under this contract up to seven clear working days from delivery by returning, at your own cost, the item to the promoter.'

Question: How do I express the right to substitute other goods?

Answer: I suggest something along the following lines: 'The promoter may substitute an equivalent item if the one requested is unavailable. If you wish to cancel and return the substituted item, your costs will be refunded.'

Question: What happens if I do not comply with the requirements as to information provided by the Regulations?

Answer: The cooling-off period can be extended by three months from the date it would have expired had notice been given.

Contracts away from business premises

Question: What other statutory restrictions exist on direct selling?

Answer: In relation to consumer credit, canvassing business door-to-door requires a licence, and it is a criminal offence to canvass for what are called 'debtor–creditor agreements'—a term which covers most forms of cash loan.

Provisions under consumer credit legislation also provide for certain 'cooling-off and cancellation rights in respect of credit agreements negotiated away from business premises.

There is legislation giving a more general right to cancel in distance selling agreements in the form of The Cancellation of Contracts made in a Consumer's Home or Place of Work etc Regulations 2008.

Question: Tell me more about The Cancellation of Contracts made in a Consumer's Home or Place of Work etc Regulations 2008.

Answer: The rights under these Regulations apply when the consumer agrees to buy goods or services from a trader as a result of an unsolicited visit to the consumer's home or place of work. They also apply where a consumer, having asked the trader to call, agrees to buy other goods, the identity of which were not, at that stage, known to the consumer.

Traders are required to give their customers written notice that they have a seven-day cooling-off period during which agreements covered by the Regulations can be cancelled without penalty. The notice from the trader must also specify the name and address of the company or person against whom the right of cancellation can be exercised.

E-commerce

Question: Many contracts are now concluded electronically. What do the Regulations say?

Answer: The Electronic Commerce (EC Directive) Regulations 2002 provides that those engaged in e-commerce must provide the following general information:

- the business name, geographic address and other relevant details including e-mail address;

- details of any publicly available register in which you are entered, together with your registration number or equivalent;

- the particulars of any supervisory body if there is any relevant scheme of authorisation in place;

- details of any professional body with which the trader is registered;

- the trader's VAT registration number.

For those contracting online, customers must be given information about:

- the technical steps required to conclude the contract;

- whether the finalised contract will be filed by the trader and whether in this form it will be accessible;

- the relevant language or languages offered for the conclusion of the contract;

- any relevant codes of conduct to which the trader subscribes together with information as to how these may be accessed.

Question: What about trading disclosures?

Answer: The Companies (Registrar, Languages and Trading Disclosures) Regulations 2006 require that all companies in the United Kingdom must clearly state the company registration number, place of registration and registered office address on all company websites. If the company is being wound up, that fact needs to be made clear on the website as well.

CHAPTER 4

PRIZE PROMOTIONS

Background

Question: The law in this area changed significantly in 2007—why?

Answer: A sea change has taken place in the attitude of our society to lotteries and other games of chance. Historically, lotteries in particular, were seen as a way of exploiting the poor. In the case of *Reader's Digest v Williams* [1976], the then Lord Chief Justice observed that the purpose of the law had been to prevent those poor people who only had a few pence to buy food for their children from losing money. The law until 2007 reflected this view.

Question: Why the change?

Answer: The change has been a reflection of changed attitudes. Many factors are responsible. The launch of the National Lottery was one of the most significant because gambling ceased to be a minority pursuit and instead became an activity in which the majority of the population have participated to some degree. An activity once seen as a risk to the poor and disadvantaged had suddenly become a significant part of the leisure industry.

Question: But what about promotional marketing?

Answer: The situation was unsatisfactory. Linking games of chance directly to product purchase, as with an instant win, gave rise to the spectre of an illegal lottery. To cope with the legal problem, free entry routes were developed so that nobody was obliged to purchase. But this was never sanctioned by either statute or case law. Legally doubtful, its acceptance was simply part of a policy laid down by the Crown Prosecution Service (CPS). The public never understood why chances were given to non-purchasers. It was clear that the public did not understand why promotional games of chance linked to the purchase of goods or services were tainted with illegality and this was much of the reasoning behind the CPS policy not to challenge such promotions if there was a genuine and realistic free-entry route.

As a result of a comprehensive review of gambling legislation, the Government made the Gambling Act 2005. This came into force in 2007.

Promotional games of chance

Question: How does the Act affect promotional games of chance?

Answer: The Gambling Act redefines 'lottery' so as not to include a produce purchase obligation. For the first time, there is a statutory definition of lottery, but one based on previous case law—essentially the offer of prizes in a game of chance in which people are required to pay in money or money's worth in order to participate. However, Sch 2(2) makes it clear that an obligation to pay for goods or services will not count as payment within the definition of a lottery unless one is paying at a price or rate which reflects the opportunity to participate. In other words, it is only if the price is 'loaded' to take account of the promotion that the scheme will constitute an illegal lottery.

Question: What is the effect of this on promotional marketing?

Answer: It means that unless the price has been inflated on account of the promotion, any promotional game of chance is legal without the need for a free entry route.

Question: What about postage or telephone costs?

Answer: The Act makes it clear that the ordinary cost of postage or telephone calls will not constitute payment. However, if the cost is more than the basic, as in the case of a premium rate 'phone call, it will be regarded as payment. This reflects the understanding that grew up in relation to the previous legislation.

Question: What happens if a charge is made, not for formal entry into a prize promotion, but in order to ascertain whether one has won and, if so, the identity of the prize?

Answer: Both situations are covered in Sch 2, paras 6 and 7 to the Act. Any payment to discover whether a prize has been won or to claim a prize will be regarded as a payment to take part in the arrangement making such schemes lotteries.

Question: But what if I offered a 50% discount off the price of a world cruise? Does that mean my promotion will be an illegal lottery?

Answer: This question troubled many of us before the Bill was passed. And it is an issue that encompasses many other situations. What is the position, for example, in relation to a prize of a ticket to a pop concert where one has to pay the cost of travel to the event? And what about a car that will need to be taxed and issued before it can be driven?

     When ministers were challenged on this they argued that such arrangements did not contravene the statutory provisions. They argued that where a 50% voucher was the prize, one took possession of the prize when one received the voucher. They argued similarly in relation to the other examples. More importantly, perhaps, the Gambling Commission the dedicated enforcement body under the Act also appears to have taken this view. Since they are responsible for enforcement, one can presumably take a relaxed view of the issue.

Question: What is the difference between a prize and a gift?

Answer: I do not know of any case law defining the term 'prize' in contradistinction to 'gift'. The British Code of Advertising, Sales Promotion and Direct Marketing does not define 'prize', but says that gifts should not be described as prizes if they are given to a significant proportion of those taking part in the promotion. Accordingly, if everyone 'wins' something of comparable value, they are gifts and not prizes.

Question: What if a retailer offers, say, to refund the purchase price to all those who spend £50 or more in their shop during the month of May if England subsequently wins the World Cup that year?

Answer: It has always seemed to me that such a scheme is not caught by the legislation on lotteries, because either everyone will receive something, or everyone will receive nothing. Each purchaser stands in exactly the same position as all other purchasers. There is no drawing of lots, which would suggest that prizes are to be distributed to each winner according to chance. The outcome of the World Cup is determined by the skill of the teams and is not, therefore, a result based on chance.

This scheme clearly is not a competition, because of the absence of any skill or dexterity by participants. Neither can the participants said to be playing a game. This rules out the application of gaming legislation.

However, the conundrum lies in whether such a promotion can be said to be a wager or a bet. When the Institute of Promotional Marketing sought leading counsel's advice on this point, his advice was that such a promotion did not fit into case law definitions of 'wager' and 'bet'.

The final arbiter of such matters will be the courts. However, given the backing of leading counsel's opinion, I see no reason why promoters should be dissuaded from running such promotions.

Question: What is the situation if participants did not appreciate that they acquired a chance when they spent money?

Answer: It used to be the case that if people spent money unaware that they were obtaining a chance, that payment did not constitute contribution from the point of view of the definition of a lottery. This principle arose in the case of *Minty v Sylvester* [1915], the basis of which was if that there was no 'allurement' there was no contribution. The ruling in *Minty v Sylvester* has now been done away with as a result of Sch 2, para 4, which says 'It is also immaterial for the purposes of s 14 and this Schedule whether a person knows when he makes a payment that he thereby participates in an arrangement.'

Question: I have heard about customer lotteries. What are they?

Answer: The Government has established a new category of exempt lottery. Apart from traditional exemptions for the National Lottery, private lotteries and society lotteries, there is a new category of 'customer lottery'. This is a lottery promoted by a person who occupies business premises provided that nobody wins more than £50 as a prize and the lottery is organised in such a way as to ensure that no profits are made. It is therefore a small non-profit-making method of creating interest for customers.

Question: Does the Gambling Act apply to Northern Ireland?

Answer: No, the Act only covers Great Britain, (ie England, Wales and Scotland). This means that Northern Ireland operates on the basis of the old legal framework that previously operated in Great Britain prior to the Gambling Act 2005. That law is contained within the Betting, Gaming, Lotteries and Amusements (Northern Ireland) Order 1985. At the time of writing, a review of Northern Ireland's gambling laws is underway, but no decision has been made to extend the provisions to Northern Ireland.

Question: How then should we deal with the situation in Northern Ireland?

Answer: It is extremely unlikely that a promotion in Northern Ireland which complied with the law in the rest of the United Kingdom would be challenged. After all, to do so would be to deny the wish of the people of Northern Ireland to be an integral part of the UK and would be politically embarrassing.

In any event, recent decisions of the European Court of Justice concerning the EU Unfair Commercial Practices Directive are such that the restrictions in Northern Ireland are no longer legally valid, so there is no sound basis for objecting to promotions in Northern Ireland that meet the legal requirements of Great Britain (see detailed discussion of this point in **Chapter 11**).

Games of chance and National Lottery tickets

Question: What about games of chance and other promotions that make reference to the National Lottery?

Answer: Many promotions have referred to the National Lottery, in ways too varied to describe in detail. They range from 'Sorry you were not successful, but your ticket is worth 50p off your grocery bill this week' to 'You may not have won on the Lottery with only one number, but with us you have won…', etc. The law is stated in s 16 of the National Lottery etc Act 1993, which prohibits any false indication that a scheme is part of the National Lottery or otherwise connected with it.

The problem is what is meant by 'otherwise connected with it'. Personally, I think it means any false suggestion of an official link (eg a suggestion that Camelot has licensed the scheme in some way). It is a difficult area and each scheme has to be looked at separately.

What one can say is that if a promoter is in doubt, it is probably a good idea to institute a formal disclaimer such as 'This promotion is not connected with the National Lottery in any way whatsoever.' Such disclaimers have been used for some promotions in the tabloid press.

Question: What about National Lottery tickets as prizes and as premiums?

Answer: The thorniest issue, and the one with the greatest impact on the promotions industry, is the question of giving National Lottery tickets or scratch cards as prizes or premiums. Dealing in Lottery tickets is prohibited under the terms of Camelot's licence to run the National Lottery and under the published game rules, and the view has been taken that buying lottery tickets and giving them away in a promotion would amount to dealing in lottery tickets.

At a meeting, Camelot told me that they may not pay out in respect of prizes won on promotional lottery tickets or scratch cards. The courts have not ruled on this issue but I, for one, would not be prepared to take the risk.

Games of skill

Question: What does the Act say about competitions?

Answer: Very little in fact. The Act is solely concerned with gambling in its various forms. Accordingly s 339 provides that a prize competition is not gambling for the purposes of the Act unless it is either:

● gaming within the mean of s 6;

● participation in a lottery within the meaning of s 14; or

● betting within the meaning of ss 9–11.

Question: When will a prize promotion amount to gaming?

Answer: Section 6 tells us that gaming means playing a game of chance for a prize. Playing a game was taken by the Gaming Board, and presumably will also be taken by the Gambling Commission, to mean an active game rather than one involving merely passive participation. The former would cover, for example, a game involving throwing a dice or spinning a wheel, whereas the latter might involve merely rubbing off a scratch card.

Question: When will a prize promotion amount to a lottery?

Answer: This is more complicated. Section 14(5) provides:

'A process which requires persons to exercise skill or judgment or to display knowledge shall be treated for the purposes of this section as relying wholly on chance if:

(a)   the requirement cannot reasonably be expected to prevent a significant proportion of persons who participate in the arrange-

(b) the requirement cannot reasonably be expected to prevent a significant proportion of persons who wish to participate in that arrangement from doing so.'

Question: What does this amount to?

Answer: It means that what is supposedly a game of skill will be regarded as a game of chance if the skill required cannot reasonably be expected to prevent a significant proportion of participants from winning a prize or from wishing to participate. In other words, a competition has to have about it a sufficient deterrent effect, both in terms of people receiving a prize and people wishing to participate in the first place for there to be considered a sufficient level of skill. If there is any doubt, the Gambling Commission recommends that, before organising a competition, the promoter should run what is in effect a controlled experiment to see whether the level of skill does indeed have the necessary deterrent effect. However, in the absence of case law, there remains doubt as to how the skill test will be interpreted legally in actual cases.

Question: What about multi-stage promotions?

Answer: This was always the most difficult aspect of the old law and in many ways remains so. If the first stage relies wholly on chance, the whole scheme will be regarded as a game of chance. However, so long as the first stage meets the skill test in s 14(5) of the Act, it doesn't matter if the second stage is based on chance. Accordingly, so long as the first stage is a valid skill test, the second stage could be a draw.

Question: When will a prize promotion amount to betting?

Answer: Under the old law, the forecasting of the result of a future event or of a past event, the result of which was not yet ascertained or generally known, would make a prize promotion an illegal competition. In the new law, that element is reflected within the statutory provisions on betting. Betting, in s 9, is defined as:

'…making or accepting a bet on:

(a)   the outcome of a race, competition or other event or process;

(b)   the likelihood of anything occurring or not occurring; or

(c)   whether anything is or is not true'.

Question: What happens if a promotion involving the forecasting of, for example, a race, is free to enter?

Answer: To be covered by the sections on betting, one has to consider whether there is payment within the meaning of Sch 1 to the Act. Schedule 1, para 2 makes it clear that the definition of payment excludes paying for goods or services at a normal market price which has not been inflated to reflect the opportunity to participate.

Particular types of competition

Question: What about 'spot the ball' competitions?

Answer: The legal status of 'spot the ball' competitions was never satisfactorily and definitively settled under the old law. The problem is that whilst skill would probably get you to the general area in which the ball is located, where precisely the ball is must be a matter of pure chance.

In view of the wide preponderance of 'spot the ball'-type schemes and the absence of any clear challenge on the point of legality it is probably safe, in practice, to run such schemes. However, the best advice may be to ask competitors where the ball most logically would be, rather than where the ball actually was. However, the author believes that 'spot the ball' competitions, however they are run, are likely to satisfy the test of skill set out in s 14(5) of the Gambling Act 2005.

Question: Do ranking competitions present any special problems?

Answer: Ranking competitions, or factoral competitions as they are sometimes known, involve putting a list of factors in order of importance. They are a popular form of competition, but they pose problems for both consumers and promoters alike.

Depending on the number of factors, it can be virtually impossible to win a ranking competition due to the huge number of possible variants. Some unscrupulous competition organisers have therefore, organised ranking competitions knowing the chances of winning are very small. They then offer a substantial prize, say £1 million, and cover the very slight risk of winning by means of an insurance policy.

To deal with this problem, the Committee of Advertising Practice has advised that, if some advertised prizes may not be won, this fact should be made clear, and if the winning of a prize is distinctly unlikely, that fact should be given special prominence.

It is advisable for a promoter to give a small pen picture of the sort of person whose judgment would be relevant to the list of factors. So, instead of saying 'List these factors in order of importance', one should be more specific: 'List these factors in order of importance from the point of view of the modern busy housewife.' This makes the competition more focused. It is then less open to the danger of the scheme being regarded as an illegal lottery, as happened in the case of *Hobbs v Ward* [1929] where the court concluded that all one could do to take part was to make a guess at the right order.

Finally, in ranking competitions promoters should ensure, if they are awarding prizes to nearly correct listings, that this is to be judged in descending order. There is a lot of difference between the transposing of the bottom two factors and the transposing of the top two.

Question: And what about estimating-type competitions?

Answer: Competitions that involve estimating distances and amounts are particularly problematic in that their judging is much more likely to be challenged. One professional 'comper' regularly challenged the judging of estimating-type questions, particularly when they involved distances between two points. There is no reason in law why a promoter should not run such a competition, but it should be aware of the risks. It is very important to avoid describing the outcome of the judges' deliberation as 'the right answer' or 'the correct answer': there will be people who will have bought thousands of bars of chocolate just to see how many fit into the back of a Mini. Accordingly, promoters should make it clear that the answer is as determined by the panel of judges, and that the judges' decision is final.

The position of free entry routes

Question: How important were the changes?

Answer: It would be no exaggeration to say that it was one of the most profound changes to the regulatory framework affecting promotional marketing. Certainly, by effectively allowing lotteries in sales promotion, it has had major consequences for the business. Most importantly it meant the end of the necessity for free entry routes in relation to on-pack games of chance such as instant wins. This change has further diminished the use of skill competitions in the industry, particularly since, as a rule, games of chance can be easier to administer and bring a greater response.

In fact, the legislation creates for promotional marketing a very unrestricted environment. As we have seen, the consequence of not meeting the skill test in the Act is that a promotion is seen totally as chance and not skill. Similarly, where the first stage is chance the whole promotion is seen as chance. However, as we have also seen, provided the price of a product or service is not 'loaded', such promotions are legal in any event. What this means is that provided the price of a product is not increased because of the promotion, then any combination of skill or chance will be legal.

Question: What about premium rate promotions?

Answer: In any case where under the terms of the Act there will still be payment to take part, a game of chance will constitute a lottery. The best example of this is the case of a premium rate promotion. Not being the basic cost of a telephone call, the additional cost will be regarded as payment and in the context of a game of chance such as a draw this will make the scheme a lottery. The only way to avoid a lottery arising is to institute a free entry route.

Question: I thought free entry routes were no longer needed?

Answer: For most purposes, yes. But in a few cases it will be the only way to prevent a scheme constituting an illegal lottery. Paragraph 8 of Sch 2 provides that an arrangement is not to be regarded as a lottery if there is a genuine choice to pay or not to pay. The promoter's alternative route must not involve charging more than the ordinary cost of a letter. Alternatively, it can involve another method of communication, neither more expensive nor less convenient than paying to enter the promotion. Some might reasonably argue that a free entry route is always less convenient than buying a product. The Gambling Commission and the courts have called for a practical view.

Unfair Commercial Practices

Question: I understand there are new regulations affecting commercial practices generally. What are they?

Answer: In 2005, the EU promulgated the Unfair Commercial Practices Directive (UCPD) on the basis that the countries of the EU needed a more general approach to unfair commercial practices to be able to deal effectively with fast moving changes in the market place. As far as the UK is concerned, the approach in the past has been very much a case of having sector-specific legislation dealing with abuses as and when they arise.

The Directive has been implemented in the UK in the form of The Consumer Protection from Unfair Trading Regulations 2008. These Regulations introduce a general prohibition on traders in all sectors engaging in unfair commercial practices against consumers.

They do this by introducing a general prohibition on traders treating consumers unfairly and by banning misleading actions, misleading omissions, aggressive practices and a number of specific prohibitions listed in the schedule to the Regulations.

Question: Are any of these specific prohibitions related to prize promotions?

Answer: Yes, there are three specific prohibitions that have a relevance to prize promotions.

'Claiming that products are able to facilitate winning in games of chance'—I have no doubt that this is about products (ie books etc) that claim to be able to increase people's chance of winning, say the National Lottery. Sometimes, these advertisers claim to have some sort of method that increases peoples' chances of winning. That I feel sure is what is aimed at, and rightly so.

'Claiming in a commercial practice to offer a competition or prize promotion without awarding the prizes described or a reasonable equivalent'—This is clearly aimed at scams where prizes are promised and they are simply not awarded. But what about an instant win scheme on-pack where although the chances are in the pack, some of those chances are not redeemed? In some cases, something like 40% of in-can chances are not redeemed. And then we have the problem of a competition where prizes are offered to those who answer certain questions or complete a skill test and nobody successfully answers the skill test, therefore the prize isn't awarded.

I believe that the key to interpreting this is the word 'Awarding'. I would argue that in all these genuine cases the prizes have been awarded, or are available to be awarded, but through no fault of the promoter circumstances arise which result in them not being claimed.

'Creating the false impression that the consumer has already won, will win, or will on doing a particular act win, a prize or other equivalent benefit, when in fact either: (a) there is no prize or other equivalent benefit; or (b) taking any action in relation to claiming the prize or other equivalent benefit is subject to the consumer paying money or incurring a cost'— The particular problem here is in relation to (b). I understand the scams for which this is designed. But what about a prize that involves a concert ticket and which necessarily involves the cost of a train fare to the location of the concert? Is that paying money in order to claim the prize, and, if so, would such a promotion be automatically unfair under the new regulations? When the Gambling Bill was going through Parliament, Ministers argued that the prize was the ticket and one took possession of the prize when one received the ticket.

I believe that this view is the correct interpretation of the Regulations and it is clearly the view of the Gambling Commission, as well.

Contractual issues

Question: The Gambling Act 2005 gives rise to a criminal prosecution. Are there no civil law implications in respect of competitions?

Answer: Yes. When people enter a competition there is a contract between the participant and the promoter. This is one reason why it is so important to spend time on drafting the rules of the competition. Even free-entry competitions can create a contractual relationship if some 'consideration' is involved. Breach of contract could be occasioned by a failure to run the competition properly, (eg by failing to follow the published methodology for selecting winners). For instance, in the case of *Chaplin v Hicks* [1911] a woman was awarded damages for the loss of a chance to win a beauty contest; she had lost that chance because of a breach of contract by the organisers.

Since the rules set out the basis of the contract between the promoter and the consumer it is important to ensure total accuracy. Promoters have come unstuck by claiming that a panel of judges was independent when only one member was. And do not say

'Proof of postage will not be taken as proof of delivery' if what you mean is 'Proof of posting will not be taken as proof of delivery'.

Another area of civil law that may be relevant is product liability. If a product supplied as a prize is defective and causes injury then a civil action will lie.

Competition rules

Question: Now I have established the basic legality of my promotion. What's next?

Answer: You must next make sure that the scheme meets all the requirements of the British Code of Advertising, Sales Promotion and Direct Marketing ('the Code').

Question: What about the rules of the promotion?

Answer: Rules 8.17 and 8.28 of the Code give guidance on the construction of rules for competitions and other promotions with prizes. Getting the rules right is critical for the interests of the promoter, as well as the consumer. Many subsequent arguments can be avoided if more attention is given to making sure that the rules are set out clearly, comprehensively and unambiguously. The issues that should be covered by the rules are as follows:

(a)   the closing date;

(b)   any restriction on the number of entries or prizes that may be won;

(c)   any requirements for proof of purchase;

(d)   description of prizes;

(e)   any age or other personal restrictions, or any geographical restrictions;

(f)   how and when winners will be notified and results published;

(g) the criteria for judging entries;

(h) where appropriate, the ownership of copyright in entries;

(i) whether and how entries are returnable by the promoter;

(j) how participants may obtain any supplementary rules which may apply—although these should not be rules which would reasonably affect the decision to purchase in the first place;

(k) if a cash alternative to any prize is available;

(l) any permissions required (eg from parent or employer);

(m) any intention to use winners in related publicity.

Finally, in common with all promotions there should be a clear statement of the promoter's name and normal business address unless this is clear from the context.

Question: Can I short-circuit the process?

Answer: Sometimes it may not be possible to include all the necessary rules, and competitors may have to be directed towards an address from which they can get the full rules. If this is done, the rules given 'up-front' must be those that have a direct bearing on whether the consumer decides to purchase and participate in the promotion. The Code says that the items that should be made clear before purchase or participation are:

(a) the closing date for receipt of entries;

(b) any geographical or personal restrictions such as location or age;

(c) any requirements for proofs of purchase;

(d) the need, if applicable, to obtain permission to enter from parents, employers or others;

(e) the nature of the prize(s);

(f) the identity of the promoter.

Changing the goal posts

Question: What happens if I realise that I have misjudged things after the promotion has started?

Answer: Usually there is little that can be done. Sometimes the competition does not generate enough interest, for any number of reasons. Even so, the competition must be completed and prizes awarded—even if all the entrants qualify for prizes. Slippage of dates may be excusable if there is some good reason for it. Although it will rarely, if ever, be acceptable to delay the closing date, the date by which winners will be notified may slip because of unforeseeable circumstances. However, unless there is a very good reason indeed, such slippages could result in an infringement of the Code.

In addition, it is worth remembering, as we have already noted, that when competitors take part in a promotional competition there is a legally binding contract between the participants and the promoter. The rules are part of the contract and failure to abide by them is a breach of contract.

A single prize

Question: Should a promoter continue to advertise a prize promotion, such as an instant win, knowing that the only prize has already been claimed and is therefore no longer available to be won?

Answer: This is a difficult question in practice. It is the reason why some promoters have been known to make sure that the winning scratch card only makes its appearance towards the end of the promotion. What one can say is that there should be several other valuable prizes within the promotion so that if a main prize is claimed there is still a legitimate reason to continue with the promotion.

Publicity

Question: How can I try to ensure that I get a publicity return from my promotion?

Answer: Two rules are particularly relevant here:

(1) It is important to state, as required by the Code, whether or not there is a cash alternative to the prize. Failure to make it clear that there is no cash alternative to a prize has in the past led some competitors to refuse to attend a ceremony for the award of a prize.

(2) The rules should, if appropriate, state that winners may be, or will be, required to take part in related publicity.

CHAPTER 5

DATA PROTECTION ISSUES

Introduction

Question: What, in a nutshell, is the objective of data protection legislation?

Answer: Concern about the use of computers for the collecting, storing, processing and distribution of personal information lay behind the establishment of a European Convention on Data Protection. The purpose of UK data protection legislation was therefore to enable the UK government to meet its obligations under the European Convention, as well as addressing growing concerns about computers and personal information.

Question: What does the Data Protection Act 1998 (the 1998 Act) cover?

Answer: Broadly speaking, the 1998 Act covers information relating to identifiable living people, whether held in a computer or a manual filing system as long as it is relatively easy to extract information about the individuals. The 1998 Act applies both to data controlled by individuals as well as by organisations. Those who control the processing of personal data are, not surprisingly, known as 'data controllers'. And those who process data on behalf of a data controller are termed 'data processors'.

Question: What is meant by notification?

Answer: The 1998 Act provides for a system of 'notification'. If you control the processing of personal data you must notify the Information Commissioner; this involves setting out where you obtained the data from and the uses to which you intend to put it.

Question: How does this affect particular elements in the list business?

Answer: There are several players in the creation and use of mailing lists. First, there is the list owner, who creates the list and makes it available. Secondly, there are the third parties to whom the list is made available, such as a list broker. Thirdly, there may be a direct marketing agency involved. Fourthly—last but not least— is the advertiser whose mailing shot is to be sent to those on the list.

As far as the 1998 Act is concerned, it applies first to the list owner, since it will normally have created the list and, having computerised it, will be its controller. List brokers may need to notify under the Act depending on whether they control the contents of the list. If brokers only arrange the use of lists and have no control over them, they do not need to notify, and the same is true of the direct marketing agency. It is also true of the advertiser unless the advertiser comes to control the list—and an advertiser can quite easily come to control a list if it keeps a bought-in list on computer and operates a suppression mechanism. They would then have the same responsibilities as a list owner.

Finally, mailing houses, because they are processing automatically personal data for third parties, may need to notify.

Question: Who is the Information Commissioner?

Answer: The Information Commissioner is appointed by the Queen on the recommendation of the government of the day. The Information Commissioner must give an annual report to Parliament. The Information Commissioner's functions under the 1998 Act are, principally, to compile and maintain the Register of Data Controllers and to promote compliance with the Data Protection Principles. In addition, the Information Commissioner has the role of encouraging codes of practice in particular sectors, and of assisting in compliance with the Data Protection Principles. Finally, there is certain enforcement action that the Information Commissioner can take, which may involve enforcement notices in relation to the Data Protection Principles, or criminal prosecutions (eg in relation to a failure to notify under the Act).

Question: Are there any exclusions?

Answer: Yes. There are both primary exemptions and miscellaneous exemptions. The primary exemptions broadly
cover:

(a) the safeguarding of national security;

(b) the prevention or detection of crime and the
assessment and collection of taxes;

(c) the physical or mental health of the data subject;

(d) processing of personal data in respect of regulatory functions exercised by public enforcement
agencies;

(e) journalistic uses and also artistic and literary
purposes;

(f) research purposes;

(g) information made public by law (eg the electoral
list), but the exemption only applies in the hands
of the person who is required to make it public;

(h) disclosures required by law;

(i) disclosures in connection with legal proceedings;

(j) domestic purposes.

In addition, there are a number of miscellaneous
exemptions covering such items as legal professional
privilege, corporate finance, management planning
and confidential references given by the data controller.

Question: OK, so how do I notify under the Act?

Answer: Forms can be obtained from the Information Commissioner at Wycliffe House, Water Lane, Wilmslow,
Cheshire SK9 5AF (0303 123 1113). Online forms
and further details can also be obtained from the
Information Commissioner's website: www.ico.gov.uk

At first sight, the forms can look somewhat forbid-
ding, but they are quite easy to complete once one
understands the basic format. One starts by a descrip-

tion of the data subjects; in other words, the types of individuals about whom personal data are to be held. Then one goes on to identify the classes of personal data which are to be held about the data subjects identified previously; and then identify the sources of personal data relating to the data subjects, and to whom disclosures are to be made. Finally, there is a section on overseas transfer of data.

All this is done by means of a series of boxes that need to be ticked and, if one follows the guidance notes, this operation is, as I have said above, much easier than would seem at first sight.

Question: So what happens when I have notified the Information Commissioner?

Answer: First, one has to make sure that the notification is kept up-to-date, and is renewed every three years. Failure to notify, or to keep the notice up-to-date or to renew, would give rise to a criminal offence. Once having notified, one also has to make sure that one's processing of data complies with the eight Data Protection Principles that are set out in Sch 1 to the 1998 Act (see below).

The Data Protection Principles

Question: What are the Data Protection Principles?

Answer: The eight Data Protection Principles as set out in Sch 1 to the 1998 Act are:

(1) Personal data shall be obtained and processed fairly and lawfully.

(2) Personal data shall be obtained only for one or more specified and lawful purposes, and shall not be further processed in any manner incompatible with that purpose or those purposes.

(3) Personal data shall be adequate, relevant and not excessive in relation to the purpose or purposes for which they are processed.

(4) Personal data shall be accurate and, where necessary, kept up-to-date.

(5) Personal data processed for any purpose or purposes shall not be kept for longer than is necessary for that purpose or those purposes.

(6) Personal data shall be processed in accordance with the rights of data subjects under the 1998 Act.

(7) Appropriate technical and organisational measures shall be taken against unauthorised or unlawful processing of personal data and against accidental loss or destruction of, or damage to, personal data.

(8) Personal data shall not be transferred to a country or territory outside the European Economic Area unless that country or territory ensures an adequate level of protection for the rights and freedoms of data subjects in relation to the processing of personal data.

Question: So what happens if I fail to abide by one of these Principles?

Answer: Failure to comply with a Data Protection Principle is not, in itself, a criminal offence, but the Information Commissioner can take action. The Information Commissioner can use an enforcement notice requiring a data controller to take, or refrain from taking, specified steps, or even to stop processing any personal data generally or data of a specified description or for a specified purpose.

Question: Tell me more about enforcement notices.

Answer: In an enforcement notice, the Information Commissioner will set out the Principle or Principles that he believes have been contravened, and the basis for the allegation. It will go on to stipulate the steps that the Information Commissioner requires to be taken, and the relevant time-period. Finally, it will remind the addressee of a right of appeal to the Data Protection Tribunal.

There is also a notice which the Information Commissioner can issue known as an 'information notice'. This notice requires information from the data controller so that the Information Commissioner can decide whether or not the data controller has complied with the Data Protection Principles. An appeal against an information notice can also be made to the Data Protection Tribunal.

Question: Supposing I do not agree with the notice from the Information Commissioner?

Answer: First, one could take the view that the enforcement notice is unfounded, and simply demand that the Information Commissioner brings a prosecution, where the Information Commissioner would have to prove his or her case in the normal way before the criminal courts. However, since the only defence open to the data controller is that he or she has exercised all due diligence to comply, or there is some legal defect in the notice, it is generally an unwise course. It would be more appropriate is to use the right of appeal under the 1998 Act to the Data Protection Tribunal, a course of action which will have been highlighted in the notice. The Tribunal consists of a legally qualified chairman, together with lay members, and was set up to consider appeals against the Information Commissioner's decision, and it can overturn the Information Commissioner's decision or substitute another decision, if it thinks that more appropriate.

Question: When can personal data be disclosed?

Answer: The principal situation in which data can be disclosed is where the disclosure is made in accordance with the Disclosures section of the data controller's notification entry, and the disclosure is not in breach of the first Data Protection Principle.

However, as we have seen, data can also be disclosed when it is required by law, or needed for an investigation into a potential criminal offence where a failure to disclose would be likely to prejudice the prevention or detection of crime. Disclosures can be made for the purpose of obtaining legal advice or in the course of legal proceedings in which the person making the disclosure is a party or a witness. They can also be made in emergencies where the disclosure is urgently required for preventing injury or other damage to anyone's health. Finally, disclosure is allowed where it is made to employees or agents of the data user and where the disclosure is made with the data subject's consent.

Question: I understand that the first Data Protection Principle, ie that data shall be processed fairly and lawfully, is the most significant one for direct marketing. Is this so?

Answer: Yes, in practice the first Data Protection Principle is the most important one for marketing interests and, in considering whether the Principle has been complied with, the Information Commissioner will take account of all the circumstances of the obtaining, and the method by which the information was obtained. The individual must be aware of the identity of the data controller, the purposes for which personal data are to be held or not, and the disclosures of personal data to third parties. Information is always regarded as having been obtained fairly if it is obtained from a person who is authorised by law to supply it. In other situations, the Information Commissioner will make a judgment by having regard to the method by which the information was obtained, including the question of whether or not any person who provided the information was deceived or misled as to the purpose or purposes for which it was to be held, used or disclosed.

In the case of *Innovations (Mail Order) Ltd v The Data Protection Registrar* [1993], a case heard before the Data Protection Tribunal, it was held that any non-obvious purpose or purposes for which the data is being collected should be made clear to the individual before the information is obtained. The Tribunal said that where information comprised names obtained for a particular purpose, and is subsequently used for another purpose that the data subjects were not told about, the data user must seek the positive consent of the data subjects if use is to be made of their data for that non-obvious purpose.

Question: Tell me more about the *Innovations* case.

Answer: The case related largely to the point at which consumers should be told of an intention by a mail order company to make use of names and addresses for list broking purposes. In this case, 'Innovations' included a note on an acceptance of order form to the effect that they made customer lists available to other companies, and that consumers could avoid further mailings by sending an exact copy of their address label to an address set out on the note.

The Data Protection Registrar, the predecessor of the Information Commissioner concluded that the notice should have been given to the data subject (ie the consumer, before his or her name and address were supplied in connection with the order). The Data Protection Tribunal agreed with the Registrar and made these comments:

> "We conclude that a later notice may be a commendable way of providing a further warning, but whether it does so or not, we conclude that the law requires in the circumstance we have here that when possible the warning must be before the obtaining.

> This can best be done by including the warning in the advertisement itself. Where it may not be possible (eg the use of existing names for a new purpose) we consider that the obligation to obtain the data subject's positive consent for the non-obvious use of their data falls upon the data user."

Question: How does one overcome the problem of a non-obvious purpose?

Answer: When personal information is collected, for example, as part of a sales promotion, it is clear that the information can be considered fairly obtained for the fulfillment of that promotion, and the Information Commissioner takes the view that, within reason, it should be obvious to an individual respondent that the data controller might use the personal data for future direct marketing of its own related goods and services. It was, after all, the reason for which the consumer gave their personal data. If, however, there is the intention of using the data for other mailings, or for transfer to third parties, then it is important to have an appropriate statement which informs the consumers that this will happen, and give them the option of saying no.

There is a growing use of data capture in promotions, and sometimes promotional techniques, such as draws, are used solely to incentivise data capture exercises. Normally, this is done by means of what is termed an 'opt-out box'. Something along the following lines is needed:

'From time to time we may pass your details to other companies so that they can write to you about their products or services. If you do not wish to receive such mailings, please tick this box.'

E-mail and text are treated differently—see later in the chapter.

Question: What about sensitive data?

Answer: There are certain pieces of information that are stated to be 'sensitive personal data' and processing of such material is tightly controlled. 'Sensitive data' is defined as information relating to racial or ethnic origin, political opinions, religious or other similar beliefs, membership of a trade union, physical or mental health, sex life and criminal records.

In relation to such data the data subject has to give explicit consent. Processing is also allowed in certain other situations, such as where it is necessary in relation to legal advice, medical purposes and the administration of justice. Regulations also permit the processing of sensitive personal data in relation to ten specific situations, including confidential counselling, insurance and pension payments, protection of the public from crime, political parties and research and archive material.

Question: What about host mailings?

Answer: There are a number of ways in which host mailings can arise in direct marketing—one of the most common being where a mail order trader inserts a third party's leaflet in mailings to its own customers. The Information Commissioner takes the view that, where personal data are used for 'package insert' host mailings and everyone receives the same insert, data users are not generally required to provide a notification. A notification is, however, needed if the host mailing is to be selective or if 'solus' host mailings are to be carried out.

Rights

Question: What rights are individuals given under the 1998 Act?

Answer: Perhaps the most important right is for the data subject to secure access, subject to limited exceptions, to the relevant data, on payment of a modest fee of up to £10. This enables data subjects to know what data is kept in respect of them.

Individuals have the right to prevent processing of personal data for the purposes of direct marketing—a right which we discuss below. Additionally, any person may ask the Information Commissioner to carry out an assessment of whether any processing of personal data has been carried out in compliance with the Act. Where the data subject believes data will be processed in a way that is likely to cause him or her damage or distress, the data subject can serve a 'data subject notice' on the data controller requiring the processing to cease or not to begin. If the data controller takes no action, the data subject can seek a court order.

In addition, a data subject can secure compensation from the courts for damage and associated distress caused by any contravention of the requirements of the 1998 Act entitling them to compensation. The court can also order the rectification, blocking or destruction of any data that has been the subject of a successful claim under this provision.

Finally, an individual may feel that the user of his or her data is in breach of one or more of the eight Data

Protection Principles and is entitled to complain to the Information Commissioner who can issue, in appropriate cases, an enforcement notice.

Question: Tell me about the right to prevent direct marketing?

Answer: An individual has the right, under the 1998 Act, to prevent direct marketing. To do this, an individual must send a notice in writing to a data controller asking for the processing of any personal data relating to him or her that is to be used for direct marketing purposes to cease. The data controller must comply, failing which the Information Commissioner can issue an enforcement notice on the basis that the data controller has breached the sixth Data Protection Principle.

Question: So what rights are conferred by The Privacy and Electronic Communications (EC Directive) Regulations 2003?

Answer: These Regulations provide for four basic rights:

(1) Private individuals must not receive direct marketing faxes without positive consent.

(2) There should be no telephone calls to private individuals if they have objected to receiving them.

(3) No direct marketing faxes should be sent to businesses if they have objected to receiving them.

(4) No e-mails or text marketing communications without positive consent.

Question: Tell me more about the position in respect of e-mail when used for direct marketing purposes—does there need to be an opt-in box?

Answer: Under The Privacy and Electronic Communications (EC Directive) Regulations 2003, a data subject must give express consent to the receipt of marketing communications by e-mail or text. That consent could be given by means of a box which must be ticked in order to opt-in to receiving such communications. This is not, however, necessary if it is made clear that by giving their e-mail address or mobile 'phone number, they will then receive future marketing communications. It must, however, be clear. Hiding a statement about future marketing communications within the small print will not suffice. It must be in close proximity to where an e-mail address is to be given. Alternatively, positive consent could be given by asking data subjects to click on an icon.

Question: What happens if they are existing customers?

Answer: You do not need prior consent if you have already obtained the recipients' e-mail or text details in the course of the sale or the negotiations for the sale of a product or service and the proposed marketing communications are in respect of similar products and services. However, every subsequent communication will have to have an opt-out facility. This exception to the normal rule is colloquially known as the 'Soft opt-in'.

Children

Question: Finally, what about data protection and children?

Answer: This is a sensitive area and one can only point to advice from the Information Commissioner. In his guidance, the Information Commissioner endorses the view that personal data must only be collected from children with the explicit and verifiable consent of the child's parent/guardian unless that child is 12 years or over, the information collected is restricted to that necessary to enable the child to be sent further, but limited, online communications and it is clear what is involved.

Additionally, as far as members of the Direct Marketing Association (DMA) are concerned, the DMA Code states:

'When collecting data in an online environment from minors under 16 years of age, members must secure consent from that minor's parent or guardian. When collecting data in an offline environment from minors under 14 years of age, members must secure consent from that minor's parent or guardian'.

As far as promotional activity is concerned, it is probably wise to say that parental consent is needed for those under 18. Indeed, such requirements are common in promotional rules and, apart from anything else, they demonstrate on the part of the promoter a socially responsible approach and one that lays marketing to children less open to criticism. Given the considerable opposition to marketing to children particularly in some European countries, that has to be a sensible approach.

Question: Has the Information Commissioner issued any advice about the situation where children are asked to provide information about a third party?

Answer: The Information Commissioner has given the following guidance:

> 'Sometimes children are asked to provide information about other people, for example their friends or family members. Generally you should only request such information for the purpose of obtaining parental consent. The Committee of Advertising Practice advises that children under 16 should never be asked to provide information about anyone else for marketing purposes. This is good advice, but more generally it is for organizations to assess the level of risk associated with asking a child to provide personal data about a third party. In some cases, the risk is low because the information collected is relatively innocuous, for example where a child provides another person's e-mail address to transmit a newsletter and where the address isn't retained or used for any other purpose.'

Question: How does the CAP Code approach this issue?

Answer: At the time of writing, CAP has agreed to amend the Code to add a new rule 10.16 which will read as follows:

'Marketers must not knowingly collect personal information about other people from children under 16 unless that information is the minimum required to make a recommendation for a product, is not used for a significantly different purpose from that originally consented to, and the marketer can demonstrate that the collection of that information was suitable for the age group targeted.'

Data about third parties collected from children must not be kept for longer than is necessary.

CHAPTER 6

INTELLECTUAL PROPERTY

Definitions

Question: What is 'intellectual property'?

Answer: Intellectual property is the name we give to the branch of law that covers copyright, trade marks and patents.

Question: What do we mean by 'copyright'?

Answer: Copyright is essentially a right of the creator of original material to control the reproduction of that material for as long as the material stays within copyright. Copyright exists basically in every original piece of literary, artistic, dramatic or musical work, and in sound recordings, films, television broadcasts, cable programmes and published editions.

Question: What is *not* subject to copyright protection?

Answer: The main exception to copyright protection is in respect of ideas and concepts. Although the tangible expression of an idea will be copyright, the idea itself is not copyright—although it may be protected in other ways, as we shall see later.

Another important exclusion from copyright protection relates to names, titles and slogans. In a well-known case early in the last century, no copyright was held to subsist in the slogan 'Beauty is a social necessity, not a luxury' *(Sinanide v La Maison Kosmeo* [1928]). However, the possibility that, exceptionally, copyright might exist in slogans has been raised in the recent (2010) case of *NLA v Meltwater and PRCA.*

However, it is interesting to note that copyright does exist in such items as train timetables and football fixture lists, not so much on the basis of the originality of the information, but on the basis of the work involved in gathering and presenting the material.

Such documents are held to be compilations and the legislation specifically provides that they are subject to copyright protection as literary works.

Ownership of copyright

Question: Who owns the copyright and for how long?

Answer: The copyright belongs to the author of the copyright work, with the one exception that in the case of work created by employees in the course of their employment, the copyright belongs to their employer unless otherwise agreed. So, with work created in-house by employees of an advertising agency or sales promotion consultancy, the copyright would belong to the agency—but not work created by freelancers. The author of a work is normally the person who created it, though the rules are different for films and sound recordings.

Copyright in literary, artistic, dramatic or musical works currently lasts for life of the author plus 70 years from the end of the calendar year in which the author dies.

Question: How do you copyright something?

Answer: It is a widely held belief that one can go through some process of registration and thereby 'copyright' a piece of work. However, in the UK there is no process of registration that needs to be undertaken because copyright protection arises automatically once a piece of work has been created to which copyright protection applies.

Question: I understand there are regulations on databases?

Answer: Yes. The Copyright and Rights in Databases Regulations 1997 provide that there is a copyright to protect the structure of a database so long as the database contents satisfy an 'intellectual creativity' test.

Separately, there is a database right to protect substantial work in obtaining, verifying or presenting the database contents. The right lasts for 15 years.

A recent High Court decision found that the annual fixture lists of the English and Scottish Premier Football Leagues are protected by database copyright.

Ideas and concepts

Question: The most valuable part of a promotion is often the idea or concept. Are you really saying that this cannot be protected?

Answer: As we have already seen, there is no copyright in an idea or concept, so copyright protection cannot be used to protect a creative idea. However, that does not mean that the idea is not capable of some protection by using other legal devices. The main way this can be done is by invoking what is known as the 'law of confidentiality'. The law requires the following aspects to be present:

(a) The circumstances in which the information was communicated import an obligation of confidence, in particular by making it clear to the other party that the material is copyright.

(b) The content of the idea is a clearly identifiable original, of potential commercial attractiveness and capable of reaching fruition.

This was well illustrated by what has become known as the *Rock Follies* case (*Fraser v Thames Television* [1983]). Three members of the pop group Rock Bottom went to Thames Television and outlined their ideas for a new television series. They did so in circumstances which made it clear that the ideas were being communicated in confidence and this was also tied-up in a contract by which Thames paid £500 for an option. Thames Television at that stage said they were not interested in the idea, but three years later a series was run by Thames Television based on the idea that had been presented to them. Since the ideas and concepts had been presented in circumstances that imposed a duty of confidentiality on Thames Television, the suit against them was successful and the three individuals were awarded damages of £500,000.

Question: What if the idea is commonplace?

Answer: There is an old saying, 'you can't make a silk purse out of a sow's ear'. In this context, it means you cannot make a promotional idea or concept confidential if it is very much public property. So the idea of an instant win promotion could not be made confidential, unless the proposed use was highly innovative or presented in a very original way.

Moral rights

Question: I have heard about 'moral rights'—what are they?

Answer: Moral rights belong to the author of a copyright literary, dramatic, musical or artistic work and to the director of a copyright film. Under the Copyright, Designs and Patents Act 1988, such rights cannot be assigned to anyone else, because they are personal rights. They can, however, be waived. So what are those moral rights?

(1)   *The right to be identified as author or director.* The right does not apply unless it has been asserted, either generally or specifically in relation to a particular use of the material. Such an assertion must be in writing, signed by the author or director or contained in a document that assigns the copyright.

There are a number of exceptions to this right, the most important of which, for agencies, is where use is made of copyright material by the copyright owner or with his or her consent, and where the copyright belongs to the author's or director's employer. In an agency situation, this would mean no moral rights would apply to employees and their work, provided that any usage was by the agency or with the agency's consent. Again, this would not include freelancers, and in their case agencies need to think about waivers of moral rights.

(2) *The right to object to derogatory treatment of work.* The law provides that an author or film director has the right not to have his or her work subjected to derogatory treatment. What does this mean?

(a) 'Treatment' means any addition to, deletion from or alteration to, or adaptation of the work, other than a translation of a literary or dramatic work, or an arrangement or transcription of a musical work involving no more than a change of key or register.

(b) 'Derogatory' means any treatment that amounts to distortion or mutilation of the work, or is otherwise prejudicial to the honour or reputation of the author or director.

The right to object to derogatory treatment of work will not apply to employees unless they were identified at the time of the derogatory treatment or were previously identified in or on published copies of the work.

Practical issues

Question: What must I consider in relation to copyright?

Answer: First, you must remember that most creative material will be copyright and, except for material created in-house in the course of employment, it will be necessary to make sure that the necessary assignments or usage licences are obtained. Also, you must remember to secure waivers of moral rights in respect of externally commissioned creative work.

Secondly, you need to protect your own creative material. As I have said, material is either subject to copyright protection or it is not. However, there are certain steps that one can take to reinforce one's claim to ownership of the copyright. It is important to keep copies of original drawings and other original creative material, in order to be ready for any challenge on ownership. It is also advisable to consider putting a 'C' in a circle and the word 'Copyright' against it and perhaps the name of the copyright owner and the date; this should be used as a way of indicating that a particular piece of material is copyright and to act as something of a warning that the copyright owner will be likely to protect their interests.

Trade marks

Question: Where do trade marks fit in?

Answer: Under the Trade Marks Act 1994 (the 1994 Act), registration is possible for 'any sign capable of being represented graphically which is capable of distinguishing goods or services of one undertaking from those of other undertakings'.

The possibilities for registration under the 1994 Act are extensive.

Under the 1994 Act, the following can be registered: sounds, shapes, slogans and smells. Slogans will only be registered where they can be shown to be distinctive. Most slogans are not distinctive and never will be because they are, to coin a phrase, 'here today, gone tomorrow'. And one should remember that it is no use going through the time and expense of an application for trade mark registration if the likelihood is that a new slogan will be in use by the time the procedural formalities have been completed.

The 1994 Act has a provision that allows unauthorised use of a registered trade mark where it is used for identification purposes, so long as it is in accordance with honest industrial and commercial practices. This is a provision designed to facilitate comparative advertising.

Question: Do we have any decisions from the courts on when the use of trade marks for identifying the goods of another trader is to be regarded as acceptable?

Answer: A series of cases have thrown up robust decisions from the courts. In *Barclays Bank Plc v RBS Advanta* [1996], Barclays Bank attempted to stop a comparative advertisement relating to credit cards and interest rates. The court took the view that the facts as stated were correct, the advertisement was not misleading to the people to whom it was addressed, and therefore the use of the trade mark was in accordance with honest industrial practices.

In the case of *Vodafone Group Plc v Orange Personal Communications Services Ltd* [1997], the claimant sued over the use of their trade mark in an advertisement which claimed that Orange users saved £20 over Vodafone's tariffs. The court concluded that the comparison was a fair one and not misleading. The trade mark infringement claim therefore failed.

Accordingly, one can say with some confidence that the use of other companies' trade marks will be allowed unless it is in the context of an unfair and misleading advertisement.

Question: When can trade marks be used?

Answer:
(a) The most obvious circumstance in which a registered trade mark can be used is where there is permission or authority to use the mark. Sometimes that will be express permission, although there are many circumstances in which there is implied consent. For example, if the purpose of a promotion is to promote the sales of the goods which have the mark on them, then it is reasonable to assume that there is implied permission for that exposure and use of the mark because it is necessary to assist in the marketing of the relevant goods.

(b) As we have seen already, a trade mark can be used to identify the goods or services of another, but it must be in accordance with honest industrial or commercial practices. If not, the use will be treated as infringing the trade mark if the use takes unfair advantage of, or is detrimental to, the distinctive character or repute of the mark.

Question: How can I check out trade marks?

Answer: If there is any doubt about whether a mark is registered, then the easiest course is to go online to the

Patents Office website (www.patent.gov.uk) and do a search. Alternatively, one can ask a trade mark agent to conduct a search and prepare a report. The existence of an 'R' in a circle will indicate a registered mark—to use such a device when a mark is not registered is a criminal offence. Sometimes, one will see the letters 'TM' in a circle. This indicates an unregistered or common law trade mark. As long as there is no confusion, there is little the owner of an unregistered trade mark can do to stop unauthorised use.

Question: What are the consequences of an infringement of copyright or registered trade mark?

Answer: Damages are possible as compensation for an infringement of copyright or a registered trade mark although, if the damage suffered is relatively slight in commercial terms, it is unlikely that the amount of damages that a court would award would make it worthwhile pursuing a case to full trial. In most cases, the only remedy worth having for an infringement of copyright or a registered trade mark is an injunction, which puts an end to the relevant infringement. An application for an injunction can be made before a full trial but, if the application for an injunction is unsuccessful, in most cases the matter does not proceed to a full hearing.

Patents

Question: What are patents?

Answer: Patents were first granted in the reign of Elizabeth I to facilitate the growth of new industries. Patents encourage industrial innovation by giving the inventor of an industrial technique a monopoly right to exploit that invention for a period of 20 years—after which the invention is considered to be in the public domain.

However, patent protection does not protect innovative design but only the essential function.

Question: When do patents become relevant?

Answer: 1.   In relation to the production of promotional mer-
                    chandise, it is important to make sure that no
                    existing patents are infringed. This is particularly
                    important given the widespread importation of
                    promotional merchandise from countries in the
                    Far East, such as China and Korea.

               2.   Occasionally, in developing a new promotional
                    technique or developing a novel way of present-
                    ing an existing promotional technique, a device
                    is produced which is patentable. One example
                    that has come my way over the years is related to
                    a drinks can with a device that enabled money
                    to pop out when winning cans were opened. This
                    was an invention, and an application was made
                    to patent this device. This does not happen very
                    often, but sales promotion practitioners should
                    be aware of the possibility.

CHAPTER 7

PRICE PROMOTIONS AND PRICE CLAIMS

Introduction

Question: Where is the law on price claims to be found?

Answer: The relevant law covering price promotions and price claims is to be found principally in The Consumer Protection from Unfair Trading Regulations 2008. The Regulations have introduced a general prohibition on traders in all sectors engaging in unfair commercial practices against consumers—providing a comprehensive framework for dealing with sharp practices and rogue traders who have in the past set out to exploit loopholes in existing legislation.

The Regulations achieve their objective by introducing a general prohibition on traders not to treat consumers unfairly and by banning misleading actions, misleading omissions, aggressive practices and a number of specific prohibited practices listed in Sch 1 to the Regulations.

There are three categories of Unfair Commercial Practices.

(1) Those that are always unfair in all circumstances. This involves 31 practices that are delineated in the Schedule to the Regulations.

(2) Those that are unfair if they cause or are likely to cause the average consumer to take a transactional decision they would not have taken otherwise as a result of a misleading action or false information, a misleading omission, such as leaving out key information or an aggressive practice such as persistent sales calls.

(3) Those that are generally unfair if, contrary to the requirements of professional diligence (the standard of special skill and care which one may reasonably expect from that trader) and also the situation where the practice materially distorts, or is likely to distort, the economic behaviour of the average consumer.

Question: Are there any banned practices in Sch 1 that are relevant to price promotions and price claims?

Answer: Yes. The following practices are relevant:

(1) Making an invitation to purchase products at a specified price without disclosing the existence of any reasonable grounds the trader may have for believing that he will not be able to offer for supply, or to procure another trader to supply, those products or equivalent products at that price for a period that is and in quantities that are, reasonable having regard to the product, the scale of advertising of the product and the price offered (bait advertising).

(2) Making an invitation to purchase products at a specified price and then—

(a) refusing to show the advertised item to consumers;

(b) refusing to take orders for it or deliver it within a reasonable time; or

(c) demonstrating a defective sample of it,

(d) with the intention of promoting a different product (bait and switch).

(3) Falsely stating that a product will only be available for a very limited time, or that it will only be available on particular terms for a very limited time, in order to elicit an immediate decision and deprive consumers of sufficient opportunity or time to make an informed choice.

Question: I understand there has been an issue over free gifts with purchase?

Answer: It was the author's view that the wording of banned practice number 20 effectively outlaws free gifts with purchase and there are member states of the European Union who take the same view.

However, the authorities, including the European Commission, appear to be taking the view that this doesn't eliminate free gifts with purchase and this now seems to have been borne out by one of the three cases this year before the European Court of Justice concerning the interpretation of the Unfair Commercial Practices Directive.

The Office of Fair Trading and the British Government support this view and given that the new edition of the British Code of Advertising, Sales Promotion and Direct Marketing proceeds on the basis that free gifts with purchase remain legal, there is no need in practice to take a different view at the present time.

Question: What has happened to the Code of Practice for Traders on Price Indications last issued in 2005?

Answer: Under the old law, the Code had a specific status, which allowed its provisions to be taken into consideration in the event of a prosecution. That status has now been removed and under the 2008 Regulations the Code has no official status. However, it still exists and in the author's view provides a most useful guide to making price claims. It is certainly true to say that anyone complying with the Code is extremely unlikely to fall foul of the 2008 Regulations because everything in the Code is designed to help business to create fair and meaningful price indications.

Indications that a price is less than it actually is

Question: We have often heard of self-service retailers being prosecuted for selling goods at a higher price than indicated. Is that an offence and can it affect goods subject to promotions?

Answer: The offence of charging a higher price at the checkout than appears on the goods or on a shelf-edge marker is one of the oldest pricing problems for retailers. It is known in the trade as 'buncing'. It was first prohibited by the Trade Descriptions Act 1968 and since then many retailers have fallen foul of it. Rarely is it done deliberately; most often it is simply carelessness in failing to alter marked prices or barcodes on old stock when prices are increased. Charging a higher price than is suggested by the price indication would clearly contravene the 2008 Regulations.

Question: How can incentive goods be caught by the suggestion that the price is less than it actually is?

Answer: It is most likely to arise where prices have changed immediately before or after a promotion with stock of the promoted goods remaining on display simultaneously with standard non-promoted packs. It is basically a question of controlled stock rotation.

Reductions from a previous price

Question: How can genuine reductions in prices be indicated?

Answer: This is the most straightforward of all price comparisons, provided it complies with the following basic rules:

(a) the higher and the reduced price must be shown;

(b) the higher price must be the last price at which the goods were offered in the previous six months;

(c) the product should have been available to consumers at the higher price for at least 28 days in the preceding six months;*

(d) the previous price should have been offered for that period at the same shop where the reduced price is now being offered.

* *Note:* The 28-day rule does not apply to food and drink or non-food perishables if they have a shelf life of less than six weeks.

For full guidance as to reduced prices, see para 1.2 of the Prices Code (in **Appendix 2** below).

Question: If it is impossible to satisfy these rules, can a disclaimer be used?

Answer: To avoid committing an offence, positive statements rather than disclaimers are required in order that price comparisons be fair and reasonable.

Question: (a) What positive statement would suffice if the 28-day rule had not been complied with?

(b) What positive statement would suffice if the goods had not been previously offered at the higher price in the same shop?

Answer: (a) The actual period during which the higher price had been on offer should be stated (eg 'SALE: £25—Previous price £30—Offered from 1 to 15 December')*

(b) An indication of the shops where they had been offered is required (eg 'These goods were on sale at the higher price in our five largest stores)*

* Note: These examples of positive statements would not be acceptable in all cases. If, to take an extreme case, a higher price had only been on offer for a very short period indeed (say, one hour), the price indication may be misleading even though a positive statement had been made. The same might be the case if a very large company with 300 stores had offered the goods at the higher price in only one or two of those stores. In all cases the comparison must be fair and reasonable, notwithstanding the use of positive statements.

Question: How do these rules apply to catalogue or mail order traders?

Answer: Any comparison with a previous price should be with the price in the trader's own last issued catalogue, advertisement or leaflet. If the product is offered in both catalogues etc and shops, the higher price should be the last price at which the goods were offered. In all other respects the rules given above apply.

Question: Can we offer a series of reductions on the same goods?

Answer: Yes. The Prices Code makes allowance for circumstances where it is wished to make further reductions during the same sale or special offer period. Only the highest price need comply with the 28-day rule. See para 1.2.6 of the Prices Code (in **APPENDIX 2** below).

Question: Are there any restrictions as to how a genuine previous price must be indicated?

Answer: The expressions used must be clear. Thus 'normal price', 'regular price' or 'usual price' should not be used alone. They should be qualified to show that they are the seller's own previous price (eg 'our normal price').

Question: I understand there has been a recent case involving the Officer's Club in which previous prices was an issue. What does it tell us?

Answer: In this case, the retailer's own price discount advertisements took the general form of '70% off everything'. The court found that the advertisements were misleading as the higher prices used for the basis of the comparison were not, in the court's opinion, genuine higher prices. As a result of this case, the Office of Fair Trading (OFT) has advised that to be genuine, a higher price must satisfy the following criteria:

●   The seller must honestly believe that the price is an appropriate sale price for the goods. In other words, he must honestly believe that the goods could be sold in significant numbers at that price.

●   The seller must have placed a significant quantity of the goods on sale at the higher price. In this context, this involves a snapshot comparison at a particular moment in time between what had previously been offered for sale at the higher price and what at that later snapshot moment was offered for sale at the discounted price.

- The goods must be offered for sale at the higher price for a period at least sufficient to be a genuine offer of sale to the section of the public likely to be interested in purchasing such goods, that is, sufficient time for knowledge of the availability of the goods to be acquired by that section of the public, and sufficient time for them to view the goods, make up their minds whether to purchase them, and, if so, to complete the purchase of them.

'Significant quantity' and 'sufficient time' are not defined but the OFT says that this will allow retailers, regulators and the courts to apply a commonsense judgment.

Recommended prices

Question: Can we compare our selling prices with genuine manufacturers' recommended prices?

Answer: Yes, provided you comply with the following rules:

(a) Initials or abbreviations may not be used except for 'RRP' to describe a recommended retail price and 'man rec price' to indicate a manufacturer's recommended price. In all other cases the basis of the comparison with a recommended price must be spelt out in full.

(b) The recommended price must have been recommended to the retailer by the manufacturer or supplier as a price at which the product might be sold to consumers.

(c) The retailer must deal with the manufacturer or supplier on normal commercial terms.

(d) The recommended price is not significantly higher than prices at which the product is generally sold at the time the comparison is first made.

Question: How can we judge whether a recommended price is not significantly higher than prices at which the product is generally sold?

Answer: Commonsense is the best guide to what is a reasona-
                ble recommended price, particularly when supported
                by a survey of prices charged for comparable goods.

Question: What is the difference between a 'recommended
                price' and 'resale price maintenance'?

Answer: Resale price maintenance occurs when a manufac-
                turer or supplier seeks to compel retailers to sell goods
                supplied to them at a minimum price. The Competition
                Act 1998 makes such practices unlawful. Whenever a
                manufacturer or supplier wishes to recommend retail
                selling prices it must make it clear that it is merely a
                recommendation and not a minimum price.

Question: It is often the case that manufacturers print a sell-
                ing price on packs. How can a retailer sell below
                that price if he does not wish to obliterate it from the
                pack?

Answer: The Prices Code recognises this problem and pro-
                vides that such printed prices may be regarded as
                recommended prices by the retailer without the need
                to indicate that they are recommended prices. The
                retailer is therefore free to offer the goods at a lower
                price and to mark that lower price on the packs with-
                out first obliterating the manufacturer's marked price.
                This does not apply to retailers' own-label packs.

Question: Are there any bans on RRPs?

Answer: The Restrictions on Agreements and Conduct (Speci-
                fied Domestic Electrical Goods) Order 1998 prohib-
                its suppliers from notifying RRPs to dealers in respect
                of camcorders, dishwashers, freezers, fridges, hi-fi
                systems, tumble dryers, televisions, video cassette
                recorders and washing machines. For Prices Code
                requirements as to recommended prices, see paras
                1.6 and 1.7 thereof (in **Appendix 2** below).

Introductory offers

Question: Introductory offers are important for the launching of
                new products or businesses. What are the rules?

Answer: A promotion must not be called an introductory offer unless it is the intention to continue to offer the product for sale after the offer period is over and at a higher price. The offer must have a reasonably short life or it could become misleading to call it an intro-ductory offer. The period may vary depending on the nature of the product and its shelf life. It is, however, very unlikely that an offer would be deemed to be misleading if an expiry date is given and the price that will pertain after that date is quoted.

However, the Prices Code suggests that an after-promotion price should only be given if the trader is certain that, subject only to circumstances beyond its control, identical products will continue to be offered at the higher price for at least 28 days in the three months after the end of the offer period or after the offer stocks run out. This suggestion has been criticised because the purpose of many introductory offers is to test public response to a new product and if demand is heavy it may be impossible to honour the 28-day period. It must be assumed, until a court rules otherwise, that heavy and unexpected demand would be deemed to be circumstances beyond con-trol.

Question: If demand is lower than expected may an introduc-tory offer be extended?

Answer: Yes. The Prices Code requires a positive statement such as 'Extended for a further two weeks until 1 June' to make it clear that the period has been extended.

For the suggestions as to introductory offers, see para 1.3 of the Prices Code (in **APPENDIX 2** below).

Question: Can we avoid the rules on introductory offers by call-ing the offer an 'after-promotion price'?

Answer: No, the rules are the same for both types of pro-motion. It is also necessary to state in full what is meant whenever future prices are quoted (ie 'after-sale price' not 'ASP' and 'after-promotion price' not 'APP').

Comparisons with other traders' prices

Question: Can comparisons be made with other traders' prices?

Answer: The government recognises that competition in the market is beneficial to consumers and it is therefore necessary to permit fair comparisons with other traders' prices. The Prices Code, however, makes it difficult to do so without risking the commission of an offence. The rules are:

(a)   The quoted 'other trader's price' must be accurate and up-to-date. This is nearly impossible to achieve because as soon as the other trader learns of the comparison it is likely to reduce its price, thereby making the comparison misleading.

(b)   The name of the other trader must be clearly and prominently stated with the price comparison.

(c)   The shop where the other trader's price applies must be identified if the other trader is in fact trading from a shop.

(d)   The other trader's price must relate to the same products or substantially similar products. Any differences between the products must be stated clearly.

Question: Can general statements about prices charged by other traders be made?

Answer: The Prices Code refers to price promise statements such as 'If you can buy this product elsewhere for less, we will refund the difference', and requires that such statements should not be made in relation to 'own-brand' products which other traders do not stock unless the offer will also apply to other traders' equivalent goods. Further, if there are any conditions attached to such offers they must be clearly stated.

Comparisons with other traders' prices are always difficult and, to some extent, dangerous. They are more likely to succeed in relation to mail order offers where the other traders' prices are quoted in a catalogue and cannot be easily changed.

Question: Are there any other problems with comparisons with other traders' prices?

Answer: If another trader's price is incorrectly stated, not only would the trader making the comparison face the possibility of criminal proceedings but the offended trader may sue for damages for loss of business. It is a technique that should be used with the greatest care.

'Basket of goods' comparisons can create problems where one retailer compares a range of its goods with those of another retailer. In such cases, it is important to make sure that one is comparing like with like. It is also important to make it clear when the comparison was made. Prices change quickly and the comparison needs to be presented as a snapshot in time. Guidance on 'basket of goods' comparisons can be obtained from the Committee of Advertising Practice Copy Advice Service.

References to value or worth

Question: What about general statements concerning the value or worth of goods offered?

Answer: The Prices Code prohibits comparisons of selling prices with amounts described only as 'worth' or 'value'. General advertising slogans and statements about general trading practice, such as 'Low prices is our policy', or innocuous statements such as 'Unbeatable value' or 'The greatest value in town' are considered to be advertisers' puffery and are not seen as price claims.

The test to be considered in each case is whether the slogan or words used are likely to suggest a comparison with another price in the minds of consumers. All price comparisons should be capable of substantiation.

Sales and special events

Question: In a 'sale' is it necessary that all goods offered should have been previously offered at a higher price?

Answer: There is nothing to prevent reduced goods being sold side-by-side with other goods that have not been reduced or further goods which have been brought in specially for the sale, provided that each group of goods is clearly identified. Goods which have been reduced should be marked with the original higher price; the reduced price; and be distinguished from other goods which have not been reduced. Merchandise being sold at its normal price should be separately displayed so that there can be no doubt that it is not a part of the sale. Goods brought in for the event should be marked 'special purchase' or something similar, and should not be double priced.

Question: Is it in order to use general price statements such as 'half-marked price'?

Answer: Yes, provided you also indicate the higher and lower prices on each item of merchandise and take care that all reductions are in fact at least 50%.

Question: What about statements such as 'up to 50% off?

Answer: The Prices Code requires that at least 10% of the range of products on offer should have been reduced by 50%. For sales and special events, see para 1.9 of the Prices Code (in **APPENDIX 2** below).

Price comparisons in different circumstances

Question: Is it still permitted to quote different prices for different quantities of goods?

Answer: Yes. You can offer, for example, '£1 each, 4 for £3.50'.

Question: What about different prices for goods in different condition?

Answer: It is acceptable to quote 'Seconds £20, when perfect £30' etc. The 'when perfect' price should have been previously charged by the trader concerned and the 28-day rule and the rules as to different shops should be followed. If the 'when perfect' price is a recommended price, then the rules on recommended prices should be followed and, if it is another trader's price, then the rules on comparisons with other traders' prices should be followed.

Question: Can different prices be charged depending on the availability of the goods?

Answer: It is in order to quote different prices such as 'Price £50—when specially ordered £60'. The test is whether the different circumstances are clearly stated.

Question: What are the rules for different prices for goods in a different state?

Answer: This usually applies to goods available both in kit-form and ready-assembled form. The rules are that it is in order to quote 'Price in kit-form £50, price ready assembled £70', but the Prices Code suggests that one-third of the total stock should be in the different state (eg one-third ready assembled and two-thirds in kit-form, or vice versa, in the same shop). If another trader's price for one or other of the different states is being used as a basis for comparison, then the rules on comparisons with other traders' prices should be followed.

Question: Is it still in order to quote different prices for different groups of people?

Answer: Yes, this is another principle that has not been changed. It is in order to quote, for example, 'Senior citizens' price £2.50—others £5'. The Prices Code, however, gives further advice by stating that words such as 'our normal price' or 'our regular price' should not be used to describe the higher price unless it applies to at least half of the trader's customers.

For Prices Code requirements as to different circumstances see para 1.4 (in **APPENDIX 2** below).

Post, packing and ancillary charges

Question: Must prices quoted to consumers always include postage, packing and other ancillary charges?

Answer: Yes. The Prices Code is quite specific about this and
                it applies to mail order traders and shops that offer
                a delivery service (see paras 2.2.4 and 2.2.5 of the
                Prices Code in **APPENDIX 2** below). The Price Mark-
                ing Order 2004 requires prices to be all-inclusive of
                non-optional ancillary charges, or for their cost to be
                clearly shown.

VAT

Question: Do the same rules apply to VAT-inclusive prices?

Answer: Where transactions with consumers are concerned,
                all quoted prices should be VAT-inclusive. For busi-
                ness contracts see para 2.2.8 of the Prices Code (see
                APPENDIX 2 below). If rates of VAT should change, the
                correct VAT-inclusive price should be communicated
                to consumers before they are committed to a pur-
                chase. As with ancillary charges, the Price Marking
                Order 2004 requires consumer prices to be shown
                inclusive of VAT and other taxes.

Mail order trade

Question: How long do prices in mail order catalogues remain
                current?

Answer: The Prices Code is quite specific that prices that
                are correct at the time they are given can become
                misleading later and thus constitute an offence. This
                applies if consumers could reasonably be expected
                still to be relying on prices quoted in catalogues and
                the mail order trader had not taken all reasonable
                steps to prevent them from doing so.

                Consequently, if prices stated in a current catalogue
                have to be changed, the very least which should be
                done is to ensure that anyone who orders goods at
                the old price is advised of the new price before being
                committed to the purchase. See para 3.1 of the Prices
                Code (in **APPENDIX 2** below).

Newspaper and magazine advertisements

Question: For how long are prices quoted in newspaper and magazine advertisements expected to remain current?

Answer: The Prices Code suggests that the period should be a reasonable one and generally not less than seven days. Much would depend on the frequency of publication and whether any indication of possible changes in price was given in the advertisement. See para 3.2 of the Prices Code (in **APPENDIX 2** below).

Method of payment

Question: What is the position with prices when people pay with credit cards?

Answer: A trader does not have to charge the same price to cash and credit card customers. However, if the price varies depending on the method of payment, the Price Indications (Method of Payment) Regulations 1991 require that a clear explanatory statement be given.

Vouchers and coupons

Question: What are the rules about offering vouchers or coupons as an alternative to price promotions?

Answer: The offer of vouchers, coupons, container attachments etc is a useful alternative to direct reductions in price or comparisons with other prices. It is only in certain very unlikely circumstances that there could be a breach of criminal law in relation to a coupon etc promotion. For example, if a collection of a number of bottle tops were offered as a discount against the price of a further purchase of the product and that discount was not honoured, it could be argued that there was an offence in that there was a misleading indication of the price to be paid for the further purchase. To the best of my knowledge, there has never been such a case but it is possible that such an offence could be committed.

One must also remember that regard must be had to the provisions of the British Code of Advertising, Sales Promotion and Direct Marketing which requires that the following should be easily seen and understood by consumers:

(a)   the method of making use of the opportunity presented by the sales promotion, or of obtaining the goods, services, facilities or refunds on offer;

(b)   the nature and number of any proofs of purchase required; and

(c)   the cost and conditions of participation in the promotion, including methods of payment and amounts of any additional postage or delivery charges.

Any instructions as to how a consumer may participate in a sales promotion should give the full name of the promoter and the address at which it can be contacted during normal business hours. When such instructions require participants to detach and return a response coupon, the address of the promoter should appear in the material which can be retained by the participant.

There are notes for guidance on best practice in respect of coupons from the Institute of Promotional Marketing and endorsed by all the key organisations concerned with the creation and use of coupons. These notes for guidance are set out as APPENDIX 3 below.

CHAPTER 8

FREE AND EXTRA VALUE INCENTIVES

This chapter deals with the offer of free additional goods or services and extra value offers, such as additional quantity in the pack.

Free offers

Question: If goods or services are offered 'free' does this mean that they must be wholly free or can minor ancillary charges, such as postage and packing, be made?

Answer: The unqualified use of the word 'free' in a promotion means that there can be no charges of any kind. The British Code of Advertising, Sales Promotion and Direct Marketing (the CAP Code) requires that offers should not be described as free if:

- the consumer has to pay packing, packaging, handling or administration charges for the 'free' product;

- the cost of response, including the price of a product that the consumer must buy to take advantage of the offer, has been increased, except where the increase results from factors that are unrelated to the cost of the promotion; or

- the quality of the product that the consumer must buy has been reduced.

In all cases, the consumer's liability for such costs should be made clear, and there should be no additional charges for packing or handling. Misleading statements about free offers may also be unlawful under the Consumer Protection from Unfair Trading Regulations 2008. The Code of Practice for Traders on Price Indications (the Price Indications Code) (see

CHAPTER 7) says that consumers should be told exactly what they must buy to get the free offer.

Question: Is it necessary to be specific about the finish dates for free offers?

Answer: Yes. The date on which free offers end should always be stated clearly in advertising material.

Question: The offer of free goods sometimes involves fitting the free goods before they can be used by consumers. How can misunderstandings about this be prevented?

Answer: By making it absolutely clear in the promotional material what is offered. A statement such as 'Special offer—windows fitted free' leaves the consumer in doubt as to whether the whole deal (ie windows and fitting) is free, or whether it is intended to offer free fitting only. If words such as 'Windows purchased during our special offer period will be fitted free' had been used, the problem would not arise.

Question: Sometimes goods are of a type rarely fitted by consumers themselves. Is it still necessary to make it clear that a free offer applies only where fitting is carried out?

Answer: Of course. The Advertising Standards Authority (ASA) has upheld complaints on this very point. In one case a buyer who responded to an advertisement stating 'Free offer—gas effect fire or equivalent fire-side items if you buy a design fireplace now' was refused the gas effect fire on the grounds that it only applied where the advertiser fitted the fireplace. The ASA upheld the complaint because the offer was not sufficiently specific. If the words 'fitted by us' had been added to the offer, all would have been well.

Question: Are there any other problematic areas in regard to free incentives?

Answer: One phenomenon has been the offer of such things as free travel and accommodation in relation to time-share business. By their very nature, such promotions tend to be rather complex and require very careful drafting to ensure that consumers can easily understand each feature of the offer. The offer of free travel and accommodation is now also subject to the Package Travel, Package Holidays and Package Tour Regulations 1992.

Question: Can a value be ascribed to free goods, such as 'A valuable set of wine glasses worth £40, free when you buy a case of Nuit St Georges'?

Answer: No. The Price Indications Code (see **APPENDIX 2**) says that where any value is ascribed to a free offer it must be done as if the free offer were itself being sold. This means that the trader would have to state its usual selling price for the free goods, a recommended price or another trader's price etc. Unsupportable references to 'worth' or 'value' would not be acceptable.

Extra value packs

Question: What are the rules about adding additional quantities to a standard pack of a product, and flashing '10% extra'?

Answer: This is entirely in order, provided that the additional quantity is included in the declaration of contents, if required. The additional quantity could also be indicated by a band around the top of the container which fairly represents 10% of the capacity of the standard pack.

Question: You refer to declarations of quantity above as being necessary 'if required'. Are such declarations not necessary on all packaged goods?

Answer: Regulations made under the Weights and Measures Act 1985 (the 1985 Act) provide that certain classes of goods must be marked with a statement of quantity, either by weight, volume, capacity, measurement, length or number, whilst others may be so marked if required. Yet, other goods are wholly exempt from such declarations or are partially so when packed with other goods or in multiple packs. If goods are marked with a declaration of quantity either because they must be or because the packer wishes to do so, that declaration must be for the net contents of the pack including the additional quantity. The presence of the additional quantity could be declared separately in addition to the statutory declaration, (eg '250g + 25g—now 275g').

Question: Are there any additional considerations if we wish to claim that the extra quantity is free?

Answer: It is necessary to ensure that there has been no recent increase in the price of the standard pack immediately before or coincidental with the introduction of the extra quantity pack so that an allegation that the price has been increased to pay for the additional quantity cannot be made. The extra quantity pack should be offered by each retailer at the same price as the standard pack; ideally that price should have prevailed for a continuous period of at least 28 days before the introduction of the extra quantity pack.

Question: What are the problems about offering extra quantity in products subject to prescribed pack ranges?

Answer: Where a product is required to be made up in prescribed pack sizes there is a danger that a pack with a certain amount extra may not fall into the next highest prescribed pack size. For example, biscuits are required to be made up in quantities of 100g, 125g, 150g, 200g, 250g, 300g or a multiple of 100g up to 5kg; packs of 85g or less are exempted. If it the decision was taken to offer 10% extra on a 250g pack, for example, the new pack would be 275g and that is not a permitted pack size. The pack would thus be unlawful. The only alternatives are to pack to the next prescribed size above the standard pack (ie 300g in the example given, thus offering 20% extra, or to offer a small pack of 25g banded to the standard pack, thus keeping the extra quantity to the desired 10%.

Question: Which products are subject to prescribed pack sizes?

Answer: Mainly foodstuffs, including these product categories: barley, rice and similar cereals, certain biscuits, bread, cereal breakfast foods, chocolate products, cocoa products, coffee and coffee mixtures, dried fruits, dried vegetables, edible fats, flour, honey, jams and similar products, jelly preserves, milk, molasses, syrup and treacle, oat products, pasta, potatoes, salt, sugar and tea.

It is recommended that professional advice be sought on all extra quantity promotions for products subject to prescribed pack sizes.

Multiple packs

Question: Are there any problems with the 'Get one extra free' or 'Three for the price of two', etc type of promotion with packs banded together?

Answer: The advice above about recent price increases should be observed. In multiple packs the compulsory labelling requirements of regulations made under the 1985 Act and/or the Food Safety Act 1990 should be borne in mind.

For food products it is necessary that the product name, the list of ingredients, the minimum durability date, the name and address of the packer or seller, the indication of origin and instructions for use or storage if required and the statement of quantity must be clearly visible. For non-foods the basic requirement is the statement of quantity but there are special additional labelling requirements in relation to cosmetics, medicinal products and certain dangerous products.

If all of the information required by law can be seen through the banding, all is well. If it cannot, then the information must be repeated on the banding or outer packaging. In most cases, it will be necessary to give an overall statement of quantity (eg '5 × 250g', in addition to the weight marking of '250g' on each individual pack).

CHAPTER 9

BRIBERY

Bribery legislation

Question: What legislation covers this field?

Answer: The legislation in this field has been comprehensively updated and consolidated into the Bribery Act 2010. This came into force in April 2011.

Question: What are the main offences under the Act?

Answer: There are two general offences:

(1) *Paying bribes.* This makes it an offence to offer or give a financial or other advantage with the intention of inducing the person receiving the advantage to perform a 'relevant function or activity' 'improperly' or to give that person some reward for doing so.

(2) *Receiving bribes.* As well as being an offence to offer or give a financial or other advantage, it is also an offence to receive a financial or other advantage with the intention that the 'relevant function or activity' should be performed 'improperly' in consequence.

Question: What is meant by 'relevant function or activity'?

Answer: This very wide term covers any function of a public nature and also any activity connected with a business.

Question: What is meant by improperly?

Answer: This has to be approached from the point of view of the standard one would reasonably expect in relation to the performance of the type of function or activity in question.

Question: I understand there is an offence affecting commercial organisations?

Answer: Yes, there is a new offence that increases the potential liability of a commercial organisation. It applies where a person who is associated with the relevant commercial organisation engages in bribery and the organisation cannot show that it had adequate procedures in place to prevent such conduct.

Question: What is meant by 'an associated person'?

Answer: This is another very wide term. It covers employees, agents of the commercial organisation and related third parties.

Lessening the risk

Question: How are commercial organisations to judge what is meant by 'adequate procedures'.

Answer: The Ministry of Justice has published guidance to help commercial organisations understand their responsibilities. In particular, the Ministry has drawn attention to the need for organisations to conduct a proper risk assessment.

Question: Does the value of the incentive make any difference?

Answer: In practice it does, because if the value is not significant it is unlikely to be sufficient to encourage an employee to disregard his or her employer's interests. Accordingly, small gifts such as Christmas bottles of spirits are usually acceptable, but they should be carefully monitored, with an eye to avoiding any hint of a calculated effort to secure business favours.

Question: Is there any action I can take to lessen the risk of trouble?

Answer: Yes. First, it will help considerably if the employer is made aware of the incentive and gives consent. It is hard to see how an offence would arise if the employer is made aware of the scheme and does not object.

Secondly, the terms of the incentive should state that participation is dependent on the participants having the permission of the senior management.

Thirdly, it is important to make sure that the incentive is delivered to the company address and not a private residence.

Fourthly, where possible the incentive should be presented as a corporate benefit rather than an individual one.

Prosecutions

Question: What are the penalties?

Answer: On conviction at the Crown Court, a person is liable to imprisonment for a term not exceeding ten years. A company convicted of failing to prevent bribery could receive an unlimited fine.

Question: Does the British Code of Advertising, Sales Promotion and Direct Marketing (the Code) have anything to say on this?

Answer: Yes. Rules 8.30–8.32 cover trade incentives and it sets out a number of important rules. The important principle in the Code is that no trade incentive to employees should be such as to cause any conflict with the duty of employees to their employer, and that participating employees should normally secure the prior agreement of the employer or responsible manager. Trade incentives should not compromise the obligation of those employees giving advice to the public to give honest advice. Finally, promoters should observe any procedures adopted by any companies for their employees—including any rules for participating in promotions.

Question: Are there any controls which directly apply to those working in procurement ?

Answer: Yes. Members of the Chartered Institute of Purchasing and Supply (CIPS) are required, as a condition

of membership, to comply with the Institute's Professional Code of Ethics, which is designed to ensure
that members never use their authority or office for
personal gain and continually seek to uphold and
enhance the purchasing and supply profession

Tax

Question: Are there any tax implications?

Answer: An additional concern for promoters devising trade
incentive schemes is the tax implications. Regard
should be had, for example, to s 577 of the Income
and Corporation Taxes Act 1988, which deals with
business entertaining expenses.

The terms of the incentive should make clear to participants that there may be a tax liability, and that
they should check their position.

Question: What about business gifts?

Answer: As we saw earlier, business gifts present the same
potential problems as incentives. One must use
common sense and consider certain factors, such as
the position and remuneration level of the recipient,
whether the recipient can provide business favours
for the donor, and whether the gift has a business use.

Note: See also 'Tax and VAT' in **CHAPTER 10**.

MISCELLANEOUS LEGAL ISSUES

Age discrimination

Question: What relevance does age discrimination have to promotional marketing?

Answer: The Equality Act 2010 prohibits direct or indirect age discrimination. In particular, the rules cover employment benefits, employment rules, or any other practices that have the effect, without objective justification, of discriminating against people of a particular age. This has a particular relevance to incentive or motivation schemes.

Question: What about loyalty incentives?

Answer: The Act allows genuine schemes to continue which reward loyalty and experience and motivate staff. Their existence would not, therefore, constitute *unlawful* discrimination. However, any benefits offered under such schemes should not suggest an intention to discriminate on the basis of age.

Question: What action should I take to avoid contravening the law?

Answer: Companies should have a policy that relates to all anti-discrimination law. That policy should ensure that the range of benefits on offer do not unwittingly, and without objective justification, discriminate in favour of a particular age group. In most cases, this will be a matter of commonsense. For example, a company whose loyalty benefits consisted wholly or largely of extreme sports activities might be seen to have discriminated indirectly against older employees. Help and advice can be obtained from the Advisory Conciliation and Arbitration Service (ACAS). It can be contacted on 08457 474747.

Charity promotions

Question: Is there any special legislation affecting charity promotions?

Answer: Charity promotions are affected by the Charities Act 1992 (as amended by the Charities Act 2006) and the Charitable Institutions (Fundraising) Regulations 1994. There are a number of implications for promoters, or commercial participators, as they are styled in the legislation. In any promotion that represents that charitable contributions are to be made, there has to be a clear statement indicating:

(a) the name or names of the institution or institutions concerned;

(b) if there is more than one institution concerned, the proportions in which the institutions are respectively to benefit; and

(c) (in general terms) the method by which it is to be determined as the case may require:

- what proportion of the consideration given for goods or services sold or supplied by him, or of any other proceeds of a promotional venture undertaken by him, is to be given to or applied for the benefit of the institution or institutions concerned, or

- what sums by way of donations by him in connection with the sale or supply of any such goods or services are to be so given or applied,

as the case may require.

The 1994 Regulations require a comprehensive written agreement between the charity and the promoter, covering all aspects of the promotion, including how the charity is to benefit and the obligations of the promoter.

Companies Act 2006

Question: Surely companies' legislation has nothing to tell us about the legality of sales promotion schemes?

Answer: Yes, it does. Although the Companies Act 2006 cannot be thought of as mainstream sales promotion legislation, it does have its implications. Section 82 of the Act provides power for the Secretary of State to make regulations requiring every company, *inter alia*, to include its name and specified information in specified documents and communications. Using these powers, the Secretary of State has made the Companies (Registrar, Languages and Trading Disclosures) Regulations 2006. The Regulations require all companies in the United Kingdom to include the following information on their websites and on electronic business letters and order forms:

- name of the UK registered company;

- place of registration;

- company registration number;

- registered office address.

This requirement extends to electronic business communications, the rules which have operated previously under the 1985 Act in respect of non-electronic communications.

Consumer credit

Question: How does consumer credit law control credit-linked promotions?

Answer: The Consumer Credit Act 1974, as amended by the Consumer Credit Act 2006 and the Regulations made thereunder include strict controls on advertising and other activities seeking business. The controls are as follows:

(a) it is an offence to advertise goods or services on credit when it is not intended also to offer them for cash;

(b) it is an offence to advertise credit facilities in a manner which is false or misleading in a material respect;

(c) where an advertiser commits one of the offences given above, the publisher of the advertisement, any person who devised the advertisement and any person who procured the advertisement are also, subject to certain defences and exemptions, liable to prosecution;

(d) it is an offence to canvass credit business off-trade premises;

(e) it is an offence to send a document to a minor inviting him or her to borrow money, obtain goods or services on credit, or to apply for information or advice on borrowing money.

Question: Most credit-linked promotions concern either a low or a no deposit credit deal or 0% interest finance. Are there any particular difficulties with this type of promotion?

Answer: Under the Consumer Credit (Advertisements) Regulations 2010, credit advertisements must give a fully representative example if the advertisement includes a rate of interest or an amount relating to the cost of the credit. The representative example has to comprise:

- the rate of interest, whether fixed, variable or both;

- the nature and amount of any other charge included in the total charge for credit;

- the total amount of credit;

- a representative annual percentage rate (APR);

- in the case of credit relating to a deferred payment for specific goods and services or land or other things, the cash price and the amount of any advance payment;

- except where the consumer credit agreement is an open-ended agreement, the duration of the agreement and the total amount payable by the debtor and the amount of each repayment of credit.

Question: Does the advertisement need to specify an address?

Answer: The advertisement needs to specify a postal address unless it is a television or radio advertisement, on the premises of a dealer or creditor (but not leaflets that can be taken away) and also excludes any advertisement that includes the name and address of a dealer, or which includes the name and address of a credit broker.

Question: Are there any requirements in terms of presentation?

Answer: Yes, every credit advertisement must be in plain and intelligible language, be easily legible—or audible in the case of radio advertisements, and also specify the name of the advertiser.

Disability discrimination

Question: Do I need to worry about the disability provisions of the Equality Act 2010?

Answer: The Equality Act 2010 makes it unlawful to discriminate against disabled persons in a number of ways. Discrimination is defined as the situation where, for reasons that relate to the disabled person's disability, he or she is treated less favourably than others. There is an exception where it can be shown that the treatment is justified by reference to a set of conditions.

Informational requirements in direct response advertisements

Question: In a mail order advertisement or in a self-liquidating offer, people do not have the opportunity to inspect the goods before purchase. What effect does that have?

Answer: This means that legislation will apply that requires the provision of certain consumer information. For example, the Textile Products (Indications of Fibre Content) Regulations 1986, as amended by the Textile Products (Indications of Fibre Content)(Amendment) Regulations 2008 and the Textile Products (Determination of Composition) Regulations 2008, require details of fibre content to be given on labels attached to a product so that they can be seen before purchase. Obviously, if one is ordering goods on the strength of an advertisement or a promotional leaflet one cannot inspect the goods first. Accordingly, under reg 6, one is required to give the information in the advertisement. The Regulation refers to advertisements 'intended for retail customers describing textile products with sufficient particularity to enable the products to be ordered by reference only to the description in the advertisement'.

The same regime applies to direct response advertisements for nightwear. The Nightwear (Safety) Regulations 1985 require such advertisements to give information about the flammability of the product advertised.

Major sporting events

Question: We have been told that we can no longer offer tickets to major sporting events if we are not official sponsors or licensees. Is this true?

Answer: It has been common in the past for promoters to offer tickets to major sporting events without a formal relationship with the event. Tickets could be bought from a number of sources and then made the centrepiece of a promotion. Except in relation to the Olympics (see below), the legal position has not changed but the practical environment has. This is as a result of increased litigiousness and the growth in official sponsorship and licensing. The position now is that, increasingly, the use of tickets from unauthorised sources will bring a challenge.

Question: Would any challenge be successful?

Answer: There is an absence of case law because the major events are generally unwilling to risk legal action in case they are unsuccessful. Far better from their point of view to exaggerate the legal rights available to event organisers and to bully as many promoters as possible who are running unauthorised promotions to pay some sort of licence fee. We do know, however, that in one case UEFA challenged a promotion involving a high street name and went so far as to go to court for an injunction. A central part of UEFA's argument was that the promoter was inducing a breach of contract. By approaching a person selling a ticket, the promoter was encouraging the seller to break the terms on which they had originally received the ticket, the point being that the official terms of ticket distribution forbade unauthorised use in promotions.

The case was never concluded because the promoter abandoned the promotion and settled the claim; the terms have been kept confidential.

Although the case never received a judicial ruling, it demonstrates an increased willingness by bodies such as UEFA to move beyond threats to actual court action. Therefore, the only safe advice to give the industry now is that no use should be made of tickets in a promotion unless they have been come by lawfully and their use is consistent with the terms under which the tickets were originally issued.

Question: Are there any other legal issues involved?

Answer: Yes. Use of tickets which are unauthorised, or indeed any promotion that dovetails into a major sporting event, raises several legal issues.

First, there is the possibility of a challenge on the grounds of passing off. Basically, the argument would be that the promotion amounts to a misleading representation of a connection in the course of business between the promoter and the event—most usually on the basis that people would think that the promoter must be an official sponsor or licensee.

Secondly, there is the risk of an action for breach of copyright if some design work is shown, which attracts copyright protection such as the logo of the event.

Thirdly, there is also the possibility of an action for trade mark infringement which would probably be run in association with a claim for passing off. If the advertisement is misleading, the promoter would not be allowed to rely on the exception for what I would call 'honest identification use' in s 10(6) of the Trade Marks Act 1994.

Question: What about the Olympic Games?

Answer: The Olympic Games is in a somewhat special position because it is the subject of specific legislation. First, there is the Olympic Symbol etc (Protection) Act 1995. No use whatsoever can be made of the Olympic symbol and the Olympic motto unless one is an official licensee. There are also certain 'protected words' including: Olympiad', 'Olympiads', 'Olympian', 'Olympians', 'Olympic', 'Olympics', Paralympic, Paralympics, Paralympian, Paralympians, Paralympiad, Paralympiads and any word similar to the foregoing. However, as long as the words are used in a way that fairly represents a connection with the Olympic Games and are presented honestly, the use of any of these words will not infringe the rights of the Olympics Association. This means that a hotel can describe itself as 'Handy for the Olympics'.

Secondly, we now have to contend with the London Olympic Games and Paralympic Games Act 2006 (the 2006 Act). This imposes a draconian regime on those who are not official sponsors or licensees.

Question: How does the 2006 Act affect promotions?

Answer: The Act prohibits any attempt to make, in the course of business, any representation in a manner likely to create in the public mind an association with the London Olympics. This is a wide concept and one likely to be interpreted widely. To reinforce this, there are a number of words, the use of which will raise the possibility that such an association has been created.

These words are in two groups, the first being 'games', 'Two Thousand and Twelve', '2012' and 'twenty twelve'. The second being 'gold', 'silver', 'bronze', 'London', 'medals', 'sponsor' and 'summer'.

Any combination of the expressions in the first group or any of the expressions in the second group when used with one or more expressions from the first group would give rise under the Act to the possibility of an infringement of the London Olympics Association Right. What this means is that it is going to become increasingly difficult for promoters to relate their promotions to the Olympic Games unless they are official sponsors or licensees.

Question: Can any further guidance be obtained?

Answer: The London Organising Committee of the Olympic Games (LOCOG) has issued very helpful guidance on the requirements in relation to the 2012 Olympics. In March 2010, they issued a publication entitled 'Brand Protection'.

Origin marking

Question: Must imported promotion goods be marked with an indication of origin?

Answer: No. However, where an indication is likely to create the impression that the goods were produced or manufactured in a country other than that in which they were manufactured or produced, that statement should include a statement of the country where they were in fact manufactured or produced.

These requirements also apply to goods offered free of charge by way of promotions.

Package holidays

Question: If we organise a package holiday within a promotion, does this raise any special problems?

Answer: Yes. In certain circumstances, a holiday arranged as part of the promotion will be subject to the Foreign Package Holidays (Tour Operators and Travel Agents) Order 2001. Under the Order, it is unlawful for travel agents to discriminate in the price charged for a foreign package holiday or to impose an additional charge for travel insurance for those who do not wish to buy insurance from that travel agent.

"'Travel agent" is defined as "a person who supplies or offers for supply a foreign package holiday put together by a tour operator"'. It will be seen that this definition potentially affects a number of those organising overseas travel arrangements as part of a promotion. They should take note of the most important lesson of the Order, which is that one should not make insurance from a particular supplier obligatory. It is however fine to require that the travellers concerned organise their own insurance.

Safety of promotional goods

Question: Are promotional goods subject to the law on consumer safety and if so, what are those laws?

Answer: Yes. The law on consumer safety is now contained in Pts I and II of the Consumer Protection Act 1987 (the 1987 Act), which has been extended by the General Product Safety Regulations 2005. That law relates to the 'supply' of dangerous goods, so goods offered free as incentives are subject to the law.

Part I of the 1987 Act imposes strict product liability. That means that any person who suffers damage to his or her person or to property can sue the producer of the product for unlimited damages without the need to prove the existence of a contract or negligence.

Part II of the Act, which has been amended by the General Product Safety Regulations 2005, requires that all consumer goods shall comply with the 'general safety requirement' (ie they shall be as safe as may be reasonably expected). Any producer or distributor who supplies goods contrary to the general safety requirement is liable to prosecution.

Question: Who is liable if a person is injured by an incentive product?

Answer: The producer or distributor is liable. Where a retailer offers own-label products, the retailer is deemed to be 'holding himself out to be the producer' and is liable, unless the retailer makes it clear that the product is supplied to, or manufactured for, him or her.

Question: Who is liable in respect of the general safety requirement?

Answer: The position is quite different from Part I of the Act. Failure to comply with the general safety requirement is a criminal offence and any producer or distributor who supplies consumer goods, offers or agrees to supply such goods, or exposes or possesses such goods for supply which then do not conform to the general safety requirement, is liable to prosecution.

Question: What is the general safety requirement?

Answer: Goods are deemed to fail to comply with the requirement if they are not reasonably safe, having regard to all the circumstances.

Tax and VAT

Question: What about tax implications?

Answer: There is a particular issue for incentive award schemes because the award is usually taxable. HM Revenue and Customs define an incentive award scheme as 'A way of rewarding employees and others with cash, goods or holidays rather than increases in pay.' They take a variety of forms and are usually linked to sales performance.

Question: How is tax liability arrived at?

Answer: In the case of cash awards, the amount chargeable to tax is the full amount of the award. For non-cash awards, the tax liability depends on the nature of the award. In the case of vouchers, the charge will be the cost to the provider of making the award.

Question: What if the employer or third party wishes to absorb the tax?

Answer: An arrangement can be made called a 'Taxed award scheme' in which it is agreed to pay the tax on a grossed-up basis.

Question: How do I find out more?

Answer: Readers may be interested to know that guidance can be obtained from HM Revenue and Customs Incentive Awards Unit, whose details are: 4th Floor, Trinity Bridge House, 2 Dearmans Place, Salford M3 5BH. Tel: 0161 261 3373.

Question: And VAT?

Answer: VAT is a complex subject in its own right, but it is worth mentioning the case of *Boots Company v The Commissioners of Customs and Excise* [1990]. The court decided that money-off coupons, obtained by consumers when they bought goods, are not a consideration when they are used to buy other goods. They are simply evidence of entitlement to a discount. Output VAT is therefore due only on the net amount that the consumer actually pays for the goods.

Tobacco advertising and promotion

Question: What is the position in respect of promotions for tobacco products?

Answer: The Tobacco Advertising and Promotion Act 2002 prohibits all advertising and promotion of tobacco products. There are very limited exceptions mainly applying to point of sale in relation to the premises of specialist tobacconists.

Alcohol promotions

Question: I believe there are restrictions on alcoholic drinks promotions that apply only in Scotland?

Answer: The devolved Government in Scotland has intro-
                 duced major restrictions on alcoholic drinks promo-
                 tions in relation to licenced premises. The relevant
                 provisions of the Licensing (Scotland) Act 2005 came
                 into operation on 1 September 2009.

Question: What is the main requirement of the Act?

Answer: The main requirement is that if the price of any alco-
                 hol sold on licenced premises is varied, that variation
                 must be brought into effect at the beginning of any
                 one period of licenced hours and cannot be varied
                 before the expiry of 72 hours from that time. This
                 also prevents any variation of the price of any other
                 alcohol sold on the premises during that period. This
                 means that if the licenced hours start from, say, 10
                 am, then that is the point at which the price must
                 be changed and that price must be maintained effec-
                 tively for three days for that alcohol product and for
                 all other alcohol products being sold on the licenced
                 premises.

Question: I understand there is a ban on 'irresponsible drinks
                 promotions'. How does the Act define 'irresponsible
                 drinks promotions'?

Answer: The Act specifies the following:

                 (1) Any drinks promotion involving an alcoholic
                     drink likely to appeal largely to persons under
                     the age of 18.

                 (2) The supply of an alcoholic drink free of charge or
                     at a reduced price on the purchase of one or more
                     drinks. This appears to outlaw Buy One, Get One
                     Free (BOGOF) and Two for the Price of One.

                 (3) Supplying free of charge or at a reduced price
                     one or more extra measures of an alcoholic drink
                     on the purchase of one or more measures of the
                     drink. This again would outlaw BOGOF's and
                     Two for the Price of One in relation to drinks
                     dispensed in measures.

                 (4) The supply of unlimited amounts of alcohol for
                     a fixed charge. This eliminates, for example,

charging £10 and inviting customers to then drink as much as they like.

(5) Encouraging a person to buy or consume a larger measure of alcohol than the person had otherwise intended to buy or consume. This would prevent people from being given a larger serving than that for which they initially asked.

(6) Basing a claim on the strength of any alcohol.

(7) Giving any sort of reward or encouragement to drink alcohol quickly. This may prevent certain collector-type mechanics where the number of points to be collected is significant and the time given to collect them is relatively short.

(8) Offering alcohol as a reward or prize unless it's in a sealed container to be consumed off the premises.

Question: I understand there are also restrictions affecting the retail trade?

Answer: Alcohol sold for consumption off the premises must be displayed in a single area which is agreed between the Licensing Board and the holder of the licence, or else a single area of the premises which is inaccessible to the public. If the area is one agreed with the Licensing Board, then no other product must be displayed with the alcoholic drinks, other than a non-alcoholic drink or an item packaged with an alcoholic drink which can only be purchased together with that drink.

Question: What is the role of the Portman Group?

Answer: The Portman Group, supported by the UK's leading drinks producers, is concerned with the social responsibility issues surrounding alcohol. It is responsible for a Code of Practice on the naming, packaging and promotion of alcoholic drinks (now in its fourth edition). The Portman Group's Code of Practice can be downloaded from its website: www.portmangroup.org.uk.

Using products in promotions

Question: Are there any risks in showing other company's products in a promotion?

Answer: Offering other company's products in promotions, particularly prize promotions, has been commonplace within the industry. However, as a result of an increased trend towards litigiousness, the use of other company's products within a promotion have to be seen as more risky today than before. The main risks are in relation to passing off and in relation to trade mark and copyright infringement.

Question: What are the copyright implications in showing another company's product?

Answer: Fortunately, s 51 of the Copyright, Designs and Patents Act 1988 tells us that it is not an infringement to copy an article if it has resulted from a design document or model recording or embodying the design. Since most products will start from a design document, it will not therefore normally be an infringement of copyright to feature such a product in a promotion. However, this does not apply to artistic works or to any surface decoration on the product. The product packaging will not be covered by s 51 nor will the logo of the company, which will also be a copyright work as well as possibly being a registered trade mark.

Question: Would it help if I took the brand name off the product?

Answer: In my view, one should only take the brand name off the product if in so doing the product looks like a generic item rather than one from a specific manufacturer; otherwise it may annoy the manufacturer to see that their brand name has been removed. In any event, s 10(6) of the Trade Marks Act 1994 allows what I would call honest identification use. As long as one is simply identifying the trade mark as that of the manufacturer and it is in the context of honest marketing communication, there will not be a trade mark infringement.

Question: What about the issue of passing off?

Answer: Passing off involves a misrepresentation that effectively 'piggybacks' the commercial reputation of another trader. If a product is presented in such a way as to imply that the other company is a joint promoter or has in some way licenced or approved the use of the product in the promotion, there can be an argument about passing off. Promoters must therefore make sure that their copy does not suggest any such association with the company that manufactured the relevant goods.

CHAPTER 11

EUROPEAN ISSUES

Background

Question: What do people mean by the 'European Union' (EU)?

Answer: The Maastricht Treaty, or the Treaty on European Union to give it its formal title, was signed on 7 February 1992, and came into operation on 1 November 1993. The Treaty created the EU and the concept of 'citizen of the Union'. However, contrary to popular view, the 'Union' is not a new name for the European Community (EC) or the European Economic Community (EEC).

In fact, the EU, when it was created, was like an umbrella under which the three original Treaties making up the EC continued. They were:

- the European Coal and Steel Community Treaty (which expired in July 2002);

- the European Atomic Energy Community Treaty (Euratom); and, most importantly,

- the EEC Treaty (now renamed the EC Treaty).

The EU also embraces provisions on co-operation in the fields of justice and home affairs, on a common foreign and security policy and special rules on social policy.

At the time of writing, the EU consists of 27 Member States, although there is the possibility for further expansion in the future.

Question: Tell me more about the EC Treaty.

Answer: The EC is the successor to the EEC, which it replaced as a result of the Maastricht Treaty. The EC Treaty, which, as the EEC Treaty, was signed in Rome in 1957, is the bedrock of economic integration within Europe and it contains most of the important Treaty provisions that affect business and commerce within Europe. For example, it contains the rules on European competition law and the fundamental provisions on free movement of persons, goods and capital. As we shall see later on, the EC Treaty has also been the basis for the development of the principles on freedom of movement of goods, which became so powerfully expressed in the famous *Cassis de Dijon* case.

Question: What are the main institutions of the EC?

Answer: The EC shares the same institutions with Euratom. These institutions are as follows:

(1) *The Council of the EU*: The Council consists of a government minister from each Member State of the Community. The identity of that minister depends on the subject matter under discussion so that periodically there are meetings (eg of agriculture ministers, transport ministers and consumer ministers). The chairmanship is taken in turns, giving each Member State six months in rotation.

(2) *The EC*: The Commission is somewhat analogous to the UK civil service in that its functions are to develop proposals and implement agreed Community policies. Twenty-seven commissioners are appointed by the Member States—one for each country—and there is a staff of 24,000 civil servants. Unlike the Council, where national interests are paramount, the Commission is intended to operate in the interests of the Community as a whole. Each commissioner has a five-year term, which may be renewed, and each assumes responsibility for a particular area, or 'portfolio', of Community business. The President of the Commission is chosen by the governments of EU Member States, subject to approval by the European Parliament.

(3) *The Court of Justice of the European Communities*: The EU has its own legal order, arising from the treaties, and this takes precedence over the

domestic law of each Member State. At the time of writing, the Court of Justice consists of 27 judges and eight advocates-general, and is the final arbiter on matters of European law. Based in Luxembourg, the Court is frequently asked to give 'preliminary rulings' on points of European law referred to it by various national courts.

(4) *The European Parliament*: The role of the Parliament is largely consultative, although its influence has been growing since direct elections. Its 736 members serve for five years and they form their own political groupings. It is based in Luxembourg although it sometimes meets elsewhere, particularly in Brussels, where committee meetings are held. Plenary sessions are held in Strasbourg. Amongst other rights, it has the right to be consulted about Community legislation, to question members of the Commission and to reject the Community budget.

(5) *The European Economic and Social Committee*: The Committee, based in Brussels, is an advisory body designed to involve representatives of the various economic and social interest groups by giving them a vehicle for the expression of their views. Under the EC Treaty, the Council and the Commission must seek the views of the Committee on a wide range of issues. It has 344 members.

Commission involvement in marketing

Question: Why did the Commission get involved in the area of marketing?

Answer: There are two reasons why the EC is involved in the area of marketing.

First, there was the pressure to give the Community a human face in a Europe that appeared to be characterised by wine lakes and butter mountains. Accordingly, the EC launched its first Consumer

Action Programme in 1974 and a number of further consumer action programmes have followed over the years. This has led to a number of measures in the consumer protection field that have had a major impact on marketing, such as the Directives on Misleading Advertising, Distance Selling, and Product Liability. As a result of the Maastricht Treaty, consumer protection has been given a greatly enhanced role, and the Commission's Consumer Policy Service has been busy on a number of areas of concern to those in marketing (eg consumer guarantees).

Secondly, the involvement of the Commission in the field of marketing is a natural consequence of the whole notion of an economic community in which there is the progressive elimination of barriers. The push towards 1992 and the completion of the Internal Market involved the consideration of barriers to cross-frontier trade. For this reason, the EC produced a Green Paper on Commercial Communications. This examined comprehensively the restrictions that still exist on pan-European marketing in all the relevant marketing disciplines and proposed a methodology for dealing with those restrictions.

Question: Tell me more about the Commercial Communications Green Paper.

Answer: In 1994, the EC began a massive review of the restrictions on marketing communications with the Single European Market. The Green Paper made its appearance in early 1996. It was a comprehensive study of all forms of advertising, direct marketing, sponsorship, sales promotions, and public relations promoting products and services within the EU.

There were five principal conclusions from the Green Paper:

(1) Cross-border commercial communication services in the Internal Market were a growing phenomenon.

(2) Differing national regulations created obstacles for companies wanting to offer such services across national borders and also created problems

for consumers seeking redress against unlawful cross-border commercial communication services.

(3) Some of these divergences between the regulatory frameworks of Member States could give rise to barriers as more commercial communication services circulate across borders.

(4) The risk of such regulatory differences giving rise to barriers may be accentuated with the advent of the new services developed in the Information Society.

(5) The availability of information about regulatory measures and market developments was becoming increasingly important at the national and community level.

The Green Paper made three important proposals. The first established a proportionality assessment procedure to gauge compatibility with European law. The second established a committee of representatives from the Member States to review such problems. The third established a central contact point to receive complaints and provide information on all Community law in this field.

European legislation

Question: I understand about UK legislation, but I am confused about the legislation that comes from Brussels and the form it takes.

Answer: There are two main forms of legislation emanating from the EU: Directives and Regulations.

(a) *EC Directives*: Article 249 of the consolidated EC Treaty says: 'A Directive shall be binding as to the result to be achieved, upon each Member State to which it is addressed, but shall leave to the national authorities the choice of form and methods.' The Member States are given a period of time, usually two years, in which to give effect to the Directive. The European Court has considerably extended the importance of directives so that in certain circumstances individuals can claim damages for their non-implementation.

(b) *EC Regulations*: Article 249 says: 'A Regulation shall have general application. It shall be binding in its entirety and is directly applicable in all Member States.' Unlike a Directive, a Regulation lays down immediate legal obligations throughout the Community. Regulations are usually made where it is necessary to have common European rules, usually on technical issues.

Cassis de Dijon

Question: Much has been made over the years of the *Cassis de Dijon* case in the context of European marketing. Why?

Answer: Article 29 of the EC Treaty is the legal bedrock of free circulation of goods within the Community. It forbids Member States from instituting quantitative restrictions on imports or any measures having equivalent effect. A long line of cases on this article has arisen in the Court of Justice over the years—the most famous of which is *Cassis de Dijon* [1979].

The *Cassis* case involved the famous French black-currant liqueur. As produced in France, it contained 15–20% alcohol by volume. Problems arose in relation to its importation into Germany, because German law required such a product to have at least 32% alcohol. It could be imported into Germany, but it was not possible to market it as 'Creme de Cassis'.

The European Court held that such indirect discrimination fell foul of Art 29 (as it now is) and, since the German rule could not be justified on other grounds, it was contrary to the Treaty. Accordingly, the case opened up the markets of Europe to cross-frontier trade, even where the national marketing restrictions applied to imports and domestic industry alike.

Although the case law of the European Court on Art 29 has varied over the years—sometimes in a seemingly contradictory way—the present position appears to be that an obstacle to the free movement of goods is unlawful under European law unless the restrictions apply equally to domestic as well as imported goods. Such restrictions must also be necessary to genuinely satisfy requirements relating to such matters as consumer protection and must be proportionate to the intended purpose. So, for example, in a case in 1990, a Belgian supermarket was able to overturn a conviction under Luxembourg law relating to the distribution of leaflets that offered a reduced price offer and gave the original higher prices.

Different national rules

Question: Is it correct to say that existing national rules in the United Kingdom on sales promotion and direct marketing have been the most liberal in Europe?

Answer: Yes, although Ireland's rules have been very similar.

Germany has traditionally had the most restrictive rules although some liberalisation has taken place, particularly as a result of the new Competition Act. Traditionally, premiums have only been allowed if a reasonable price is charged, the premium is of insignificant value, or it can be regarded as a product accessory.

Other EU countries have serious restrictions on promotions. For example, France has limits on the value of premiums—7% of the selling price of the purchased article. Free draws and instant win mechanics are sometimes not allowed in Germany, Austria and Switzerland. Depending on the value, free gifts can also be a problem in those countries, and in France a nominal price has to be charged for the 'free gift' unless certain limited exceptions apply.

Generally speaking, more northerly countries are more restrictive than the southern ones. Those countries like Germany, which heavily restrict sales promotion, do so because they believe that promotional techniques have the effect of deflecting the consumer's attention from rational purchasing decisions based on an objective analysis of a product's characteristics.

Question: I understand Ireland has been a problem on prize promotions?

Answer: Yes. The Irish legislation is the Gaming and Lotteries Act 1956—a very similar piece of legislation to the UK's Lotteries and Amusements Act 1976. However, in relation to instant wins and similar schemes, the Irish Supreme Court has concluded that most, if not all, such schemes are illegal lotteries in Ireland.

In *Flynn and Denieffe v Independent Newspapers Plc* [1992], the Court concluded that as the overwhelming majority of people had bought a newspaper in order to participate, it did not matter that they could have entered without purchase. Blayney J concluded:

> 'The fact that persons who had not purchased a newspaper could take part in no way prevented the scheme being a lottery vis-à-vis those whose participation resulted from purchasing a newspaper.'

This decision creates a substantial difference between what is regarded as acceptable in the United Kingdom and what is acceptable in the Irish Republic. It has made prize promotions aimed at both the United Kingdom and the Irish Republic problematic and professional advice is needed.

Question: What about other European countries?

Answer: As we have seen, the national rules on sales promotion have varied considerably across the EU. However, as the next question and answer demonstrate, many national rules on sales promotion are now invalid.

Question: I have heard that there have been some European Court decisions. What were they about?

Answer: Three cases have come before the European Court of
                    Justice concerning the interpretation and application
                    of the EU Unfair Commercial Practices Directive.
                    They involved Germany, Austria and Belgium. Two
                    involved prize promotions and one involved a free
                    gift with purchase.

                    The main case in which the court made its judgment
                    on 10 January was a preliminary ruling in the case of
                    Bekampfung unlauteren Wettbewerbs e V. The case
                    concerned a German retailer who offered points
                    for purchases, which then went into a draw. Under
                    German law, this was illegal but the Court of Justice
                    of the European Communities ruled that German law
                    could not prevent such schemes operating on the
                    basis of the following reasoning.

                    (1) Sales promotions schemes were subject to the
                        EU Directive on Unfair Commercial Practices.

                    (2) The Directive was a Maximum Harmonisation
                        Directive and therefore national law could not
                        go further than the restrictions in the Directive.

                    (3) A sales promotion scheme had to be judged
                        against the terms of the Directive and on that
                        basis the German law was invalid because
                        it constituted an automatic ban on games of
                        chance linked to purchase.

                    (4) European law takes precedence over national
                        law.

Question: So does this mean many restrictions on sales promo-
                    tion in Europe are now invalid?

Answer: Yes, clearly these judgments from the European Court
                    mean that promotions have to be judged against the
                    requirements of the Directive and any requirements
                    that go further than the Directive are invalid. So it
                    is quite clear, for example, that automatic bans in
                    national law against games of chance linked to prod-
                    uct purchase are invalid. In the author's view, this also
                    means that not only are the restrictions against pro-
                    motional techniques largely invalid, but also attend-
                    ant administrative requirements. In the author's view,

the requirements in some European countries for notification or licences are invalid because they too impose requirements over and beyond the requirements of the Directive.

Question: Why are promoters not operating on the basis that many national restrictions are now invalid?

Answer: In the author's experience, despite the clear legal position that has emerged, promoters are reluctant to run promotions which conflict with national regulations and restrictions until such time as the relevant national law has been formally changed to recognise the effect of the European Court decisions. Such changes are not required for promotions to be legally acceptable, but many promoters are waiting for formal changes to be made in national law to reflect the new legal position.

European self-regulation

Self-regulation in Europe operates principally on the basis of national systems and national codes. There is a great deal of similarity between these codes, not least because they owe much of their inspiration to the Codes of Marketing Practice produced by the International Chamber of Commerce (ICC). These Codes were consolidated in 2006 into one ICC Code entitled 'Advertising and marketing communication practice' which, at the time of writing, is being reviewed.

However, a measure of co-ordination of national self-regulation is achieved through the European Advertising Standards Alliance (EASA).

The EASA brings together 33 self-regulatory advertising organisations and 15 industry associations. It has developed a system that makes it possible for consumers to complain about a cross-border advertisement or sales promotion simply by writing to the complainant's own national advertising self-regulatory body (eg the ASA in the United Kingdom).

If the complaint turns out to be a cross-border complaint, it is passed to the relevant self-regulatory body in the country of origin of the medium in which the advertisement appeared. It is then checked for compliance with the rules set out in that country's code of practice on marketing communications.

Question: Is there any European equivalent of copy advice or pre-clearance?

Answer: In 2009, EASA established a European copy advice/ pre-clearance facility in association with ClearCast UK. This pre-publication advice on compliance with the various national systems of self-regulation covers, at the time of writing, 17 European countries.

CHAPTER 12

PROMOTIONAL MARKETING ADMINISTRATION CHECKLIST

There is an old saying that a chain is as strong as its weakest link. Nowhere is this more true than in the world of promotional marketing. A lot of links in the chain must hang together effectively for a promotion to be a success. So, many of the promotional marketing schemes that feature in the case reports of the Advertising Standards Authority (ASA) are not the result of a failure by the promoter and its agency to appreciate the law and the codes; rather they are the result of various failures of administration.

Another thought to concentrate the mind is that the cost of a failure of administration can be truly colossal. Potentially, a promotion that goes wrong can be much more expensive to a company than an advertising campaign which goes wrong. As someone put it to me: 'The ending of a promotion can require just as much thought as the beginning of one.'

This book is not the place for a detailed consideration of such issues, but I have taken the opportunity to set out a checklist of some of the major issues affecting the administration of a promotion. From experience, I know how crucial such issues are to a promotion's success.

- *Taking promotional marketing seriously*: Within marketing departments of major companies, there has been a tendency to regard promotional marketing as the Cinderella of the marketing mix. Some years ago, an advertising agency executive said to me that, whereas promotional marketing was a mechanical operation, advertising was a cerebral activity. This snobbish view means that decisions relating to promotional marketing have all too often not been taken at a senior enough level within the company, and this in itself can lead to problems of administration.

  Fortunately, the growth of promotional marketing as a marketing discipline has necessitated a re-evaluation of its importance by other marketing disciplines, and by those in the marketing departments of major companies. This is crucial, as one of the prime considerations in promotional marketing schemes being effective is that companies take promotional marketing as a marketing discipline as seriously as they do advertising and other marketing disciplines.

● *Taking administration seriously*: Quite rightly, many in the industry see creativity as the key to a successful promotion. And creativity is important in making an impact in a highly competitive marketplace. But a successful promotion also needs to be professionally administered in all its stages if consumers are not to be disadvantaged. It may not be glamorous and it may not win industry awards, but its importance cannot be underestimated.

● *Outside suppliers*: Inevitably, promoters frequently need to use outside suppliers in order to fulfil the needs of a promotion, whether it is a sourcing company, a travel company or a handling house. It is crucial that the promoter makes sure that the outside companies that they use to fulfil the promotion are up to the job. Many promoters take little interest in the standing and position of outside suppliers, or supervising their work, with the result that the reputation of the promoter itself suffers.

  Promoters must institute appropriate checks into the standing and effectiveness of the outside companies that they use and, in appropriate cases, they should use only those companies that are members of an association with a recognised code of practice. For example, in the case of handling houses it is important that promoters use only those companies that are willing to adhere to the IPM's 'Guidelines for briefing fulfilment houses' (reproduced in Appendix 4 below).

● *Contracts*: In order to run a successful promotion, a great many relationships need to function effectively and this is where careful drafting of contracts becomes important. Apart from the contract between agency and promoter, there will be many others with those who are responsible for fulfilling the promotion, such as printers, sourcing companies and handling houses. Particularly important are the fundamental questions of who does what and when. Issues of quality are fundamental, particularly in contracts with sourcing companies.

  There are, of course, many other issues to consider but the fundamental point is that the good administration of a promotion requires clear and comprehensive contracts.

● *Effective communication*: Time and time again, a promotion fails and falls foul of the British Code of Advertising, Sales Promotion and Direct Marketing (CAP Code) because of inadequate briefing.

It is no good for the marketing department to be clear in their own mind what needs to happen for a promotion to be legally sound and in compliance with the Code, if the people who need to operate the promotion down the line are not properly briefed. Effective communication and briefing of all those involved in a promotion is therefore crucial.

- *Careful estimations*: A successful promotion requires a careful estimate of likely consumer demand from the promotion, and proper arrangements to meet that demand. This is by far one of the most important administrative aspects of running a promotion. Indeed, the CAP Code requires promoters to make a reasonable pre-estimate of likely demand. This is not just a Code requirement; it is also a commercial necessity.

- *Realistic budgets*: Akin to making a careful estimate of likely demand is to make sure the budget for the promotion is adequate to the likely demand.

- *Realistic timetables*: So often, unrealistic timetables are included within a promotion. This is particularly true of competitions that involve a lengthy judging process. A timetable for judging and awarding of prizes needs to be instituted, and not infrequently this cannot be met and, therefore, there is a problem of slippage of dates. It is crucial that realistic dates are set for a promotion (ie dates that the promoter knows can be complied with, and which make allowances for absences and the natural delaying factors which arise in everyday life).

- *Check and double-check*: So many promoters have come adrift over the years because assumptions have been made, particularly assumptions that other people have done what is required of them.

  It is important for promoters to check and re-check every aspect of a promotion to make sure that everything that should happen, does happen, and that everybody who has a role to play meets his or her obligations. Some of the worst catastrophes in sales promotion have arisen because assumptions have been made, particularly assumptions that people can be relied on, when they cannot.

- *Complaints*: Dealing with complaints in respect of the promotion is an important challenge for promoters. One should always deal positively with complaints, whether they are justified or unjustified; there is nothing worse than a weak and vacillating response.

  If the complaint is justified, then by far the best way to defuse the issue is to apologise and make an appropriate gesture of amends.

Nothing keeps an issue alive more effectively than for a company to prevaricate and make excuses when it is patently obvious to an independent observer that some mistake has been made and the company is trying to cover up. At the end of the day, the company gains more credit from an open acknowledgement and apology.

If, on the other hand, the complaint is groundless, then it is important that a firm and resolute response is given, and important that no token is given which could be interpreted as an acknowledgement of weakness on the part of the promoter. If the promoter's position is sound, then the promoter must stand firm.

- *Keep records*: There are a number of competition enthusiasts, known in the trade as 'compers'. Some are prepared to challenge the adjudication on competitions—in some cases several years after the competition has been run. In addition, there are growing numbers of people prepared to challenge the way in which promotions are organised and administered.

  In order to deal properly with these challenges, a promoter must keep proper records and for a reasonable period of time. It is difficult to say what that period should be, but in my view in the case of prize competitions and games of chance I would recommend two years and I would recommend at least one year from the end of the promotion in the case of other promotional mechanics.

  Some concern has been expressed as to whether keeping promotion records for any length of time conflicts with Data Protection Principle 5: 'Personal data processed for any purpose or purposes shall not be kept longer than is necessary for that purpose or purposes.' We have no guidance on this point from the Information Commissioner's office, nor are there are relevant cases to which we can refer. It is therefore a commonsense judgment that we need to apply. This, in my view, means keeping records for as long as is reasonably necessary to see whether any challenge is made. If any challenge is made, the records should then be kept for a much longer period.

- *Checklist*: It is important for those in the promotional marketing industry to develop their own checklists in order to ensure a systematic approach to the creation, planning and administration of each promotion. The issues we have discussed here should provide a basis for such a checklist.

- *'The secretary test'*: Those who give professional advice about promotions know only too well that the most valuable service that can be rendered in respect of a promotion is often the provision of an independent view. We often cannot see clearly something that we are closely involved in, and we need an independent third party to look at what we are doing.

Accordingly, there is much to be said for getting such an independent person to read through the material for a promotion, because he or she can look at a promotion very much through the eyes of an ordinary consumer, without the inside knowledge and experience of those who put the promotion together. So often agencies and promoters have persuaded themselves that a particular piece of wording is clear. Yet the moment that material is seen by a third party it is patently obvious that it is far from clear, and is actually highly ambiguous, to say the least.

That independent third-party can be anybody, but I call this test 'the secretary test' because secretaries are often blessed with a considerable degree of common sense and this makes them peculiarly well suited to giving a view about the wording and presentation of a promotion.

APPENDICES

THE CAP CODE: THE UK CODE OF NON-BROADCAST ADVERTISING, SALES PROMOTION AND DIRECT MARKETING

Published by TSO (The Stationery Office) and available from: TSO, PO Box 29, Norwich, NR3 1GN. Telephone orders/General enquiries: 0870 600 5522. Fax orders: 0870 600 5533. E-mail: customer.services@tso.co.uk. Textphone 0870 240 3701. http://www.tsoshop.co.uk

Published by kind permission of the Committee of Advertising Practice

Preface

In the UK, The UK Code of Non-broadcast Advertising, Sales Promotion and Direct Marketing (the Code) is the rule book for non-broadcast advertisements, sales promotions and direct marketing communications (marketing communications). The Code is primarily concerned with the content of marketing communications and not with terms of business or products themselves. Some rules, however, go beyond content; for example, those that cover the administration of sales promotions, the suitability of promotional items, the delivery of products ordered through an advertisement and the use of personal information in direct marketing. Editorial content is specifically excluded from the Code, though it might be a factor in determining the context in which marketing communications are judged.

The Committee of Advertising Practice (CAP) is the self-regulatory body that creates, revises and enforces the Code. CAP's members include organisations that represent the advertising, sales promotion, direct marketing and media businesses. Through their membership of CAP member organisations, or through contractual agreements with media publishers and carriers, those businesses agree to comply with the Code so that marketing communications are legal, decent, honest and truthful and consumer confidence is maintained.

Some CAP member organisations, for example, the Direct Marketing Association and the Proprietary Association of Great Britain, also require their members to observe their own codes of practice. Those codes may cover some practices that are not covered in this Code.

The Code supplements the law, fills gaps where the law does not reach and often provides an easier way of resolving disputes than by civil litigation or criminal prosecution. In many cases, self-regulation ensures that legislation is not necessary. Although advertisers, promoters and direct marketers (marketers), agencies and media may still wish to consult lawyers, compliance with the Code should go a long way to ensuring compliance with the law in areas covered by both the Code and the law.

By creating and following self-imposed rules, the marketing community produces marketing communications that are welcomed and trusted. By practising self-regulation, it ensures the integrity of advertising, promotions and direct marketing.

The value of self-regulation as an alternative to statutory control is recognised in EC Directives, including those on misleading and comparative advertising (Directives 2005/29/EC and 2006/114/ EC). Self-regulation is accepted by the Department for Business, Innovation and Skills and the Office of Fair Trading as a first line of control in protecting consumers and the industry.

The Advertising Standards Authority (ASA) is the independent body that endorses and administers the Code, ensuring that the self-regulatory system works in the public interest. The ASA's activities include investigating and adjudicating on complaints and conducting research. Full information about the ASA's complaints procedure is available on www.asa.org.uk.

The vast majority of advertisers, promoters and direct marketers comply with the Code. Those that do not may be subject to sanctions. Adverse publicity may result from the rulings published by the ASA weekly on its website. The media, contractors and service providers may withhold their services or deny access to space. Trading privileges (including direct mail discounts) and recognition may be revoked, withdrawn or temporarily withheld. Pre-vetting may be imposed and, in some cases, noncomplying parties can be referred to the Office of Fair Trading for action, where appropriate, under the Consumer Protection from Unfair Trading Regulations 2008 or the Business Protection from Misleading Marketing Regulations 2008.

The successful track record of the self-regulatory system meant that the ASA was recognised as the natural co-regulatory partner when Ofcom was required to give effect to European Union legislation governing advertising content on relevant on-demand services. The ASA was designated by Ofcom as the co-regulator of advertising content included in on-demand services with effect from August 2010. The statutory requirements applying to certain on-demand services are reflected in the rules set out in **APPENDIX 2** in this document.

The system is structured so that it does not operate in an unfair or anti-competitive manner or restrict free speech unjustifiably. ASA decisions are subject to independent review, including in exceptional cases by the Administrative Division of the High Court.

The full text of the Code is available on www.cap.org.uk.
Mid City Place
71 High Holborn
London
WC1V 6QT

CAP: t 020 7492 2200 f 020 7404 3404 e enquiries@cap.org.uk
www.cap.org.uk

ASA: t 020 7492 2222 f 020 7242 3696 e enquiries@asa.org.uk
www.asa.org.uk

Copyright The Committee of Advertising Practice 2010

Contents

Introduction

This twelfth edition of the Code comes into force on 1 September 2010. It replaces all previous editions.

As well as this Code, non-broadcast marketing communications are subject to legislation. See www.cap.org.uk for a non-exhaustive list. The advertising rules that apply to video-on-demand services which are subject to statutory regulation are reflected in the rules set out in Appendix 2.

I   The code applies to:

a.   advertisements in newspapers, magazines, brochures, leaflets, circulars, mailings, e-mails, text transmissions (including SMS and MMS), fax transmissions, catalogues, follow-up literature and other electronic or printed material

b.   posters and other promotional media in public places, including moving images

c.   cinema, video, DVD and Blu-ray advertisements

d.   advertisements in non-broadcast electronic media, including but not limited to: online advertisements in paid-for space (including banner or pop-up advertisements and online video advertisements); paid-for search listings; preferential listings on price comparison sites; viral advertisements (see III l); in-game advertisements; commercial classified advertisements; advergames that feature in display advertisements; advertisements transmitted by Bluetooth; advertisements distributed through web widgets and online sales promotions and prize promotions

e.   marketing databases containing consumers' personal information

f.   sales promotions in non-broadcast media

g.   advertorials (see III k).

II   The code does not apply to:

a.   broadcast advertisements (The BCAP Code sets out the rules that govern broadcast advertisements on any television channel or radio station licensed by Ofcom)

b. the contents of premium-rate services, which are the responsibility of PhonepayPlus; marketing communications that promote those services are subject to PhonepayPlus regulation and to the CAP Code

c. marketing communications in foreign media. Direct marketing communications that originate outside the United Kingdom and sales promotions and advertisements in paid-for space that are published on non-UK-registered websites, if targeted at UK consumers, are subject to the jurisdiction of the relevant authority in the country from which they originate if that authority operates a suitable cross-border complaint system. If it does not, the Advertising Standards Authority (ASA) will take what action it can. Most members of the European Union, and many non-European countries, have a self-regulatory organisation that is a member of the European Advertising Standards Alliance (EASA). EASA co-ordinates the cross-border complaints system for its members (which include the ASA)

d. claims, in marketing communications in media addressed only to medical, dental, veterinary or allied practitioners, that relate to those practitioners' expertise

e. classified private advertisements, including those appearing online

f. statutory, public, police and other official notices or information, but not marketing communications, produced by public authorities and the like

g. works of art exhibited in public or private

h. private correspondence, including correspondence between organisations and their customers about existing relationships or past purchases

i. live oral communications, including telephone calls and announcements or direct approaches from street marketers

j. press releases and other public relations material not covered by part I above

k. editorial content; for example, of the media or of books and regular competitions such as crosswords

l. flyposting (most of which is illegal)

m. packages, wrappers, labels, tickets, timetables and price lists unless they advertise another product or a sales promotion or are visible in a marketing communication

n. point-of-sale displays, except those covered by the sales promotion rules or the rolling paper and filter rules

o. political advertisements as defined in Section 7

p. website content not covered by I d, including (but not limited to) editorial content, news or public relations material, corporate reports and natural listings on a search engine or a price comparison site

q. sponsorship; marketing communications that refer to sponsorship are covered by the Code

r. customer charters and codes of practice.

III These definitions apply to the code:

a. product encompasses goods, services, ideas, causes, opportunities, prizes or gifts

b. consumer is anyone who is likely to see a given marketing communication, whether in the course of business or not

c. the United Kingdom covers the Isle of Man and the Channel Islands

d. a claim can be implied or direct, written, spoken or visual; the name of a product can constitute a claim

e. the Code is divided into numbered rules

f. a marketing communication includes all forms of communication listed in part I

g. a marketer includes an advertiser, promoter or direct marketer

h. a supplier is anyone who supplies a product that is sold by a distance-selling marketing communication (and can be the marketer)

i. a child is anyone under 16

j.   a corporate subscriber includes corporate bodies such as limited companies in the UK, limited liability partnerships in England, Wales and Northern Ireland or any partnerships in Scotland.

It also includes schools, hospitals, Government departments or agencies and other public bodies. It does not include sole traders or non-limited liability partnerships in England, Wales and Northern Ireland. See rule 10.14

k.   An advertorial is an advertisement feature, announcement or promotion, the content of which is controlled by the marketer, not the publisher, that is disseminated in exchange for a payment or other reciprocal arrangement

l.   A viral advertisement is an e-mail, text or other non-broadcast marketing communication designed to stimulate significant circulation by recipients to generate commercial or reputational benefit to the marketer. Viral advertisements are usually put into circulation ("seeded") by the marketer with a request, either explicit or implicit, for the message to be forwarded to others. Sometimes they include a video clip or a link to website material or are part of a sales promotion campaign.

IV   These criteria apply to the code:

a.   the ASA Council's interpretation of the Code is final

b.   if it is not clear whether a communication falls within the remit of the Code, the ASA will be more likely to apply the Code if the material complained about is in paid-for space

c.   compliance with the Code is assessed according to the marketing communication's probable impact when taken as a whole and in context. That will depend on the medium in which the marketing communication appeared, the audience and its likely response, the nature of the product and any material distributed to consumers

d.   the Non-broadcast ASA Council may have regard to decisions made by the Broadcast ASA Council under the BCAP Code and, similarly, the Broadcast ASA Council may have regard to decisions made by the Non-broadcast ASA Council under the CAP Code. Factors that help to determine whether an ASA adjudication is likely to apply across media include, but are not limited to, the characteristics of the medium, how the advertisement is targeted, the context in which a claim is made and the extent to which the relevant CAP Code provisions correspond to those in the BCAP Code

e.   the Code does not have the force of law and its interpretation will reflect its flexibility. The Code operates alongside the law; the Courts may make rulings on matters covered by the Code

f.   an indication of the statutory rules governing marketing communications is given on www.cap.org.uk; professional advice should be taken about their application

g.   no spoken or written communication from the ASA or CAP should be understood as containing legal advice

h.   the Code is primarily concerned with the content of advertisements, promotions and direct marketing communications and not with terms of business or products. Some rules, however, go beyond content; for example, those that cover the administration of sales promotions, the suitability of promotional items, the delivery of products ordered through an advertisement and the use of personal information in direct marketing. Editorial content is specifically excluded from the remit of the Code (see II k) although it might be a factor in determining the context in which a marketing communication is judged (see IV c)

i.   the Code makes due allowance for public sensitivities but will not be used by the ASA to diminish freedom of speech unjustifiably

j.   the ASA does not arbitrate between conflicting ideologies

k.   in assessing compliance with the Code, the ASA may take account of honest market practices and the general principle of good faith in the traders' field of activity.

01   Compliance

Principle

The central principle for all marketing communications is that they should be legal, decent, honest and truthful. All marketing communications should be prepared with a sense of responsibility to consumers and society and should reflect the spirit, not merely the letter, of the Code.

Background

Marketers should use the ASA website, www.asa.org.uk, or the CAP website, www.cap.org.uk, to inform themselves of recent ASA adjudications, the latest text of the Code and CAP guidance on the Code.

The fact that a marketing communication complies with the Code does not guarantee that every publisher will accept it. Media owners can refuse space to marketing communications that break the Code and are not obliged to publish every marketing communication offered to them.

The ASA/CAP self-regulatory system is recognised by the Government, Office of Fair Trading and the Courts as one of the "established means" of consumer protection in non-broadcast marketing communications. Any matter that principally concerns a legal dispute will normally need to be resolved through law enforcement agencies or the Courts.

The ASA and CAP will treat in confidence any genuinely private or secret material supplied unless the Courts or officials acting within their statutory powers compel its disclosure.

Rules

1.1   Marketing communications should be legal, decent, honest and truthful.

1.2   Marketing communications must reflect the spirit, not merely the letter, of the Code.

1.3   Marketing communications must be prepared with a sense of responsibility to consumers and to society.

1.4   Marketers must comply with all general rules and with relevant sector-specific rules.

1.5   No marketing communication should bring advertising into disrepute.

1.6   Marketing communications must respect the principles of fair competition generally accepted in business.

1.7   Any unreasonable delay in responding to the ASA's enquiries will normally be considered a breach of the Code.

   1.7.1   The full name and geographical business address of the marketer must be given to the ASA or CAP without delay if requested.

1.8   Marketing communications must comply with the Code. Primary responsibility for observing the Code falls on marketers. Others involved in preparing or publishing marketing communications, such as agencies, publishers and other service suppliers, also accept an obligation to abide by the Code

1.9   Marketers should deal fairly with consumers.

Legality

1.10   Marketers have primary responsibility for ensuring that their marketing communications are legal. Marketing communications should comply with the law and should not incite anyone to break it.

1.10.1   Marketers must not state or imply that a product can legally be sold if it cannot.

02   Recognition of marketing communications

Background

Other sections of the Code contain product-specific or audience-specific rules that are intended to protect consumers from misleading marketing communications. For example, the Charity-linked Promotions and Children sections of the Code contain rules that apply, as well as the general rules, to marketing communications that fall under those sections.

Rules

2.1   Marketing communications must be obviously identifiable as such.

2.2   Unsolicited e-mail marketing communications must be obviously identifiable as marketing communications without the need to open them (see rule 10.6).

2.3   Marketing communications must not falsely claim or imply that the marketer is acting as a consumer or for purposes outside its trade, business, craft or profession; marketing communications must make clear their commercial intent, if that is not obvious from the context.

2.4   Marketers and publishers must make clear that advertorials are marketing communications; for example, by heading them "advertisement feature".

03   Misleading advertising

Background

The ASA may take the Consumer Protection from Unfair Trading Regulations 2008 into account when it adjudicates on complaints about marketing communications that are alleged to be misleading. See Appendix 1 for more information about those Regulations.

The ASA will take into account the impression created by marketing communications as well as specific claims. It will adjudicate on the basis of the likely effect on consumers, not the marketer's intentions.

Other sections of the Code contain product-specific or audience-specific rules that are intended to protect consumers from misleading marketing communications. For example, the Children and Medicines sections of the Code contain rules that apply, as well as the general rules, to marketing communications that fall under those sections.

Rules

General

3.1   Marketing communications must not materially mislead or be likely to do so.

3.2   Obvious exaggerations ("puffery") and claims that the average consumer who sees the marketing communication is unlikely to take literally are allowed provided they do not materially mislead.

3.3   Marketing communications must not mislead the consumer by omitting material information. They must not mislead by hiding material information or presenting it in an unclear, unintelligible, ambiguous or untimely manner.

Material information is information that the consumer needs to make informed decisions in relation to a product. Whether the omission or presentation of material information is likely to mislead the consumer depends on the context, the medium and, if the medium of the marketing communication is constrained by time or space, the measures that the marketer takes to make that information available to the consumer by other means.

3.4   For marketing communications that quote prices for advertised products, material information [for the purposes of rule 3.3] includes:

3.4.1   the main characteristics of the product

3.4.2   the identity (for example, a trading name) and geographical address of the marketer and any other trader on whose behalf the marketer is acting

3.4.3   the price of the advertised product, including taxes, or, if the nature of the product is such that the price cannot be calculated in advance, the manner in which the price is calculated

3.4.4   delivery charges

3.4.5   the arrangements for payment, delivery, performance or complaint handling, if those differ from the arrangements that consumers are likely to reasonably expect

3.4.6   that consumers have the right to withdraw or cancel, if they have that right (see rule 3.55). Cross-reference: If the marketing communication encourages a consumer to buy a product through a distance-selling mechanism, please refer to Section 9: Distance Selling.

3.5   Marketing communications must not materially mislead by omitting the identity of the marketer.

Some marketing communications must include the marketer's identity and contact details. Marketing communications that fall under the Distance Selling, Database Practice or Employment sections of the Code must comply with the more detailed rules in those sections.

Marketers should note the law requires marketers to identify themselves in some marketing communications. Marketers should take legal advice.

3.6   Subjective claims must not mislead the consumer; marketing communications must not imply that expressions of opinion are objective claims.

Substantiation

3.7   Before distributing or submitting a marketing communication for publication, marketers must hold documentary evidence to prove claims that consumers are likely to regard as objective and that are capable of objective substantiation. The ASA may regard claims as misleading in the absence of adequate substantiation.

3.8 Claims for the content of non-fiction publications should not exaggerate the value, accuracy, scientific validity or practical usefulness of the product. Marketers must ensure that claims that have not been independently substantiated but are based merely on the content of a publication do not mislead consumers.

CAP has published a Help Note on the Marketing of Publications.

Qualification

3.9   Marketing communications must state significant limitations and qualifications. Qualifications may clarify but must not contradict the claims that they qualify.

3.10   Qualifications must be presented clearly. CAP has published a Help Note on Claims that Require Qualification.

Exaggeration

3.11   Marketing communications must not mislead consumers by exaggerating the capability or performance of a product.

3.12   Marketing communications must not present rights given to consumers in law as a distinctive feature of the marketer's offer.

3.13   Marketing communications must not suggest that their claims are universally accepted if a significant division of informed or scientific opinion exists.

Prohibited claims

These rules apply regardless of any substantiation presented in support of the claims:

3.14   Marketing communications must not claim that products can facilitate winning in games of chance.

3.15   Marketing communications must not explicitly claim that the advertiser's job or livelihood is in jeopardy if the consumer does not buy the advertised product.

3.16   No marketing communication may promote a pyramid promotional scheme. Pyramid promotional schemes are those in which consumers pay for the opportunity to receive payments derived primarily from the introduction of other consumers into the scheme, not from the sale or consumption of products.

Prices

Background

Price statements in marketing communications should take account of the Department for Business Innovation & Skills (BIS) Pricing Practices Guide.

Definition

Price statements include statements about the manner in which the price will be calculated as well as definite prices.

3.17   Price statements must not mislead by omission, undue emphasis or distortion. They must relate to the product featured in the marketing communication.

3.18   Quoted prices must include non-optional taxes, duties, fees and charges that apply to all or most buyers. VAT-exclusive prices may be given only if all or most consumers pay no VAT or can recover VAT; marketing communications that quote VAT-exclusive prices must prominently state the amount or rate of VAT payable if some consumers are likely to pay VAT.

3.19   If a tax, duty, fee or charge cannot be calculated in advance, for example, because it depends on the consumer's circumstances, the marketing communication must make clear that it is excluded from the advertised price and state how it is calculated.

3.20   Marketing communications that state prices must also state applicable delivery, freight or postal charges or, if those cannot reasonably be calculated in advance, state that such charges are payable.

3.21   If the price of one product depends on another, marketing communications must make clear the extent of the commitment the consumer must make to obtain the advertised price.

3.22   Price claims such as "up to" and "from" must not exaggerate the availability or amount of benefits likely to be obtained by the consumer.

Free

Principle

Marketing communications must not describe a product as "free", "gratis", "without charge" or similar if the consumer has to pay anything other than the unavoidable cost of responding and collecting or paying for delivery of the item.

3.23   Marketing communications must make clear the extent of the commitment the consumer must make to take advantage of a "free" offer.

3.24   Marketing communications must not describe items as "free" if:

3.24.1   the consumer has to pay packing, packaging, handling or administration charges for the "free" product

3.24.2   the cost of response, including the price of a product that the consumer must buy to take advantage of the offer, has been increased, except where the increase results from factors that are unrelated to the cost of the promotion, or

3.24.3   the quality of the product that the consumer must buy has been reduced.

CAP and BCAP have published joint guidance on the use of "free".

3.25   Marketers must not describe an element of a package as "free" if that element is included in the package price unless consumers are likely to regard it as an additional benefit because it has recently been added to the package without increasing its price.

3.26   Marketers must not use the term "free trial" to describe "satisfaction or your money back" offers or offers for which a non-refundable purchase is required.

Availability

3.27   Marketers must make a reasonable estimate of demand for advertised products.

3.28   Marketing communications that quote a price for a featured product must state any reasonable grounds the marketer has for believing that it might not be able to supply the advertised (or an equivalent) product at the advertised price within a reasonable period and in reasonable quantities. In particular:

3.28.1   if estimated demand exceeds supply, marketing communications must make clear that stock is limited

3.28.2   if the marketer does not intend to fulfil orders, for example, because the purpose of the marketing communication is to assess potential demand, the marketing communication must make that clear

3.28.3   marketing communications must not mislead consumers by omitting restrictions on the availability of products; for example, geographical restrictions or age limits.

3.29   Marketers must monitor stocks. If a product becomes unavailable, marketers must, whenever possible, withdraw or amend marketing communications that feature that product.

3.30   Marketers must not use the technique of switch selling, in which their sales staff decline to show the advertised product, refuse to take orders for it or to deliver it within a reasonable time or demonstrate a defective sample of it to promote a different product.

3.31   Marketing communications must not falsely claim that the marketer is about to cease trading or move premises. They must not falsely state that a product, or the terms on which it is offered, will be available only for a very limited time to deprive consumers of the time or opportunity to make an informed choice.

3.32   Marketing communications must not mislead the consumer about market conditions or the possibility of finding the product elsewhere to induce consumers to buy the product at conditions less favourable than normal market conditions.

Comparisons

Principle

The ASA will consider unqualified superlative claims as comparative claims against all competing products. Superiority claims must be supported by evidence unless they are obvious puffery (that is, claims that consumers are unlikely to take literally). Objective superiority claims must make clear the aspect of the product or the marketer's performance that is claimed to be superior.

Comparisons with Identifiable competitors

3.33   Marketing communications that include a comparison with an identifiable competitor must not mislead, or be likely to mislead, the consumer about either the advertised product or the competing product.

3.34   They must compare products meeting the same need or intended for the same purpose.

3.35   They must objectively compare one or more material, relevant, verifiable and representative feature of those products.

3.36   They must not create confusion between the marketer and its competitors or between the marketer's product, trade mark, trade name or other distinguishing mark and that of a competitor.

3.37   Certain EU agricultural products and foods are, because of their unique geographical area and method of production, given special protection by being registered as having a "designation of origin". Products with a designation of origin must be compared only with other products with the same designation.

Other Comparisons

3.38   Marketing communications that include a comparison with an unidentifiable competitor must not mislead, or be likely to mislead, the consumer. The elements of the comparison must not be selected to give the marketer an unrepresentative advantage.

Price comparisons

3.39   Marketing communications that include a price comparison must state the basis of the comparison. Comparisons with a competitor price must be with the price for an identical or substantially equivalent product and must explain significant differences between the products. If the competitor offers more than one similar product, marketers should compare their price with the price for the competitor's product that is most similar to the advertised product.

CAP has published a Help Note on Retailers' Price Comparisons and a Help Note on Lowest Price Claims and Price Promises.

3.40   Price comparisons must not mislead by falsely claiming a price advantage. Comparisons with a recommended retail prices (RRPs) are likely to mislead if the RRP differs significantly from the price at which the product or service is generally sold.

Imitation and denigration

3.41   Marketing communications must not mislead the consumer about who manufactures the product.

3.42   Marketing communications must not discredit or denigrate another product, marketer, trade mark, trade name or other distinguishing mark.

3.43   Marketing communications must not take unfair advantage of the reputation of a competitor's trade mark, trade name or other distinguishing mark or of the designation of origin of a competing product.

3.44   Marketing communications must not present a product as an imitation or replica of a product with a protected trade mark or trade name.

Endorsements and Testimonials

3.45   Marketers must hold documentary evidence that a testimonial or endorsement used in a marketing communication is genuine, unless it is obviously fictitious, and hold contact details for the person who, or organisation that, gives it.

3.46   Testimonials must relate to the advertised product.

3.47   Claims that are likely to be interpreted as factual and appear in a testimonial must not mislead or be likely to mislead the consumer.

3.48   Marketing communications must not feature a testimonial without permission; exceptions are normally made for accurate statements taken from a published source, quotations from a publication or references to a test, trial, professional endorsement, research facility or professional journal, which may be acceptable without express permission.

3.49   Marketers must not refer in a marketing communication to advice received from CAP or imply endorsement by the ASA or CAP.

3.50   Marketing communications must not display a trust mark, quality mark or equivalent without the necessary authorisation.

Marketing communications must not claim that the marketer (or any other entity referred to), the marketing communication or the advertised product has been approved, endorsed or authorised by any public or other body if it has not or without complying with the terms of the approval, endorsement or authorisation.

3.51 Marketing communications must not falsely claim that the marketer, or other entity referred to in the marketing communication, is a signatory to a code of conduct. They must not falsely claim that a code of conduct has an endorsement from a public or other body.

3.52 Marketing communications must not use the Royal Arms or Emblems without prior permission from the Lord Chamberlain's office. References to a Royal Warrant should be checked with the Royal Warrant Holders' Association.

Guarantees and after-sales Service

Definition

In the rules below, "guarantee" includes warranties, after-sales service agreements, care packages and similar products.

3.53 Marketing communications must not use the word "guarantee" in a way that could cause confusion about a consumer's rights.

3.54 Marketing communications must make clear each significant limitation to an advertised guarantee (of the type that has implications for a consumer's rights). Marketers must supply the full terms before the consumer is committed to taking up the guarantee.

3.55 Marketers must promptly refund consumers who make valid claims under an advertised money-back guarantee.

3.56 Marketing communications must not falsely claim or imply that after-sales service is available in an EEA member state in which the advertised product is not sold.

3.57 If a marketing communication in a language other than an official language of the EEA State where the trader is located offers after-sales service but the after-sales service is not available in the language of the marketing communication, the marketer must explain that to the consumer before the contract is concluded.

04   Harm and offence

Principle

Marketers should take account of the prevailing standards in society and the context in which a marketing communication is likely to appear to minimise the risk of causing harm or serious or widespread offence.

Rules

4.1   Marketing communications must not contain anything that is likely to cause serious or widespread offence. Particular care must be taken to avoid causing offence on the grounds of race, religion, gender, sexual orientation, disability or age. Compliance will be judged on the context, medium, audience, product and prevailing standards.

Marketing communications may be distasteful without necessarily breaching this rule. Marketers are urged to consider public sensitivities before using potentially offensive material.

The fact that a product is offensive to some people is not grounds for finding a marketing communication in breach of the Code.

4.2   Marketing communications must not cause fear or distress without justifiable reason; if it can be justified, the fear or distress should not be excessive. Marketers must not use a shocking claim or image merely to attract attention.

4.3   References to anyone who is dead must be handled with particular care to avoid causing offence or distress.

4.4   Marketing communications must contain nothing that is likely to condone or encourage violence or anti-social behaviour.

4.5   Marketing communications, especially those addressed to or depicting a child, must not condone or encourage an unsafe practice (see Section 5: Children).

4.6   Marketing communications must not encourage consumers to drink and drive. Marketing communications must, where relevant, include a prominent warning on the dangers of drinking and driving and must not suggest that the effects of drinking alcohol can be masked.

4.7 Marketers must take particular care not to include in their marketing communications visual effects or techniques that are likely to adversely affect members of the public with photosensitive epilepsy.

05   Children

Principle

Care should be taken when featuring or addressing children in marketing communications.

The way in which children perceive and react to marketing communications is influenced by their age, experience and the context in which the message is delivered. Marketing communications that are acceptable for young teenagers will not necessarily be acceptable for younger children. The ASA will take those factors into account when assessing whether a marketing communication complies with the Code.

Definition

For the purposes of the Code, a child is someone under 16.

Rules

Harm

5.1 Marketing communications addressed to, targeted directly at or featuring children must contain nothing that is likely to result in their physical, mental or moral harm:

> **5.1.1**   children must not be encouraged to enter strange places or talk to strangers

> **5.1.2**   children must not be shown in hazardous situations or behaving dangerously except to promote safety. Children must not be shown unattended in street scenes unless they are old enough to take responsibility for their own safety.

Pedestrians and cyclists must be seen to observe the Highway Code

5.1.3   children must not be shown using or in close proximity to dangerous substances or equipment without direct adult supervision

5.1.4   children must not be encouraged to copy practices that might be unsafe for a child

5.1.5   distance selling marketers must take care when using youth media not to promote products that are unsuitable for children.

Credulity and unfair pressure

5.2   Marketing communications addressed to, targeted directly at or featuring children must not exploit their credulity, loyalty, vulnerability or lack of experience:

5.2.1   children must not be made to feel inferior or unpopular for not buying the advertised product

5.2.2   children must not be made to feel that they are lacking in courage, duty or loyalty if they do not buy or do not encourage others to buy a product

5.2.3   it must be made easy for children to judge the size, characteristics and performance of advertised products and to distinguish between real-life situations and fantasy

5.2.4   adult permission must be obtained before children are committed to buying complex or costly products

5.3   Marketing communications addressed to or targeted directly at children:

5.3.1   must not exaggerate what is attainable by an ordinary child using the product being marketed

5.3.2   must not exploit children's susceptibility to charitable appeals and must explain the extent to which their participation will help in any charity-linked promotions.

Direct Exhortation and parental authority

5.4   Marketing communications addressed to or targeted directly at children:

5.4.1   must not actively encourage children to make a nuisance of themselves to parents or others and must not undermine parental authority

5.4.2   must not include a direct exhortation to children to buy an advertised product or persuade their parents or other adults to buy an advertised product for them.

5.5   Marketing communications that contain a direct exhortation to buy a product via a direct-response mechanism must not be directly targeted at children. For a definition of "direct-response mechanism", see Section 9: Distance Selling.

Promotions

5.6   Promotions addressed to or targeted directly at children:

5.6.1   must make clear that adult permission is required if a prize or an incentive might cause conflict between a child's desire and a parent's, or other adult's, authority

5.6.2   must contain a prominent closing date if applicable (see rule 8.17.4)

5.6.3   must not exaggerate the value of a prize or the chances of winning it.

5.7   Promotions that require a purchase to participate and include a direct exhortation to make a purchase must not be addressed to or targeted at children. See Section 8: Sales Promotions.

06   Privacy

Principle

Individuals should be protected from unwarranted infringements of privacy.

Rules

6.1   Marketers must not unfairly portray or refer to anyone in an adverse or offensive way unless that person has given the marketer written permission to allow it. Marketers are urged to obtain written permission before:

- referring to or portraying a member of the public or his or her identifiable possessions; the use of a crowd scene or a general public location may be acceptable without permission

- referring to a person with a public profile; references that accurately reflect the contents of a book, an article or a film might be acceptable without permission

- implying any personal approval of the advertised product; marketers should recognise that those who do not want to be associated with the product could have a legal claim.

Prior permission might not be needed if the marketing communication contains nothing that is inconsistent with the position or views of the featured person.

6.2   Members of the Royal Family should not normally be shown or mentioned in a marketing communication without their prior permission but an incidental reference unconnected with the advertised product, or a reference to material such as a book, article or film about a member of the Royal Family, may be acceptable.

07   Political advertisements

Rules

7.1   Claims in marketing communications, whenever published or distributed, whose principal function is to influence voters in a local, regional, national or international election or referendum are exempt from the Code.

7.2   Marketing communications by central or local Government, as distinct from those concerning party policy, are subject to the Code.

08   Sales promotions

Background

The sales promotion rules apply to consumer and trade promotions, incentive schemes and the promotional elements of sponsorships; they regulate the nature and administration of promotions.

Promoters should take legal advice before embarking on promotions with prizes, including competitions, prize draws, instant-win offers and premium promotions, to ensure that the mechanisms involved do not make them unlawful lotteries (see the Gambling Act 2005 for

Great Britain and the Betting, Gaming, Lotteries and Amusements (Northern Ireland) Order 1985 (as amended) for Northern Ireland).

Promoters should comply with all other relevant legislation, including data protection legislation for which guidance is available from the Information Commissioner's Office.

The sales promotion rules must be read in conjunction with all other parts of the Code, including the relevant rules in Section 5: Children and Section 18: Alcohol.

Definition

A sales promotion can provide an incentive for the consumer to buy by using a range of added direct or indirect benefits, usually on a temporary basis, to make the product more attractive. A non-exhaustive list of sales promotions includes: "two for the price of one" offers, money-off offers, text-to-wins, instant-wins, competitions and prize draws. The rules do not apply to routine, non-promotional, distribution of products or product extensions, for example one-off editorial supplements (in printed or electronic form) to newspapers or magazines.

Rules

8.1   Promoters are responsible for all aspects and all stages of their promotions.

8.2   Promoters must conduct their promotions equitably, promptly and efficiently and be seen to deal fairly and honourably with participants and potential participants. Promoters must avoid causing unnecessary disappointment.

Protection of consumers, Safety and Suitability

8.3   Promoters must do everything reasonable to ensure that their promotions, including product samples, are safe and cause no harm to consumers or their property. Literature accompanying promotional items must give any necessary warnings and safety advice.

8.4   Alcoholic drinks must not feature in promotions directed at people under 18. Alcohol must not be available on promotion to anyone under 18.

8.5   Promotions must not be socially undesirable to the audience addressed by encouraging excessive consumption or irresponsible use.

8.6   Promoters must do everything reasonable to ensure that unsuitable or irresponsible material does not reach consumers or other recipients.

8.7   No promotion or promotional item should cause serious or widespread offence to consumers.

Children

8.8   Special care must be taken with promotions addressed to children or if products or items intended for adults might fall into the hands of children. (See Section 5: Children)

Availability

8.9   Promoters must be able to demonstrate that they have made a reasonable estimate of the likely response and that they were capable of meeting that response.

8.10   Phrases such as "subject to availability" do not relieve promoters of their obligation to do everything reasonable to avoid disappointing participants.

8.11   Promoters must not encourage the consumer to make a purchase or series of purchases as a precondition to applying for promotional items if the number of those items is limited.

8.12   If, having made a reasonable estimate as in rule 8.9, it is unable to supply demand for a promotional offer because of an unexpectedly high response or some other unanticipated factor outside its control, the promoter must ensure relevant communication with applicants and consumers and offer a refund or a substitute product in accordance with rule 9.5.

8.13   If a prize promotion is widely advertised, the promoter must ensure the widespread availability of the requisite forms and any goods needed to establish proof of purchase.

Administration

8.14   Promoters must ensure that their promotions are conducted under proper supervision and make adequate resources available to administer them. Promoters, agencies and intermediaries should not give consumers justifiable grounds for complaint.

8.15 Promoters must allow adequate time for each phase of the promotion: notifying the trade, distributing the goods, issuing rules if relevant, collecting wrappers and the like and judging and announcing results.

8.15.1 Promoters must award the prizes as described in their marketing communications or reasonable equivalents.

8.16 Promoters must normally fulfil applications within 30 days in accordance with rule 9.4 and refund money in accordance with rule 9.5.

Significant conditions for promotions

Background

Please see the Children section, the Prize Promotions sub-section and the CAP Help Note on Promotions with Prizes.

8.17 Before purchase or, if no purchase is required, before or at the time of entry or application, promoters must communicate all applicable significant conditions. Significant conditions include:

8.17.1 How to participate

How to participate, including significant conditions and costs, and other major factors reasonably likely to influence consumers' decision or understanding about the promotion

8.17.2 Free-entry route explanation

Any free-entry route should be explained clearly and prominently

8.17.3 Start date

The start date, if applicable

8.17.4 Closing date

8.17.4.a A prominent closing date, if applicable, for purchases and submissions of entries or claims. Closing dates are not always necessary, for example: comparisons that refer to a special offer (whether the promoter's previous offer or a competitor's offer) if the offer is and is stated to be "subject to availability"; promotions limited only by the availability of promotional packs (gifts with a purchase, extra-volume packs and reduced-price packs) and loyalty schemes run on an open-ended basis

8.17.4.b   Unless the promotional pack includes the promotional item or prize and the only limit is the availability of that pack, prize promotions and promotions addressed to or targeted at children always need a closing date

8.17.4.c   Promoters must be able to demonstrate that the absence of a closing date will not disadvantage consumers

8.17.4.d   Promoters must state if the deadline for responding to undated promotional material will be calculated from the date the material was received by consumers

8.17.4.e   Unless circumstances outside the reasonable control of the promoter make it unavoidable, closing dates must not be changed. If they are changed, promoters must do everything reasonable to ensure that consumers who participated within the original terms are not disadvantaged

8.17.5   Proof of purchase

Any proof of purchase requirements

8.17.6   Prizes and gifts

Promoters must specify the number and nature of prizes or gifts, if applicable. If the exact number cannot be predetermined, a reasonable estimate of the number and a statement of their nature must be made. Promoters must:

8.17.6.a   distinguish those prizes that could be won, including estimated prize funds, from those prizes that will be won by someone by the end of the promotional period and

8.17.6.b   state whether prizes are to be awarded in instalments or are to be shared among recipients

8.17.7   Restrictions

Geographical, personal or technological restrictions such as location, age or the need to access the Internet. Promoters must state any need to obtain permission to enter from an adult or employer

8.17.8   Availability

The availability of promotional packs if it is not obvious; for example, if promotional packs could become unavailable before the stated closing date of the offer

8.17.9   Promoter's name and address

Unless it is obvious from the context or if entry into an advertised promotion is only through a dedicated website containing that information in an easily found format, the promoter's full name and correspondence address must be stated.

8.18   Marketing communications that include a promotion and are significantly limited by time or space must include as much information about significant conditions as practicable and must direct consumers clearly to an easily accessible alternative source where all the significant conditions of the promotion are prominently stated. Participants should be able to retain those conditions or easily access them throughout the promotion.

Prize promotions

Background

See CAP Help Note on Promotions with Prizes.

8.19   Promoters must not claim that consumers have won a prize if they have not. The distinction between prizes and gifts must always be clear: items offered to a significant proportion of consumers in a promotion should be described as gifts, not prizes, or any other term for either word likely to have the same meaning for consumers. If a promotion offers a gift to a significant proportion and a prize to those who win, special care is needed to avoid confusing the two: the promotion must, for example, state clearly that consumers "qualify" for the gift but have merely an opportunity to win the prize. If a promotion includes, in a list of prizes, a gift for which consumers have qualified, the promoter must distinguish clearly between the two.

8.20   Promoters must not exaggerate consumers' chances of winning prizes. They must not include a consumer who has been awarded a gift in a list of prize winners.

8.21   Promoters must not claim or imply that consumers are luckier than they are. They must not use terms such as "finalist" or "final stage" in a way that implies that consumers have progressed, by chance or skill, to an advanced stage of a promotion if they have not.

8.21.1   Promoters must not falsely claim or imply that the consumer has already won, will win or will on doing a particular act win a prize (or other equivalent benefit) if the consumer must incur a cost to claim the prize (or other equivalent benefit) or if the prize (or other equivalent benefit) does not exist.

8.22   Promoters must not claim that consumers must respond by a specified date or within a specified time if they need not.

8.23   Promoters must avoid complex rules and only exceptionally supplement conditions of entry with extra rules. If extra rules cannot be avoided, promoters must tell participants how to obtain them; the rules must contain nothing that could reasonably have influenced consumers against buying or participating.

8.24   Promoters of prize draws must ensure that prizes are awarded in accordance with the laws of chance and, unless winners are selected by a computer process that produces verifiably random results, by an independent person, or under the supervision of an independent person.

8.25   Participants in instant-win promotions must get their winnings at once or must know immediately what they have won and how to claim without delay, unreasonable cost or administrative barriers. Instant-win tickets, tokens or numbers must be awarded on a fair and random basis and verification must take the form of an independently audited statement that all prizes have been distributed, or made available for distribution, in that manner.

8.26   In competitions, if the selection of a winning entry is open to subjective interpretation, an independent judge, or a panel that includes one independent member must be appointed. In either case, the judge or panel member must be demonstrably independent, especially from the competition's promoters and intermediaries and from the pool of entrants from which the eventual winner is picked. Those appointed to act as judges should be competent to judge the competition and their full names must be made available on request.

8.27   Withholding prizes (see rules 8.15.1 and 8.28.2) is justified only if participants have not met the qualifying criteria set out clearly in the rules of the promotion.

8.28   Participants must be able to retain conditions or easily access them throughout the promotion. In addition to rule 8.17, prize promotions must specify before or at the time of entry:

8.28.1   any restriction on the number of entries

8.28.2   whether the promoter may substitute a cash alternative for any prize

8.28.3   if more than 30 days after the closing date, the date by which prizewinners will receive their prizes

8.28.4   how and when winners will be notified of results

8.28.5   how and when information about winners and results will be made available. Promoters must either publish or make available on request the name and county of major prizewinners and, if applicable, their winning entries. Prizewinners must not be compromised by the publication of excessive personal information

8.28.6   in a competition, the criteria and mechanism for judging entries (for example, the most apt and original tiebreaker)

8.28.7   if relevant, who owns the copyright of the entries

8.28.8   if applicable, how the promoter will return entries

8.28.9   any intention to use winners in post-event publicity.

Front-page flashes

8.29   Publishers announcing reader promotions on the front page or cover must ensure that consumers know whether they are expected to buy subsequent editions of the publication. Major conditions that might reasonably influence consumers significantly in their decision to buy must appear on the front page or cover. (see CAP Help Note on Front-page Flashes)

Trade Incentives

8.30   Incentive schemes must be designed and implemented to take account of the interests of everyone involved and must not compromise the obligation of employees to give honest advice to consumers.

8.31   If they intend to ask for help from, or offer incentives to, another company's employees, promoters must require those employees to obtain their employer's permission before participating. Promoters must observe any procedures established by companies for their employees, including any rules for participating in promotions.

8.32   Incentive schemes and relevant promotions must make clear if a tax liability might arise.

Charity-linked promotions

8.33   Promotions run by third parties (for example commercial companies) claiming that participation will benefit a registered charity or cause must:

> **8.33.1**   name each charity or cause that will benefit and be able to show the ASA or CAP the formal agreement with those benefiting from the promotion
>
> **8.33.2**   if it is not a registered charity, define its nature and objectives
>
> **8.33.3**   specify exactly what will be gained by the named charity or cause and state the basis on which the contribution will be calculated (see rule 8.34)
>
> **8.33.4**   state if the promoter has imposed a limit on its contributions
>
> **8.33.5**   not impose a cut-off point for contributions by consumers if an amount is stated for each purchase. If a target total is stated, extra money collected should be given to the named charity or cause on the same basis as contributions below that level
>
> **8.33.6**   be able to show that targets set are realistic
>
> **8.33.7**   not exaggerate the benefit to the charity or cause derived from individual purchases of the promoted product
>
> **8.33.8**   if asked, make available to consumers a current or final total of contributions made
>
> **8.33.9**   not directly encourage children to buy, or exhort children to persuade an adult to buy for them, a product that promotes charitable purposes.

8.34   Where a promotion states or implies that part of the price paid for goods or services will be given to a charity or cause, state the actual amount or percentage of the price that will be paid to the charity or cause.

> **8.34.1**   For any other promotion linked to a charity or where a third party states or implies that donations will be given to a charity or

cause, the promotion must state the total (or a reasonable estimate) of the amount the charity or cause will receive.

09   Distance selling

Background

Most distance selling contracts are subject to the Consumer Protection (Distance Selling) Regulations 2000 (as amended). These rules complement those Regulations and do not replace them.

These rules must be read in conjunction with other rules in this Code, especially the rules on availability in Section 3: Misleading Advertising.

The Direct Marketing Association (DMA) requires its members to observe the DM Code of Practice, which covers some practices that are not covered in the CAP Code.

Definition

Distance selling marketing communications are marketing communications that promote specific goods or services and include direct response mechanisms that allow readers to place orders without face-to-face contact with the marketer.

Rules

9.1   Distance selling marketing communications must make clear the marketer's identity and geographic address; that information must be given in a form that can be retained by consumers.

9.2   Distance selling marketing communications must include:

9.2.1   the main characteristics of the product

9.2.2   the price, including any VAT or other taxes payable (see "Prices" in Section 3: Misleading Advertising, and payment arrangements

9.2.3   the amount of any delivery charge

9.2.4   the estimated delivery or performance time (see rule 4.9.3) and arrangements

9.2.5 a statement that, unless inapplicable (see rule 9.6), consumers have the right to cancel orders for products. Marketers of services must explain how the right to cancel may be affected if the consumer agrees to services beginning less than 7 working days after the contract was concluded. They must, however, make it clear when the services will begin

9.2.6 any telephone, postal or other communication charge calculated at higher than the standard rate (for example, if a premium-rate call is required)

9.2.7 any other limitation on the offer (for example, period of availability) and any other condition that affects its validity

9.2.8 a statement on whether the marketer intends to provide substitute products (of equivalent quality and price) if those ordered are unavailable and one that it will meet the cost of returning substitute products on cancellation

9.2.9 if goods are supplied or services performed permanently or recurrently, the minimum duration of open-ended contracts.

9.3 At the latest by the time that goods are delivered or services begin, marketers must give consumers written information on:

9.3.1 how to exercise their right to cancel, unless inapplicable (see rule 9.6). Marketers must allow at least seven clear working days after delivery (or after the conclusion of service contracts unless the consumer agrees to an earlier start date) for consumers to cancel

9.3.2 for goods, whether the consumer has to return the goods to the suppliers on cancellation and, if so, who is to bear the cost of return or recovery of the goods (though see rule 2.8.9 for substitute goods)

9.3.3 any other guarantees and after-sales services

9.3.4 the full geographical address of the suppliers for any consumer complaints

9.3.5 the conditions that apply to the cancellation of any open-ended contract.

9.4 Marketers must fulfil orders within 30 days from the day consumers send their order unless:

9.4.1   the nature of the product or service makes it reasonable to specify a longer period in the marketing communications: for example, marketing communications for made-to-measure products, plants that are out of season, or products or services that are supplied on an instalment basis may reasonably specify a longer period, or

9.4.2   a longer performance period has been agreed with the consumer.

9.5   Marketers must refund money promptly (and at the latest within 30 days of notice of cancellation being given) if:

9.5.1   consumers have not received products within the specified period. If they prefer to wait, consumers must be given a firm dispatch date or fortnightly progress reports. Alternatively marketers may, if asked or if stated before purchase, provide a substitute of equivalent quality and price

9.5.2   products are returned because they are damaged when received, are faulty or are not as described; if so, the marketer must bear the cost of transit in both directions

9.5.3   consumers cancel within seven clear working days after delivery, unless the product is listed in rule 9.6. Consumers should assume they may try out products, except for audio or video recordings or computer software, but should take reasonable care of them before they are returned. Consumers must return the product and, unless the product is a substitute product sent instead of the ordered product, the marketer may require the consumer to pay the costs of doing so providing the marketer made that clear at the latest at the time the product was delivered.

9.5.4   an unconditional money-back guarantee is given and the products are returned within a reasonable period

9.5.5   products that have been returned are not received back, provided consumers can produce proof of posting.

9.6   If all contractual obligations to consumers are met, marketers do not have to provide a refund on:

9.6.1   services that have already begun with the consumer's agreement, if rule 9.2.5 has been complied with

9.6.2   products the price of which depends on financial market fluctuations that are outside the control of the supplier

9.6.3   perishable, personalised or made-to-measure products

9.6.4   audio or video recordings or computer software if unsealed by the consumer

9.6.5   newspapers, periodicals or magazines

9.6.6   betting, gaming or lottery services.

9.7   Marketers should take particular care when packaging products that might fall into the hands of children.

9.8   Marketers must not falsely imply that consumers have already ordered the marketed product by including in marketing material an invoice or similar document that seeks payment.

9.9   Marketers should not ask consumers to pay for or return unsolicited products, except for substitute products supplied in conformity with rules 8.12 and 9.5.1.

10   Database practice

Background

Marketers must comply with all relevant data protection legislation. Guidance on that legislation is available from the Information Commissioner's Office. Although data protection legislation has a wide application, these rules relate only to databases used for direct marketing purposes. The rules should be observed in conjunction with the legislation; they do not replace it.

Responsibility for complying with the database practice rules may rest directly not with marketers but with data controllers. Those responsible are expected to comply.

Definitions

A "data controller" is an entity that determines the purposes for which, and the manner in which, personal information is to be processed. It may be an individual or an organisation and the processing may be carried out jointly or in common with other persons or organisations.

A "preference service" is a service that, to reduce unsolicited contact, enables consumers and businesses to have their names and contact details in the UK removed from or added to lists that are used by the direct marketing industry.

Electronic mail in this section encompasses e-mail, Short Message Service (SMS), Multimedia Messaging Service (MMS) and other data transfer methods.

(See also CAP Help Notes on Mobile Marketing and Viral Marketing.)

Rules

10.1   Personal information must always be held securely and must be safeguarded against unauthorised use, disclosure, alteration or destruction.

10.2   Any proposed transfer of a database to a country outside the European Economic Area must be made only if that country ensures an adequate level of protection for the rights and freedoms of consumers in relation to the processing of personal information or if contractual arrangements provide that protection.

10.3   Marketers must do everything reasonable to ensure that, if asked in writing, consumers or the ASA (with consent of the consumer concerned) are given available information on the nature of a consumer's personal information and from where it has been obtained.

10.4   Marketers must not make persistent and unwanted marketing communications by telephone, fax, mail, e-mail or other remote media. To avoid making persistent and unwanted marketing communications, marketers must do everything reasonable to ensure that:

10.4.1   marketing communications are suitable for those they target

10.4.2   marketing communications are not sent unsolicited to consumers if explicit consent is required (see rule 10.13)

10.4.3   anyone who has been notified to them as dead is not contacted again and the notifier is referred to the relevant preference service

10.4.4   marketing communications are not sent to consumers who have asked not to receive them (see rule 10.5) or, if relevant, who have not had the opportunity to object to receiving them (see rule 10.9.3). Those consumers should be identifiable

10.4.5   databases are accurate and up-to-date and that reasonable requests for corrections to personal information are effected within 60 days.

10.5   Consumers are entitled to have their personal information suppressed. Marketers must ensure that, before use, databases have been run against relevant suppression files within a suitable period. Marketers must hold limited information, for suppression purposes only, to ensure that no other marketing communications are sent as a result of information about those consumers being re-obtained through a third party.

10.6   Marketing communications sent by electronic mail (but not those sent by Bluetooth technology) must contain the marketer's full name (or, in the case of SMS messages, a recognisable abbreviation) and a valid address; for example, an e-mail address or a SMS short code to which recipients can send opt-out requests.

10.7   Fax   and   non-live-sound   automated-call   marketing communications must contain the marketer's full name and a valid address or freephone number to which recipients can send opt-out requests.

10.8   Marketers are permitted, subject to these rules and to database rights, to use published information that is generally available if the consumer concerned is not listed on a relevant suppression file.

10.9   Unless it is obvious from the context, or if they already know, consumers must be informed in a clear and understandable manner and at the time personal information is collected:

10.9.1   who is collecting it (and the representative for data protection queries, if different)

10.9.2   why it is being collected

10.9.3   if the marketer intends to disclose the information to third parties, including associated but legally separate companies, or put the information to a use significantly different from that for which it is being provided; if so, an opportunity to prevent that from happening must be given.

10.10   The extent and detail of personal information held for any purpose must be adequate and relevant and should not be excessive for that purpose.

10.11   Personal information must not be kept for longer than is necessary for the purpose for which it was originally obtained.

10.12   If after collection they decide to use personal information for a purpose significantly different from that originally communicated, marketers must first get the explicit consent of consumers. Significantly different purposes include:

10.12.1   the disclosure of personal information to third parties for direct marketing purposes

10.12.2   the use or disclosure of personal information for any purpose substantially different from that which consumers could reasonably have foreseen and to which they might have objected.

10.13   The explicit consent of consumers (see rule 10.4) is required before:

10.13.1   processing sensitive personal data, including information on racial or ethnic origin, political opinion or religious or other similar beliefs, trade union membership, physical or mental health, sex life, criminal record or allegation of criminal activity

10.13.2   sending marketing communications by fax

10.13.3   sending marketing communications by electronic mail (excluding by Bluetooth technology) but marketers may send unsolicited marketing about their similar products to those whose data they have obtained during, or in negotiations for, a sale. Data marketers must, however, tell those consumers they may opt out of receiving future marketing communications both when they collect the data and at every subsequent occasion they send out marketing communications. Marketers must give consumers a simple means to do so

10.13.4   sending non-live-sound marketing communications by automated calling systems.

10.14   Explicit consent is not required when marketing business products by fax or by electronic mail to corporate subscribers (see III j), including to their named employees. Marketers must nevertheless comply with rules 10.4.5 and 10.5 and offer opt-outs in line with rule 10.13.3.

Children

Background

Please see Section 5: Children

10.15   Marketers must not knowingly collect from children under 12 personal information about those children for marketing purposes without first obtaining the consent of the child's parent or guardian.

10.16   Marketers must not knowingly collect personal information about other people from children under 16.

11   Environmental claims

Background

Marketers should take account of Government guidance including the Green Claims Code published by DEFRA and BIS.

Rules

11.1   The basis of environmental claims must be clear. Unqualified claims could mislead if they omit significant information.

11.2   The meaning of all terms used in marketing communications must be clear to consumers.

11.3   Absolute claims must be supported by a high level of substantiation. Comparative claims such as "greener" or "friendlier" can be justified, for example, if the advertised product provides a total environmental benefit over that of the marketer's previous product or competitor products and the basis of the comparison is clear.

11.4   Marketers must base environmental claims on the full life cycle of the advertised product, unless the marketing communication states otherwise, and must make clear the limits of the life cycle. If a general claim cannot be justified, a more limited claim about specific aspects of a product might be justifiable. Marketers must ensure claims that are based on only part of the advertised product's life cycle do not mislead consumers about the product's total environmental impact.

11.5   Marketers must not suggest that their claims are universally accepted if a significant division of informed or scientific opinion exists.

11.6   If a product has never had a demonstrably adverse effect on the environment, marketing communications must not imply that the formulation has changed to improve the product in the way claimed. Marketers may, however, claim that a product has always been designed in a way that omits an ingredient or process known to harm the environment.

11.7   Marketing communications must not mislead consumers about the environmental benefit that a product offers; for example, by highlighting the absence of an environmentally damaging ingredient if that ingredient is not usually found in competing products or by highlighting an environmental benefit that results from a legal obligation if competing products are subject to that legal obligation.

12   Medicines, medical devices, health-related products and beauty products

Background

The rules in this section are designed to ensure that marketing communications for medicines, medical devices, treatments, health-related products and beauty products receive the necessary high level of scrutiny. The rules apply to marketing communications and not the products, which are regulated by health regulators such as the Medicines and Healthcare products Regulatory Agency (MHRA), www.mhra.gov.uk, the European Medicines Agency (EMEA), www.emea.europa.eu and the Department of Health, www.dh.gov.uk. Marketing communications for those products must comply with the rules and professional codes of conduct of relevant professional bodies.

Definition

For the purposes of this Code, "licence" includes certificate, authorisation or registration.

For more information, see CAP Help Notes, especially those on: Substantiation for Health, Beauty and Slimming Claims; Health,

Beauty and Slimming Advertisements that Refer to Medical Conditions; Cosmetic Surgery Marketing and Use of Experts by the ASA and CAP.

Rules

12.1   Objective claims must be backed by evidence, if relevant consisting of trials conducted on people. If relevant, the rules in this section apply to claims for products for animals. Substantiation will be assessed on the basis of the available scientific knowledge.

Medicinal or medical claims and indications may be made for a medicinal product that is licensed by the MHRA or EMEA, or for a CE-marked medical device. A medicinal claim is a claim that a product or its constituent(s) can be used with a view to making a medical diagnosis or can treat or prevent disease, including an injury, ailment or adverse condition, whether of body or mind, in human beings.

Secondary medicinal claims made for cosmetic products as defined in the appropriate European legislation must be backed by evidence. These are limited to any preventative action of the product and may not include claims to treat disease.

12.2   Marketers must not discourage essential treatment for conditions for which medical supervision should be sought. For example, they must not offer specific advice on, diagnosis of or treatment for such conditions unless that advice, diagnosis or treatment is conducted under the supervision of a suitably qualified health professional. Accurate and responsible general information about such conditions may, however, be offered. (See rule 12.11.)

Health professionals will be deemed suitably qualified only if they can provide suitable credentials; for example, evidence of: relevant professional expertise or qualifications; systems for regular review of members' skills and competencies and suitable professional indemnity insurance covering all services provided; accreditation by a professional or regulatory body that has systems for dealing with complaints and taking disciplinary action and has registration based on minimum standards for training and qualifications.

12.3   Marketers offering individual treatments, especially those that are physically invasive, may be asked by the media and the ASA to provide full details together with information about those who supervise and administer them. Practitioners must have relevant and recognised qualifications. Marketers should encourage consumers to take independent medical advice before committing themselves to significant treatments, including those that are physically invasive.

12.4   Marketers must not confuse consumers by using unfamiliar scientific words for common conditions.

12.5   Marketers inviting consumers to diagnose their minor ailments must not make claims that might lead to a mistaken diagnosis.

12.6   Marketers should not falsely claim that a product is able to cure illness, dysfunction or malformations.

12.7   References to the relief of symptoms or the superficial signs of ageing are acceptable if they can be substantiated. Unqualified claims such as "cure" and "rejuvenation" are not generally acceptable, especially for cosmetic products.

12.8   Marketers must hold proof before claiming or implying that a minor addiction or a bad habit can be treated without effort from those suffering.

12.9   Marketers must not encourage consumers to use a product to excess and must hold proof before suggesting their product or therapy is guaranteed to work, absolutely safe or without side-effects.

12.10   Marketing communications must not suggest that any product is safe or effective merely because it is "natural" or that it is generally safer because it omits an ingredient in common use.

Medicines

The Medicines Act 1968 and secondary legislation issued under it, as well as Regulations implementing European Community Directive 2001/83/EC on the Community Code relating to medicinal products for human use, govern the advertising and promotion of medicines and the conditions of ill-health that medicines may be offered to treat. Guidance on the relevant legislation is available from the MHRA.

For more information on medicinal products and medical devices, go to: www.mhra.gov.uk. For more information on medical treatments, go to: www.healthcarecommission.org.uk.

12.11   Medicines must have a licence from the MHRA before they are marketed. Marketing communications for medicines must conform with the licence and the product's summary of product characteristics.

For the avoidance of doubt, by conforming with the product's indicated use, a marketing communication would not breach rule 12.2.

Marketing communications must not suggest that a product is "special" or "different" because it has been granted a licence by the MHRA.

12.12   Prescription-only medicines or prescription-only medical treatments may not be advertised to the public.

12.13   Marketing communications which include a product claim for a medicinal product (including legible on-pack product claims within a pack shot) must include the name of the product, an indication of what it is for, text such as "Always read the label" and the common name of the sole active ingredient, if it contains only one.

Marketing communications for a traditional herbal medicinal product or a homeopathic medicinal product must include mandatory information, which can be found in the MHRA's *The Blue Guide: Advertising and Promotion of Medicines in the UK* at www.mhra.gov. uk.

12.14   Marketers must not use fear or anxiety to promote a medicine or a recovery from illness and must not suggest that using or avoiding a product can affect normal health.

12.15   Illustrations of the effect or action of a product should be accurate.

12.16   Marketing communications for a medicine must not be addressed to children.

12.17   Marketers must not suggest that a medicinal product is either a food or a cosmetic.

12.18   Marketers must not use health professionals or celebrities to endorse medicines.

12.19   Marketing communications for a medicine may not claim that its effects are as good as or better than those of another identifiable product.

12.20   Homeopathic medicinal products must be registered in the UK. Any product information given in the marketing communication should be confined to what appears on the label. Marketing communications must include a warning to consult a doctor if symptoms persist. Marketing communications for an unlicensed product must not make a medicinal or therapeutic claim or refer to an ailment unless authorised by the MHRA to do so.

12.21   Marketers of traditional herbal medicines may advertise for the indications listed in the product's summary of product characteristics. Marketing communications for products that hold a Traditional Herbal Medicines Registration must not imply that registration is based upon clinical trials.

Cosmetics

12.22   Claims made about the action that a cosmetic has on or in the skin should distinguish between the composition of the product and any effects brought about by the way in which it is applied, such as massage. Scientific evidence must also make that distinction.

12.22.1   Some cosmetics have an effect on the type of skin changes that are caused by environmental factors. Marketing communications for them may therefore refer to temporarily preventing, delaying or masking premature ageing.

Hair and Scalp

12.23   Marketers must be able to provide scientific evidence, if relevant consisting of trials conducted on people, for any claim that their product or therapy can prevent baldness or slow it down, arrest or reverse hair loss, stimulate or improve hair growth, nourish hair roots, strengthen the hair or improve its health as distinct from its appearance.

13   Weight control and slimming

Background

The rules in this section are designed to ensure that marketing communications for slimming and weight control products receive the necessary high level of scrutiny.

See CAP Slimming Guidelines for Press Advertisements.

Definition

This section applies to marketing communications for weight control and slimming foodstuffs, aids (including exercise products that make weight-loss or slimming claims), clinics and other establishments, diets, medicines, treatments and the like. If applicable, they must comply with Section 12: Medicines, Medical Devices, Health-related Products and Beauty Products and Section 15: Food, Food Supplements and Associated Health or Nutrition Claims).

Rules

13.1   A weight-reduction regime in which the intake of energy is lower than its output is the most common self-treatment for achieving weight reduction. Any claim made for the effectiveness or action of a weight-reduction method or product must be backed, if applicable, by rigorous trials on people; testimonials that are not supported by trials do not constitute substantiation.

13.2   Obesity in adults is defined by a Body Mass Index (BMI) of more than 30 kg/m^2. Obesity is frequently associated with a medical condition and a treatment for it must not be advertised to the public unless it is to be used under suitably qualified supervision. Marketing communications for non-prescription medicines that are indicated for the treatment of obesity and that require the involvement of a pharmacist in the sale or supply of the medicine may nevertheless be advertised to the public.

13.3   Marketing communications for any weight-reduction regime or establishment must neither be directed at nor contain anything that is likely to appeal particularly to people who are under 18 or those for whom weight reduction would produce a potentially harmful body weight (BMI of less than 18.5 kg/m^2). Those marketing communications must not suggest that being underweight is desirable or acceptable.

13.4   Before they make claims for a weight-reduction aid or regimen, marketers must show that weight-reduction is achieved by loss of body fat. Combining a diet with an unproven weight-reduction method does not justify making weight-reduction claims for that method.

13.5   Marketers must be able to show that their diet plans are nutritionally well-balanced (except for producing a deficit of energy) and that must be assessed in relation to the category of person who would use them.

13.6   Vitamins and minerals do not contribute to weight reduction but may be offered to slimmers as a safeguard against any shortfall in recommended intake when dieting.

13.7   Marketers promoting Very Low Calorie Diets or other diets that fall below 800 kilo-calories a day must do so only for short-term use and must encourage users to take medical advice before embarking on them. Marketers should have regard to the guidance on "Obesity: the prevention, identification, assessment and management of overweight and obesity in adults and children" (2006) published by the National Institute for Health and Clinical Excellence.

13.8   Marketing communications for diet aids must make clear how they work. Prominence must be given to the role of the diet and marketing communications must not give the impression that dieters cannot fail or can eat as much as they like and still lose weight.

13.9   Marketing communications must not contain claims that people can lose precise amounts of weight within a stated period or, except for marketing communications for surgical clinics, establishments and the like that comply with rule 12.3, that weight or fat can be lost from specific parts of the body.

13.9.1   Marketing communications for surgical clinics, establishments and the like that comply with rule 12.3 must not refer to the amount of weight that can be lost.

13.10   Claims that an individual has lost an exact amount of weight must be compatible with good medical and nutritional practice. Those claims must state the period involved and must not be based on unrepresentative experiences. For those who are normally overweight, a rate of weight loss greater than 2 lbs (just under 1 kg) a week is unlikely to be compatible with good medical and nutritional practice. For those who are obese, a rate of weight loss greater than 2 lbs a week in the early stages of dieting could be compatible with good medical and nutritional practice.

13.10.1   Health claims in marketing communications for food products that refer to a rate or amount of weight loss are not permitted.

13.11   Resistance and aerobic exercise can improve muscular condition and tone and that can improve body shape and posture. Marketers must be able to substantiate any claim that such methods used alone or in conjunction with a diet plan can lead to weight or inch reduction. Marketing communications for intensive exercise programmes should encourage users to check with a doctor before starting.

13.12   Short-term loss of girth may be achieved by wearing a tight-fitting garment. That loss must not be portrayed as permanent or confused with weight or fat reduction.

14   Financial products

Background

Marketers must have regard to the financial promotion restriction in Section 21 of the Financial Services and Markets Act 2000 and in the Financial Services and Markets Act 2000 (Financial Promotion) Order 2005 (as amended), as reflected in the rules and guidance issued and enforced by the Financial Services Authority (FSA). The scope of that legislation, rules and guidance extends to marketing communications for: investments and investment advice; deposit taking (for example, banking); home finance transactions (regulated mortgages, home purchase plans and home finance plans); general insurance and pure protection policies (for example, term assurance). The FSA is responsible for the regulation of first-charge mortgage lending and selling, as well as certain secured loans and the activities of insurance intermediaries. The FSA does not provide pre-publication advice on proposed financial marketing communications; technical guidance is available on specific matters or rule interpretation only. For more information, contact the FSA (see www.fsa.gov.uk). The Office of Fair Trading (OFT) regulates other consumer loans under the Consumer Credit Act 1974 (as amended) and the Consumer Credit (Advertisements) Regulations 2004 (as amended). Debt management companies must ensure they comply with the Guidance for Debt Management Companies published by the OFT.

The rules that follow apply to financial marketing communications that are not regulated by the FSA or the OFT and to marketing communications for debt advice. All financial marketing communications are, however, subject to Code rules that cover non-technical elements of communications; for example, serious or widespread offence, social responsibility and the truthfulness of claims that do not relate to specific characteristics of financial products.

Rules

14.1   Offers of financial products must be set out in a way that allows them to be understood easily by the audience being addressed. Marketers must ensure that they do not take advantage of consumers' inexperience or credulity.

14.2   Marketing communications should state the nature of the contract being offered, any limitation, expense, penalty or charge and the terms of withdrawal. Alternatively, if a marketing communication is short or general in its content, free material explaining the offer must be made readily available to consumers before a binding contract is entered into.

14.3   The basis used to calculate any rate of interest, forecast or projection must be apparent immediately.

14.4   Marketing communications must make clear that the value of investments is variable and, unless guaranteed, can go down as well as up. If the value of the investment is guaranteed, the marketing communication must explain the guarantee.

14.5   Marketing communications should make clear that past performance or experience does not necessarily give a guide for the future; if they are used in marketing communications, examples of past performance or experience should not be unrepresentative.

15   Food, food supplements and associated health or nutrition claims

Principle

Public health policy increasingly emphasises good dietary behaviour and an active lifestyle as a means of promoting health. Commercial product advertising cannot reasonably be expected to perform the same role as education and public information in promoting a varied and balanced diet but should not undermine progress towards national dietary improvement by misleading or confusing consumers.

Background

These rules must be read in conjunction with the relevant legislation including the Food Safety Act 1990, the Food Labelling Regulations 1996 (as amended) - especially Schedule 6 and Regulation (EC) No 1924/2006 on Nutrition and Health Claims made on Foods.

Regulation (EC) No 1924/2006 on Nutrition and Health Claims made on Foods is complex and mandatory and seeks to protect consumers from misleading or false claims. Transitional periods apply and CAP advises advertising industry stakeholders to take advice on the effect of that Regulation. Advertising industry stakeholders might find the Guidance to Compliance with European Regulation (EC) No 1924 on

Nutrition and Health Claims Made on Foods published by the Food Standards Agency useful: www.food.gov.uk.

References to food apply also to soft drink products.

These rules should be read in conjunction with other rules in this Code, especially Section 5: Children, Section 13: Weight Control and Slimming, the Help Note on Food and Soft Drink Products and Children and the Help Note on Criteria for Nutrition Claims.

Rules

General

15.1   Marketing communications that contain nutrition or health claims must be supported by documentary evidence to show they meet the conditions of use associated with the relevant claim, as specified by the European Commission. Claims must be presented clearly and without exaggeration.

> **15.1.1**   Only Nutrition Claims listed in the Annex of EC Regulation 1924/2006 on Nutrition and Health Claims Made on Foods or claims that would have the same meaning may be used in marketing communications.

Authorised health claims in the Community Register or claims that would have the same meaning may be used in marketing communications.

Depending on the nature of the claim EC Regulation 1924/2006 contains a number of complex transitional periods, including those for health claims which are still being assessed for adoption to the EU list of permitted health claims (and which comply with existing national provisions), and for trademarks or brand names in use prior to 1 January 2005. There is no transition period for reduction of disease risk claims, which are prohibited until authorised. CAP advises advertising industry stakeholders to take advice on the effect of the Regulation.

15.2   References to general benefits of a nutrient or food for overall good health or health-related well-being are acceptable only if accompanied by a relevant authorised claim.

15.3   Comparative nutrition claims must compare the difference in the claimed nutrient to a range of foods of the same category which do not have a composition which allows them to bear a nutrition claim.

15.3.1 A marketing communication may use one product as the sole reference for comparison only if that product is representative of the products in its category.

15.3.2 The difference in the quantity of a nutrient or energy value must be stated in the marketing communication and must relate to the same quantity of food.

15.4 Marketing communications must not condone or encourage excessive consumption of a food.

15.5 Marketing communications must not condone or encourage damaging oral health care practices, especially in children.

15.6 These are not acceptable in marketing communications for products within the remit of this section:

15.6.1 Claims that state or imply health could be affected by not consuming a food

15.6.2 Claims that state or imply a food prevents, treats or cures human disease. Reduction-of disease-risk claims are acceptable if authorised by the European Commission

15.6.3 Health claims that refer to the recommendation of an individual health professional. Health claims that refer to the recommendation of an association are acceptable only if that association is a health-related charity or a national representative body of medicine, nutrition or dietetics

15.6.4 References to changes in bodily functions that could give rise to or exploit fear in the audience

15.6.5 Claims of a nutrition or health benefit that gives rise to doubt the safety or nutritional adequacy of another product

15.6.6 Health claims that refer to a rate or amount of weight loss.

Food Supplements and other Vitamins and Minerals

CAP advises marketers to ensure that claims made for dietary supplements and other vitamins and minerals are in line with the requirements of Regulation (EC) No 1924/2006 on Nutrition and Health Claims made on Foods.

15.7 Nutrition and health claims for food supplements must be permitted or authorised as provided for at rule 15.1.1 above.

Marketing communications that contain nutrition or health claims must be supported by documentary evidence to show they meet the conditions of use associated with the relevant claim, as specified by the European Commission.

15.8   Marketers must not state or imply that a balanced or varied diet cannot provide appropriate quantities of nutrients in general. Individuals should not be encouraged to swap a healthy diet for supplementation, and without well-established proof, no marketing communication may suggest that a widespread vitamin or mineral deficiency exists.

15.9   Marketing communications for foods must not claim to treat clinical vitamin or mineral deficiency.

Infant and follow-on formula

These rules must be read in conjunction with the relevant legislation including the Infant Formula and Follow-on Formula Regulations 2007 and the European Regulation (EC) No 1924/2006 on Nutrition and Health Claims made on Foods.

15.10   Except for those in a scientific publication or, for the purposes of trade before the retail stage, a publication of which the intended readers are not the general public, marketing communications for infant formula are prohibited.

15.10.1   Marketing communications must not confuse between infant formula and follow-on formula.

Food and Soft drink product Marketing communications and children

Background

See also the Help Note for food or soft drink product advertisements and children.

Diet and Lifestyle

15.11   Marketing communications must not condone or encourage poor nutritional habits or an unhealthy lifestyle in children.

15.12   Marketing communications must not disparage good dietary practice or the selection of options, such as fresh fruit and fresh vegetables, that accepted dietary opinion recommends should form part of the average diet.

Promotional Offers

15.13   Marketing communications featuring a promotional offer must be prepared with a due sense of responsibility.

15.14   Except those for fresh fruit and fresh vegetables, food product advertisements that are targeted through their content directly at pre-school or primary school children must not include a promotional offer.

> **15.14.1**   Except those for fresh fruit or fresh vegetables, marketing communications must not seem to encourage children to eat or drink a product only to take advantage of a promotional offer: the product should be offered on its merits, with the offer as an added incentive. Marketing communications featuring a promotional offer must ensure a significant presence for the product.
>
> **15.14.2**   Marketing communications featuring a promotional offer linked to a food product of interest to children must avoid creating a sense of urgency or encouraging the purchase of an excessive quantity for irresponsible consumption.
>
> **15.14.3**   Marketing communications must not encourage children to eat more than they otherwise would.
>
> **15.14.4**   Marketing communications for collection-based promotions must not seem to urge children or their parents to buy excessive quantities of food.

Licensed characters and celebrities

15.15   Licensed characters and celebrities popular with children must be used with a due sense of responsibility. Except those for fresh fruit or fresh vegetables, food advertisements that are targeted directly at pre-school or primary school children through their content must not include licensed characters or celebrities popular with children.

For the avoidance of doubt, that prohibition applies to food or drink advertisements only. The prohibition does not apply to advertiser-created equity brand characters (puppets, persons or characters), which may be used by advertisers to sell the products they were designed to sell.

Licensed characters and celebrities popular with children may present factual and relevant generic statements about nutrition, safety, education or similar.

Pressure to purchase

15.16   Although children might be expected to exercise some preference over the food they eat or drink, marketing communications must be prepared with a due sense of responsibility and must not directly advise or ask children to buy or to ask their parents or other adults to make enquiries or purchases for them. (see rule 5.4.2).

> **15.16.1**   Marketing communications must neither try to sell to children by directly appealing to emotions such as pity, fear or self-confidence nor suggest that having the advertised product somehow confers superiority; for example, making a child more confident, clever, popular or successful.

> **15.16.2**   Marketing communications addressed to children must not urge children to buy or persuade others to buy and must avoid high-pressure or hard-sell techniques. Nothing must suggest that children could be bullied, cajoled or otherwise put under pressure to acquire the advertised item.

> **15.16.3**   Products or prices must not be presented in marketing communications in a way that suggests children or their families can easily afford them.

Nutrition claims and health claims

15.17   Marketing communications must not give a misleading impression of the nutritional or health benefit of the product as a whole. Claims referring to children's development and health are acceptable if authorised by the European Commission.

16   Gambling

Principle

The rules in this section are designed to ensure that marketing communications for gambling products are socially responsible, with particular regard to the need to protect children, young persons under 18 and other vulnerable persons from being harmed or exploited by advertising that features or promotes gambling.

Background

The term "gambling" means gaming and betting, as defined in the Gambling Act 2005, and spread betting. For rules on lottery marketing communications, see Section 17.

The Gambling Act 2005 does not apply outside Great Britain. Specialist legal advice should be sought when considering advertising any gambling product in Northern Ireland or the Channel Islands.

Spread betting may be advertised as an investment under the Financial Services and Markets Act 2000, the Financial Services and Markets Act 2000 (Financial Promotion) Order 2005 (as amended) and other FSA rules and guidance (see Background, Section 14, Financial Products). A "spread bet" is a contract for difference that is a gaming contract, as defined in the glossary to the *FSA Handbook*.

The rules in this section apply to marketing communications for "play for money" gambling products and marketing communications for "play for free" gambling products that offer the chance to win a prize or explicitly or implicitly direct the consumer to a "play for money" gambling product, whether on-shore or off-shore.

These rules are not intended to inhibit marketing communications to counter problem gambling that are responsible and unlikely to promote a brand or type of gambling.

Unless they portray or refer to gambling, this section does not apply to marketing communications for non-gambling leisure events or facilities, for example, hotels, cinemas, bowling alleys or ice rinks, that are in the same complex as, but separate from, gambling events or facilities.

For the purposes of this section, "children" are people of 15 and under and "young persons" are people of 16 or 17.

Rules

16.1   Marketing communications for gambling must be socially responsible, with particular regard to the need to protect children, young persons and other vulnerable persons from being harmed or exploited.

16.2   In line with rule 1.2, the spirit as well as the letter of the rules in this section apply whether or not a gambling product is shown or referred to.

16.3   Marketing communications must not:

16.3.1   portray, condone or encourage gambling behaviour that is socially irresponsible or could lead to financial, social or emotional harm

16.3.2   exploit the susceptibilities, aspirations, credulity, inexperience or lack of knowledge of children, young persons or other vulnerable persons

16.3.3   suggest that gambling can provide an escape from personal, professional or educational problems such as loneliness or depression

16.3.4   suggest that gambling can be a solution to financial concerns, an alternative to employment or a way to achieve financial security

16.3.5   portray gambling as indispensable or as taking priority in life; for example, over family, friends or professional or educational commitments

16.3.6   suggest that gambling can enhance personal qualities, for example, that it can improve self-image or self-esteem, or is a way to gain control, superiority, recognition or admiration

16.3.7   suggest peer pressure to gamble nor disparage abstention

16.3.8   link gambling to seduction, sexual success or enhanced attractiveness

16.3.9   portray gambling in a context of toughness or link it to resilience or recklessness

16.3.10   suggest gambling is a rite of passage

16.3.11   suggest that solitary gambling is preferable to social gambling

16.3.12   be likely to be of particular appeal to children or young persons, especially by reflecting or being associated with youth culture

16.3.13   be directed at those aged below 18 years (or 16 years for football pools, equal-chance gaming [under a prize gaming permit or at a licensed family entertainment centre], prize gaming (at a non-licensed family entertainment centre or at a travelling fair) or Category D gaming machines) through the selection of media or context in which they appear

16.3.14 include a child or a young person. No-one who is, or seems to be, under 25 years old may be featured gambling or playing a significant role. No-one may behave in an adolescent, juvenile or loutish way

16.3.15 exploit cultural beliefs or traditions about gambling or luck

16.3.16 condone or encourage criminal or anti-social behaviour

16.3.17 condone or feature gambling in a working environment. An exception exists for licensed gambling premises.

16.4 Marketing communications for family entertainment centres, travelling fairs, horse racecourses and dog race tracks, and for non-gambling leisure facilities that incidentally refer to separate gambling facilities, for example, as part of a list of facilities on a cruise ship, may include children or young persons provided they are accompanied by an adult and are socialising responsibly in areas that the Gambling Act 2005 does not restrict by age.

16.5 Marketing communications for events or facilities that can be accessed only by entering gambling premises must make that condition clear.

17   Lotteries

Principle

The rules in this section are designed to ensure that marketing communications for lotteries are socially responsible, with particular regard to the need to protect children, young persons under 18 and other vulnerable persons from being harmed or exploited by advertising that features or promotes lotteries.

This section applies to marketing communications for lottery products that are licensed and regulated by the Gambling Commission, the National Lottery Commission, or in the case of small society lotteries, registered with local authorities in England and Wales or licensing boards in Scotland.

The UK National Lottery may be advertised under The National Lottery etc Act 1993 and The National Lottery Regulations 1994 (as amended). Marketing communications for the UK National Lottery are also subject to the National Lottery Advertising and Sales Promotion Code of Practice, approved by the National Lottery Commission.

Rules

17.1 Marketing communications must not portray, condone or encourage gambling behaviour that is socially irresponsible or could lead to financial, social or emotional harm.

17.2 Marketing communications must not suggest that participating in a lottery can provide an escape from personal, professional or educational problems such as loneliness or depression.

17.3 Marketing communications must not suggest that participating in a lottery can be a solution to financial concerns, an alternative to employment or a way to achieve financial security. Advertisers may, however, refer to other benefits of winning a prize.

17.4 Marketing communications must not portray participating in a lottery as indispensable or as taking priority in life; for example, over family, friends or professional or educational commitments.

17.5 Marketing communications must neither suggest peer pressure to participate nor disparage abstention.

17.6 Marketing communications must not suggest that participating in a lottery can enhance personal qualities, for example, that it can improve self-image or self-esteem, or is a way to gain control, superiority, recognition or admiration.

17.7 Marketing communications must not link participating in a lottery to seduction, sexual success or enhanced attractiveness.

17.8 Marketing communications must not portray participation in a context of toughness or link it to resilience or recklessness.

17.9 Marketing communications must not suggest participation is a rite of passage.

17.10 Marketing communications must not suggest that solitary gambling is preferable to social gambling.

17.11 Marketing communications for lotteries that can be participated in only by entering gambling premises must make that condition clear.

17.12 Marketing communications for lotteries must not exploit the susceptibilities, aspirations, credulity, inexperience or lack of knowledge of children, young persons or other vulnerable persons.

17.13 Marketing communications for lotteries must not be likely to be of particular appeal to children or young persons, especially by reflecting or being associated with youth culture.

17.14 Marketing communications for lotteries should not be directed at those aged under 16 years through the selection of media or context in which they appear.

17.15 Marketing communications for a lottery product may include children or young persons. No-one who is, or seems to be, under 25 years old may be featured gambling or playing a significant role.

17.16 Marketing communications that exclusively feature the good causes that benefit from a lottery and include no explicit encouragement to buy a lottery product may include children or young persons in a significant role.

17.17 Marketing communications for lotteries must not exploit cultural beliefs or traditions about gambling or luck.

17.18 Marketing communications for lotteries must not condone or encourage criminal or antisocial behaviour.

17.19 Marketing communications for lotteries must not condone or feature gambling in a working environment (an exception exists for workplace lottery syndicates and gambling premises).

18   Alcohol

Principle

Marketing communications for alcoholic drinks should not be targeted at people under 18 and should not imply, condone or encourage immoderate, irresponsible or anti-social drinking.

The spirit as well as the letter of the rules applies.

Definition

The rules in this section apply to marketing communications for alcoholic drinks and marketing communications that feature or refer to alcoholic drinks. Alcoholic drinks are defined as drinks containing at least 0.5% alcohol; for the purposes of this Code low-alcohol drinks are defined as drinks containing between 0.5% and 1.2% alcohol.

Where stated, exceptions are made for low-alcohol drinks. But, if a marketing communication for a low-alcohol drink could be considered to promote a stronger alcoholic drink or if the drink's low-alcohol content is not stated clearly in the marketing communications, all the rules in this section apply.

If a soft drink is promoted as a mixer, the rules in this section apply in full.

These rules are not intended to inhibit responsible marketing communications that are intended to counter problem drinking or tell consumers about alcohol-related health or safety themes. Those marketing communications should not be likely to promote an alcohol product or brand.

Rules

18.1   Marketing communications must be socially responsible and must contain nothing that is likely to lead people to adopt styles of drinking that are unwise. For example, they should not encourage excessive drinking. Care should be taken not to exploit the young, the immature or those who are mentally or socially vulnerable.

18.2   Marketing communications must not claim or imply that alcohol can enhance confidence or popularity.

18.3   Marketing communications must not imply that drinking alcohol is a key component of the success of a personal relationship or social event. The consumption of alcohol may be portrayed as sociable or thirst-quenching.

18.4   Drinking alcohol must not be portrayed as a challenge. Marketing communications must neither show, imply, encourage or refer to aggression or unruly, irresponsible or anti-social behaviour nor link alcohol with brave, tough or daring people or behaviour.

18.5   Marketing communications must neither link alcohol with seduction, sexual activity or sexual success nor imply that alcohol can enhance attractiveness.

18.6   Marketing communications must not imply that alcohol might be indispensable or take priority in life or that drinking alcohol can overcome boredom, loneliness or other problems.

18.7   Marketing communications must not imply that alcohol has therapeutic qualities. Alcohol must not be portrayed as capable of changing mood, physical condition or behaviour or as a source of nourishment. Marketing communications must not imply that alcohol can enhance mental or physical capabilities; for example, by contributing to professional or sporting achievements.

18.8   Marketing communications must not link alcohol to illicit drugs.

18.9   Marketing communications may give factual information about the alcoholic strength of a drink. They may also make a factual alcohol strength comparison with another product, but only when the comparison is with a higher strength product of a similar beverage. Marketing communications must not imply that a drink may be preferred because of its alcohol content or intoxicating effect. There is an exception for low-alcohol drinks, which may be presented as preferable because of their low alcoholic strength.

In the case of a drink with relatively high alcoholic strength in relation to its category, the factual information should not be given undue emphasis.

18.10   Marketing communications that include a sales promotion must not imply, condone or encourage excessive consumption of alcohol.

18.11   Marketing communications must not feature alcohol being handled or served irresponsibly.

18.12   Marketing communications must not link alcohol with activities or locations in which drinking would be unsafe or unwise.

Marketing communications must not link alcohol with the use of potentially dangerous machinery or driving. Marketing communications may feature sporting and other physical activities (subject to other rules in this section; for example, appeal to under-18s or link with daring or aggression) but must not imply that those activities have been undertaken after the consumption of alcohol.

18.13 Only in exceptional circumstances may marketing communications feature alcohol being drunk by anyone in their working environment.

18.14 Marketing communications must not be likely to appeal particularly to people under 18, especially by reflecting or being associated with youth culture. They should not feature or portray real or fictitious characters who are likely to appeal particularly to people under 18 in a way that might encourage the young to drink. People shown drinking or playing a significant role (see rule 18.16) should not be shown behaving in an adolescent or juvenile manner

18.15 Marketing communications must not be directed at people under 18 through the selection of media or the context in which they appear. No medium should be used to advertise alcoholic drinks if more than 25% of its audience is under 18 years of age.

18.16 People shown drinking or playing a significant role must neither be nor seem to be under 25. People under 25 may be shown in marketing communications, for example, in the context of family celebrations, but must be obviously not drinking.

18.17 Marketing communications may give factual information about product contents, including comparisons, but must not make any health, fitness or weight-control claims. The only permitted nutrition claims are "low-alcohol", "reduced alcohol" and "reduced energy" and any claim likely to have the same meaning for the consumer.

19   Motoring

Principle

Marketing communications should not condone or encourage unsafe or inconsiderate driving practices. If they make environmental claims, marketing communications for motor vehicles, fuel or accessories should comply with the rules in Section 11.

Rules

19.1 Marketing communications for motor vehicles, fuel or accessories must not depict or refer to practices that condone or encourage anti-social behaviour.

19.2   Marketing communications must not condone or encourage unsafe or irresponsible driving. If it could be emulated, marketing communications must not depict a driving practice that is likely to condone or encourage a breach of those rules of the Highway Code that are legal requirements if that driving practice seems to take place on a public road or in a public space. Vehicles' capabilities may be demonstrated on a track or circuit if it is obviously not in use as a public highway.

19.3   Marketing communications must not depict speed in a way that might encourage motorists to drive irresponsibly or to break the law.

To avoid the implication of irresponsible driving through excessive speed, care must be taken in the style of presentation of marketing communications. Particular care must be taken in, for example, cinema commercials and in marketing communications that appear in electronic media to avoid moving images that imply excessive speed. If they are shown in normal driving circumstances on public roads, vehicles must be seen not to exceed UK speed limits.

19.4   Marketers must not make speed or acceleration the main message of their marketing communications. Marketing communications may give general information about a vehicle's performance, such as acceleration and mid-range statistics, braking power, road-holding and top speed.

19.5   Safety claims must not exaggerate the benefit to consumers. Marketers must not make absolute claims about safety unless they hold evidence to substantiate them.

20   Employment, homework schemes and business opportunities

Rules

Employment

20.1   Marketing communications must distinguish clearly between offers of employment and business opportunities. Before publication, media owners normally require marketers' full details and any terms and conditions imposed on respondents.

20.2   Employment marketing communications must relate to genuine vacancies and potential employees must not be asked to pay for information.

Living and working conditions must not be misrepresented. Quoted earnings must be precise; if one has to be made, a forecast must not be unrepresentative. If income is earned from a basic salary and commission, commission only or in some other way, that must be made clear.

Employment agencies and Employment Businesses

20.3   Employment agencies and employment businesses must make clear in their marketing communications their full names and contact details. Marketing communications should state that the marketer is an employment agency or an employment business if its name does not disclose that it is.

Homework Schemes

20.4   Marketing communications for homework schemes must contain no forecast of earnings if the scheme is new. Marketers may state the likely level of earnings only if it can be supported with evidence of the experience of existing homeworkers. Marketers must not exaggerate the support available to homeworkers.

20.5   Marketing communications for homework schemes must state:

20.5.1   limitations or conditions that might influence consumers before their decision to participate

20.5.2   whether the marketers will buy any products made

20.5.3   if a financial outlay is, or might be, required.

20.6   Marketers of homework schemes must include this information in the initial marketing communication or in follow-up literature made available to all consumers before commitment:

20.6.1   the full name and geographical address of the marketer

20.6.2   a clear description of the work

20.6.3   whether participants are self-employed or employed by a business

20.6.4 charges for raw materials, machines, components, administration and the like.

Business Opportunities

20.7 Marketing communications for business opportunities must neither contain unrepresentative or overstated earnings figures nor exaggerate the support available to investors.

20.8 Marketers of business opportunities must include in their initial marketing communications or in follow-up literature made available to all consumers before commitment:

20.8.1 the full name and geographical address of the marketer

20.8.2 a clear description of the work involved

20.8.3 a statement of the extent of investors' commitments, including any financial investment or outlay.

Vocational Training and Instruction courses

20.9 Marketing communications for vocational training or other instruction courses must not give a misleading impression about the potential for employment that might follow.

Marketing communications must make clear significant conditions for acceptance onto vocational training or instruction courses, such as the level of attainment, and significant conditions likely to affect a consumer's decision to embark on a course, such as the cost or the duration of a course.

Employment, homeworking Schemes and Business Opportunities directories

20.10 Marketing communications for the sale of directories giving information about employment, homeworking schemes or business opportunities must state plainly the nature of what is being offered.

21   Tobacco, rolling papers and filters

Scope

The Rolling Papers and Filters rules govern the content of marketing communications, including point-of-sale material, for:

a. rolling papers and filters

b. any product if the marketing communication concerned features rolling papers, filters or a pack design of a recognisable brand available in the UK

c. a product displaying the colours, livery, logo or name of a rolling paper or a brand of filter in a way that promotes smoking and not that branded product.

The Rolling Papers and Filters rules do not apply to marketing communications:

d. addressed to the trade in its professional capacity in media not targeted at the public

e. for schemes, events or activities sponsored or financially supported by manufacturers or importers, including sports sponsorship, so long as undue emphasis is not placed on the rolling papers or filters as opposed to the scheme, event or activity

f. on manufacturers' or importers' websites (see Scope of the Code II q).

Other rules in the CAP Code, such as the sales promotion rules, apply to (d) and (e).

Rules

Tobacco products

21.1 Tobacco products may not be advertised to the public.

Rolling papers and filters

21.2 Marketing communications for rolling papers or filters must neither encourage people to start smoking nor encourage people who smoke to increase their consumption.

21.3 Marketing communications for rolling papers or filters must not:

21.3.1 play on the susceptibilities of those who are physically or emotionally vulnerable, especially the young or immature

21.3.2   suggest that smoking is natural, safe, popular, glamorous or aspirational or that it can lead to social, sexual, romantic or business success

21.3.3   suggest that smoking can enhance people's femininity, masculinity or appearance

21.3.4   appeal to the adventurous or rebellious or suggest that it is daring to smoke or that smoking can enhance people's independence

21.3.5   link smoking with people who are well known, wealthy, fashionable, sophisticated or successful or who possess other attributes or qualities that may reasonably be expected to command admiration or encourage emulation

21.3.6   must not suggest that smoking is healthy, can be enjoyed as part of a healthy lifestyle or that it can aid relaxation or concentration.

21.4   Marketing communications for rolling papers or filters must not depict anyone smoking.

21.5   Marketing communications for rolling papers or filters must not be targeted at, or be likely to appeal to, people under 18. Anyone depicted in a marketing communication for rolling papers or filters must be, and be seen to be, over 25. No medium may be used to advertise rolling papers or filters if more than 25% of its audience is or is likely to be males under 18 years of age or females under 24 years of age. No direct marketing communication for rolling papers or filters may be distributed to males under 18 years of age or females under 24 years of age.

21.6   Marketing communications for rolling papers or filters must not condone or encourage the use of illegal drugs. Except in exceptional circumstances, for example, in the context of an anti-drug message, any reference to illegal drugs will be regarded as condoning their use.

21.7   Marketing communications for rolling papers or filters must not be sexually titillating.

How the system works

The self-regulatory system

The self-regulatory system comprises three bodies: the Advertising

Standards Authority (ASA), the Advertising Standards Board of Finance (ASBOF) and the Committee of Advertising Practice (CAP). Their work is described below.

The strength of the system depends on the long-term commitment of all those involved in advertising, sales promotions and direct marketing. Practitioners in every sphere share an interest in seeing that marketing communications are welcomed and trusted by their audience: unless they are accepted and believed, marketing communications cannot succeed. If they are offensive or misleading, they discredit everyone associated with them and the industry as a whole.

The UK Code of Non-broadcast Advertising, Sales Promotion and Direct Marketing (the CAP Code), and the details of the guidance and training offered by CAP Services to help advertisers comply with the rules, can be found at www.cap.org. uk. The ASA publishes adjudications weekly on www.asa.org.uk.

The Advertising Standards Authority

The ASA was established in 1962 to provide independent scrutiny of the newly created self-regulatory system set up by the industry. Its chief tasks are to promote and enforce high standards in marketing communications, to investigate complaints, to identify and resolve problems through research, to ensure that the system operates in the public interest and to act as the channel for communications with those who have an interest in marketing communication standards.

The ASA is a limited company and is independent of both the Government and the marketing business. The Chairman of the ASA is appointed by ASBOF and is unconnected with the marketing business. Most of the 12-member Council appointed by the Chairman to govern the ASA is also unconnected with the marketing business. All Council members sit as individuals and are selected, as far as possible, to reflect a diversity of background and experience. Vacancies for independent members of Council are publicly advertised. Members serve for a maximum of two three-year terms.

The ASA investigates complaints from any source against marketing communications in non-broadcast media. Marketers are told the outcome of the ASA Council's rulings and, if necessary, are asked to withdraw or amend their marketing communications. The adjudications reached by the Council are published weekly on www.asa.org.uk. The ASA website contains information about the ASA's procedures for handling complaints about a marketing communication.

The ASA gives equal emphasis to conducting a substantial research and monitoring programme by reviewing marketing communications that fall within its scope. Specific media and product categories may be identified for scrutiny. In that way the ASA can identify trends and prevent future problems.

Publicising the ASA's policies and actions is essential to sustaining wide acceptance of the system's integrity. A comprehensive programme of seminars and speeches, advertising, e-mail and website updates, briefing notes on a wide range of topics, articles written for professional journals and newspaper, magazine, TV and radio coverage all augment the ASA's extensive media presence.

The Advertising Standards Board of Finance

The Advertising Standards Board of Finance sets the framework for industry policy making and is responsible for the Committee of Advertising Practice and for funding the self-regulatory system.

The self-regulatory system is funded principally by a levy on advertising and direct marketing expenditure collected by ASBOF. The separation of operation and responsibilities helps to ensure that the independent judgement of the ASA is not compromised.

ASBOF's members are advertisers, promoters and direct marketers, their agencies, the media and the trade and professional organisations of the advertising, sales promotion and direct marketing businesses.

The Committee of Advertising Practice

CAP's role is to ensure that marketing communications within the Code's remit that are commissioned, prepared, placed or published in the UK comply with the CAP Code.

CAP co-ordinates the activities of its members to achieve the highest degree of compliance with the Code. It creates, reviews and amends the Code. From time to time, it produces for the industry Help Notes that give detailed guidance on specific sectors or subjects that are covered only generally in the Code. It oversees the sanctions operated by its members. It operates a website, www.cap.org.uk, to provide information and guidance to the industry, including access to Help Notes, Advice Online and relevant Ad Alerts. It convenes *ad hoc* Working Groups for limited periods to address specific subjects arising out of the self-regulatory process.

The Code establishes a standard against which marketing communications are assessed. Other codes exist in many sectors; many require practitioners to comply with the CAP Code.

The Chairman of CAP works on a part-time basis and is appointed for an agreed period and remunerated by ASBOF.

CAP actively encourages participation in the self-regulatory system. Suggestions for improving Code rules or modifying their application should be sent in writing to the Chairman. If changes are adopted by CAP their introduction is normally deferred for a short time to give marketers an adequate opportunity to amend their marketing communications.

CAP Services

As well as writing and maintaining the rules, CAP also places great emphasis on the prevention of breaches and works to promote high compliance. CAP Services are a range of bespoke advice, training seminars and online resources to help all practitioners stay on top of advertising regulation, the requirements of the CAP and BCAP Codes, and how those are interpreted by the ASA.

Full details of CAP Services can be found at www.cap.org.uk. Practitioners are urged to register on the site and subscribe to the newsletters to help them keep up-to-date with regulatory developments, training events and updates to guidance.

The Copy Advice team

The Copy Advice team gives advice to marketers, their agencies, the media and other practitioners on the likely conformity with the CAP Code of marketing communications before they are published or distributed. It also checks marketing communications produced by marketers subject to mandatory pre-vetting (for example, those subject to the poster pre-vetting sanction).

Copy Advice is fast, free and confidential from competitors. Bespoke advice is provided by the specialist team of advisers who deal with the vast majority of written enquiries within 24 hours, although lengthy submissions can take longer, especially those that include detailed evidence that needs to be reviewed by external expert consultants. Advice is not binding either on enquirers or on the ASA. Favourable pre-publication advice does not automatically protect marketers from complaints being investigated and upheld by the ASA. It is, however, the best guide to what is likely to comply with the Code.

Online resources are available at www.copyadvice.org.uk. Visitors can register to access the most comprehensive database of guidance (AdviceOnline and Help Notes) on the CAP Code, as well as case studies and helpful checklists.

Online: www.copyadvice.org.uk
Phone: 020 7492 2100
E-mail: advice@cap.org.uk

The Compliance team

The Compliance team ensures that marketing communications comply with the Code to protect consumers and ensure a level playing-field. It enforces ASA adjudications, disseminates any ramifications of them for an industry sector and acts against marketers that persistently break the Code. Exceptionally, if a marketing communication obviously breaches the Code, for example, if it contains a claim that is blatantly misleading, the team takes immediate compliance action to stop the marketing communication from reappearing. If it seems necessary to avoid harm, the Executive may take interim action during an ASA investigation (see "Sanctions").

The team co-ordinates the sanctions operated by the Executive and by CAP members; in particular, it issues Ad Alerts to CAP members, including the media, advising them to withhold their services from non-compliant marketers or deny those marketers access to advertising space.

Information on compliance is available on www.cap.org.uk. Companies that are members of a CAP trade association or professional body can access a database of relevant Ad Alerts on a secure section of the CAP website.

The Panels

Much of the detailed work of CAP is done by its two Panels. The Sales Promotion and Direct Response Panel concentrates on sales promotions and direct marketing. The General Media Panel concentrates on all other CAP-related and BCAP-related matters. Each Panel is composed of industry experts and one ASA Council member.

The Panels guide the Executive and help the ASA and CAP to produce advice for the industry and to interpret the Code.

The Panels provide a forum to reassess recommendations and advice given by the Executive. The parties to a complaint can request a Panel assessment before the ASA Council has adjudicated; Council will take account of the Panel's opinion. Council's judgement on the interpretation of the Code is, however, final. Anyone directly affected by copy advice given by the Executive on behalf of CAP can ask for it to be considered by the relevant Panel. The Panel Chairmen can reject requests and will do so if it seems that a Panel is being used to hamper the effective running of the self-regulatory system.

The Independent review procedure

In exceptional circumstances, the ASA Council can be asked to reconsider its adjudication (including a Council decision not to investigate a complaint). Requests for a review should contain a full statement of the grounds, be in writing and be addressed to the Independent Reviewer of ASA Adjudications, 5th Floor, 21 Berners Street, London, W1T 3LP. They should be sent within 21 days of the date on the ASA's letter of notification of an adjudication. The Independent Reviewer may waive that 21-day time limit if he judges it fair and reasonable to do so.

Requests should come only from the complainant or the marketer. Those from the marketer or from an industry complainant should be signed by the Chairman, Chief Executive or equivalent; requests made only by its solicitor or agency will not be accepted. All dealings with the Independent Reviewer must be in writing.

Requests may be made on two grounds:

- If extra relevant evidence becomes available (an explanation of why it was not submitted previously, in accordance with rule 3.7, will be required).

- If the Council's adjudication or the process by which it was made is substantially flawed.

No review will proceed if the point at issue is the subject of simultaneous or contemplated legal action between anyone directly involved. Requests for review should make plain that no such action is underway or is contemplated.

The ASA will not delay publication of the relevant adjudication pending the outcome of a review save in exceptional circumstances (on the authorisation of the ASA Director General).

The Independent Reviewer will evaluate the substance of the request with advice from two Assessors (except for requests about a Council decision not to investigate a complaint). The two Assessors are the Chairman of ASBOF (or nominee) and the Chairman of the ASA.

If the Independent Reviewer decides not to accept the request (in whole or in part) because he considers that it does not meet either of the two grounds set out above, he will inform the person making the request.

If he decides to accept the request (in whole or in part) he will undertake an investigation, either by himself or with help from the ASA Executive or any other source of help or advice. He will inform the other parties to the Council adjudication or decision that he has accepted a request for review and will invite their comments on the submission made by the party requesting the review. At the end of his investigation, he will make a recommendation to the ASA Council.

The Council's decision on requests for review is final.

The Independent Reviewer will inform all parties of the Council's decision. Adjudications that are revised as a result of a review will be published on www.asa.org.uk.

Administration of the system

The ASA and CAP share a joint Executive whose duties are organised to recognise the distinct functions of the two bodies. The Executive carries out the day-to-day work of the system and acts as a channel of communication, ensuring that industry expertise, specialist advice and the decisions of the ASA Council are co-ordinated and disseminated. The ASA Council and CAP form an independent judgement on any matter reported to them after they have considered the Executive's recommendation.

Marketers bear principal responsibility for the marketing communications they produce and must be able to prove the truth of their claims to the ASA; they have a duty to make their claims fair and honest and to avoid causing serious or widespread offence. Agencies have an obligation to create marketing communications that are accurate, ethical and neither mislead nor cause serious or widespread offence. Publishers and media owners recognise that they should disseminate only those marketing communications that comply with the Code. That responsibility extends to any other agent involved in producing, placing or publishing marketing communications. They accept the rulings of the ASA Council as binding.

The ASA Council judges whether marketing communications breach the Code. Everyone responsible for commissioning, preparing, placing or publishing a marketing communication that breaches the Code is asked to act promptly to amend or withdraw it.

The law

Marketers, agencies and publishers have primary responsibility for ensuring that everything they do is legal. Since the Code was first published, the number of laws designed to protect consumers has greatly increased. More than 200 UK statutes, orders and regulations as well as several directly effective European laws affect marketing communications here (see www.asa.org.uk or www.cap.org.uk for a non-exhaustive list). The ASA maintains a rapport with those responsible for initiating or administering any law that has a bearing on marketing communications. The system is reinforced by the legal backup provided for the work of the ASA by the Consumer Protection from Unfair Trading Regulations 2008 and the Business Protection from Misleading Marketing Regulations 2008 (see Scope of the Code).

The Code, and the self-regulatory framework that exists to administer it, was designed and has been developed to work within and to complement those legal controls. It provides an alternative, and in some instances the only, means of resolving disputes about marketing communications. It stimulates the adoption of high standards of practice in matters, such as taste and decency, that are extremely difficult to judge in law but fundamentally affect consumer confidence in marketing communications.

Some important aspects are governed by legislation enforced by local authority trading standards and environmental health officers. They include product packaging (except for on-pack promotions), weights and measures, statements on displays at point-of-sale and the safety of products.

Many Government agencies administer consumer protection legislation that ranges far wider and deeper than could be enforced through self-regulatory codes of practice. Marketers who break the law risk criminal prosecution or civil action. The Code requires marketers to ensure that all their marketing communications are legal but any matter that principally concerns a legal dispute will normally need to be resolved through law enforcement agencies or the Courts.

Europe

Most member States of the European Union, and many non-EU European countries, have self-regulatory organisations (SROs) that are broadly similar to those in the self-regulatory system in the UK. Together with organisations representing the advertising industry in Europe, those SROs are members of the European Advertising Standards Alliance (EASA), the single voice of the advertising industry in Europe on advertising self-regulation. The ASA is a founder member of EASA. EASA is located in Brussels and meets regularly to co-ordinate the promotion and development of self-regulation at a European level.

Among its wide range of operations, EASA acts as a focal point for cross-border complaints investigated by individual members; consumers need complain only to the SRO in their country, no matter where the marketing communication originated. EASA is a source of information and research on self-regulation. It helps in the development and establishment of SROs in Europe and corresponds internationally.

EASA has published a statement of common principles, the core values that underpin each of its constituent SROs, and recommended standards for operating best practice in self-regulation that all SROs should seek to achieve. Both are available on www.easa-alliance.org.

Information on EASA's objectives, activities and publications, including the Alliance Update and order forms for *The Blue Book*, which contains an analysis of self-regulation in 24 European countries, is available from the EASA website, www.easa-alliance.org.

Sanctions

Compliance surveys published periodically by the Executive have demonstrated that the vast majority of marketing communications comply with the Code. By providing advice, guidance or pressure, media owners, agencies and other intermediaries play a crucial role in ensuring compliance. If a marketing communication breaks the Code, the marketer responsible is told to amend or withdraw it. Most willingly undertake to do so. If they do not, the Compliance team will consider the sanctions available to it.

The ASA and CAP do not adopt a legalistic attitude towards sanctions and they ensure that sanctions are both proportionate to the nature of the breach and effective. They focus on ensuring that noncompliant marketing communications are amended, withdrawn or stopped as quickly as possible.

The ASA and CAP are not restricted to applying sanctions only against marketers that have been subject to a formal investigation. If a marketing communication is obviously misleading or offensive, the ASA and CAP may take compliance action in the absence of complaints or during an investigation (see "The Compliance team").

Adverse publicity

Publicising the ASA's adjudications is essential to sustaining wide acceptance of the system's integrity and the principal sanction available to the ASA is the unwelcome publicity that could result from the adjudications it publishes weekly on www.asa.org.uk. Adverse publicity is damaging to most marketers and serves to warn the public. Anyone who is interested can access ASA adjudications quickly and easily on the website and can set up a profile-specific account so they are automatically notified by e-mail of relevant adjudications as soon as they are published. ASA adjudications receive a substantial amount of coverage in local, regional, national and international media.

An adverse ASA adjudications could have consequences for compliance with other codes or legal requirements. For example, personal data gathered as a result of a misleading marketing communication might not comply with the fair processing requirement in the first data protection principle of the Data Protection Act 1998.

Ad alerts

CAP may issue Ad Alerts to its members, including the media, advising them to consult the Copy Advice team before accepting advertisements for publication or, in some circumstances, to withhold their services from non-compliant marketers or deny the latter access to advertising space. Ad Alerts are issued at short notice, are carefully targeted for greatest impact, are sent electronically and, once issued, are available on a secure section of www.cap.org.uk to those who might need to consult them. They contain the name and contact details of the non-compliant marketer, a description of the compliance problem and, if possible, a scanned image of the marketing communication in question. CAP may issue Ad Alerts that cover an entire sector if it perceives a widespread problem.

Trading privileges and recognition

Many CAP trade associations and professional bodies offer their members, and others, recognition and trading privileges, which they may revoke, withdraw or temporarily withhold. For example, agency recognition offered by the print media members of CAP may be withdrawn or the substantial direct mail discounts offered by the Royal Mail on bulk mailings withheld. In exceptional cases of non-compliance, CAP members may expel companies from membership.

Pre-publication vetting

The ASA and CAP may require persistent offenders to have some or all of their marketing communications vetted by the CAP Copy Advice team until the ASA and CAP are satisfied that future communications will comply with the Code.

The poster industry members of CAP operate a poster pre-vetting sanction to deter abuse of the medium. If the ASA adjudicates against a poster on the grounds of serious or widespread offence or social irresponsibility, the poster advertiser becomes a candidate for mandatory pre-vetting. If they believe that the advertiser either is incapable of complying with the Code or seems to have deliberately flouted the Code with the intention of generating complaints, PR and subsequent notoriety, the poster industry members of CAP and the CAP Executive will compel the advertiser to check future posters with the CAP Copy Advice team for a fixed period (usually two years).

Legal backstop

The self-regulatory system is recognised by the Government, the Office of Fair Trading (OFT) and the Courts as one of the "established means" of consumer protection in non-broadcast marketing communications. If certain types of marketing communication, including those that are misleading or contain an impermissible comparison, continue to appear after the ASA Council has ruled against them, the ASA can refer the matter to the OFT for action under the Consumer Protection from Unfair Trading Regulations 2008 or the Business Protection from Misleading Marketing Regulations 2008. The OFT can seek an undertaking that the marketing communication will be stopped from anyone responsible for commissioning, preparing or disseminating it. If that is not given or is not honoured, the OFT can seek an injunction from the Court to prevent its further appearance. Anyone not complying can be found to be in contempt of court and is liable to be penalised.

The ASA and CAP maintain a rapport with the OFT and with other bodies that have a responsibility for creating, administering or enforcing laws that have a bearing on marketing communications. If necessary, they may notify those bodies of non-compliant marketers and work with them to ensure that unacceptable marketing communications are amended, withdrawn or stopped.

The OFT and other "qualified entities", such as Trading Standards Authorities, can use the Enterprise Act 2002 Part 8 to enforce consumer protection laws, including the Consumer Protection from Unfair Trading Regulations 2008 and the Business Protection from Misleading Marketing Regulations 2008. Those regulations provide that, before taking action, qualified entities should have regard to the desirability of encouraging control by the "established means".

Cross-border marketing communications

The Code does not apply to marketing communications in foreign media. If marketing communications appear in media based in countries that have self-regulatory organisations (SROs) that are members of EASA or if direct marketing originates from countries that have SROs that are members of EASA, EASA will co-ordinate cross-border complaints so the SRO in the country of origin of the marketing communication has jurisdiction; consumers need complain only to their SRO. If not, the ASA will take what action it can. The SROs with jurisdiction are formally responsible for applying any sanctions, though the ASA and CAP will, whenever they can, adopt a pragmatic approach to ensure that consumers are protected.

The ASA and CAP work closely with CAP trade associations and professional bodies, Trading Standards officers, Government departments, the OFT and other UK regulators, EASA and overseas SROs and statutory authorities to stop unacceptable marketing communications, especially misleading or offensive mailings sent direct to UK consumers from overseas. That work has achieved some success but the ASA, CAP and other authorities, whether statutory or self-regulatory, experience difficulties in enforcing the Code and laws against companies based overseas. "Qualified entities" can, however, act to ensure compliance with Directive 2005/29/EC "concerning unfair business-to-consumer commercial practices in the internal market" throughout the European Union.

To clarify what can and cannot be done, the ASA and CAP have produced a fact sheet, "Overseas Mailings", to explain how they tackle unacceptable mailings that originate outside the UK and to warn consumers to treat those mailings with the utmost caution. That fact sheet is available on www.asa.org.uk.

History of self-regulation

Self-regulation is nothing new: the medieval guilds practised self-regulation in that they inspected markets and measures, judged the quality of merchandise and laid down rules for their trades.

In advertising and marketing, self-regulation can be traced back to the poster industry in the 1880s. The first code of advertising was launched in 1925 by the Association of Publicity Clubs. And systematic scrutiny of advertising claims operated from 1926, when the newly established Advertising Association set up its Advertising Investigation Department to "investigate abuses in advertising and to take remedial action".

In 1937, the International Chamber of Commerce developed an international code of advertising practice, the first of several international marketing codes that have provided a bench mark for many national systems of self-regulation.

The Committee of Advertising Practice (or the British Code of Advertising Practice Committee, as it then was) came into existence in 1961 and was responsible for the first British Code of Advertising Practice and all subsequent Codes including this one. The Code covered all non-broadcast advertisements and, in 1962, an independent body – the Advertising Standards Authority (ASA) – was established to administer the first Code.

1974 saw the creation of a new, improved funding mechanism for self-regulation in the form of the Advertising Standards Board of Finance (ASBOF). The new system brought an automatic levy of 0.1% on all display advertisements to fund the system. With it came an increased emphasis on public awareness of self-regulation and increased staffing to facilitate pre-vetting and monitoring.

1974 also saw the establishment of the first Code of Sales Promotion Practice – a recognition of the need to expand the role of the system to encompass promotional marketing.

Since 1962, advertising self-regulation has grown in stature. It now has all-party support and enjoys a widespread acceptance of its role in protecting the consumer. That acceptance led to European legislation governing misleading advertising being implemented nationally in 1988 in a way that allowed the ASA to remain the principal regulator for misleading advertisements in non-broadcast media but with statutory reinforcement through the Office of Fair Trading (OFT). It is a measure of the success of that approach that the ASA has referred few advertisers to the OFT.

Nothing better illustrates the maturity of the self-regulatory system than the extension, in 2004, of the ASA's remit to cover broadcast advertisements. Previously, broadcast advertising had been the subject of a separate statutory regime. The change came in 2003, when the Communications Act gave the newly formed Office of Communications (Ofcom) statutory responsibility for broadcasting standards. Using its powers under the Act, Ofcom contracted out responsibility for advertising standards to the ASA in the guise of a separate, but related, body called ASA (Broadcast) in a partnership often referred to as co-regulation.

As a result, all licensed broadcast services carrying advertisements fall within the extended remit of the self-regulatory system; they include television, radio and teletext services, which were previously regulated by the Independent Television Commission or the Radio Authority. The broadcast self-regulatory system has powers to direct advertisements to be taken off air, amended or re-scheduled and broadcasters fund and use pre-vetting services. The system provides for the ASA to refer to Ofcom any broadcaster that flouts an ASA adjudication or instruction.

A separate body known as the Broadcast Committee of Advertising Practice (BCAP) took over responsibility for the existing television and radio advertising codes. Its members include representatives from the advertising and marketing industry with an interest in broadcast advertising: advertisers, agencies and television and radio broadcasters.

Today, the self-regulatory system covers non-broadcast advertising, sales promotion and many aspects of direct marketing. It is supported by a range of other self-regulatory initiatives by the industry, including the various preference services run by the Direct Marketing Association.

From its limited original remit, the UK system of self-regulation has, with the ASA as its public face, evolved into a comprehensive one-stop shop for regulating marketing communications, both broadcast and non-broadcast.

With a degree of flexibility denied to statutory controls, the self-regulatory system is constantly reviewing both the content of its codes and its remit, recently especially in relation to digital media and the challenges presented by the growth of online marketing communications.

The world of advertising and marketing has changed beyond recognition since the inception of the UK self-regulatory system in the early 1960s. Yet the purpose of self-regulation remains as it was in the beginning: to maintain, in the best way possible, the integrity of marketing communications in the interests of both the consumer and business.

Appendix 1: The CPRs and BPRs

Background

Non-broadcast marketing communications are subject to legislation as well as to this Code. See www.asa.org.uk or www.cap.org.uk for a non-exhaustive list.

The Consumer Protection from Unfair Trading Regulations 2008 (the CPRs)

One important piece of legislation that affects marketing communications is the Consumer Protection from Unfair Trading Regulations 2008 (the CPRS). For the purpose of the Regulations and in this Appendix, "consumers" refers to individuals acting outside the course of their business. The CPRs prohibit unfair marketing to consumers, including misleading or aggressive advertising. Whenever it considers complaints that a marketing communication misleads consumers or is aggressive or unfair to consumers, the ASA will have regard to the CPRs. That means it will take factors identified in the CPRs into account when it considers whether a marketing communication breaches the CAP Code. The notes below summarise those factors.

Code rules that refer to misleading marketing communications should be read, in relation to business-to-consumer marketing communications, in conjunction with these notes.

Consumers

The likely effect of a marketing communication is generally considered from the point of view of the average consumer whom it reaches or to whom it is addressed. The average consumer is assumed to be reasonably well-informed, observant and circumspect.

In some circumstances, a marketing communication may be considered from the point of view of the average member of a specific group:

- If it is directed to a particular audience group, the marketing communication will be considered from the point of view of the average member of that group.

- If it is likely to affect the economic behaviour only of a clearly identifiable group of people who are especially vulnerable, in a way that the advertiser could reasonably foresee, because of mental or physical infirmity, age or credulity, the marketing communication will be considered from the point of view of the average member of the affected group.

Unfair marketing communications

Marketing communications are unfair if they

- are contrary to the requirements of professional diligence and

- are likely to materially distort the economic behaviour of consumers in relation to the advertised goods or services.

"Professional diligence" is the standard of special skill and care that a trader may reasonably be expected to exercise towards consumers, commensurate with honest market practice and the general principle of good faith in the trader's field of activity.

Misleading marketing communications

Marketing communications are misleading if they

- are likely to deceive consumers and

- are likely to cause consumers to take transactional decisions that they would not otherwise have taken.

A "transactional decision" is any decision taken by a consumer, whether it is to act or not act, about whether, how and on what terms to buy, pay in whole or in part for, retain or dispose of a product or whether, how and on what terms to exercise a contractual right in relation to a product.

Marketing communications can deceive consumers by ambiguity, through presentation or by omitting important information that consumers need to make an informed transactional decision, as well as by including false information.

Aggressive marketing communications

Marketing communications are aggressive if, taking all circumstances into account, they

- are likely to significantly impair the average consumer's freedom of choice through harassment, coercion or undue influence and

- are therefore likely to cause consumers to take transactional decisions they would not otherwise have taken.

The Business Protection from Misleading Marketing Regulations 2008

Business-to-business marketing communications are subject to the Business Protection from Misleading Marketing Regulations 2008 (the BPRs). Business-to-business marketing communications that breach the CAP Code may be referred to the Office of Fair Trading for consideration under the BPRs. Under the BPRs, a marketing communication is misleading if it:

- in any way, including its presentation, deceives or is likely to deceive the traders to whom it is addressed or whom it reaches and by reason of its deceptive nature, is likely to affect their economic behaviour

- or, for those reasons, injures or is likely to injure a competitor.

The BPRs also set out the conditions under which comparative marketing communications, directed at either consumers or business, are permitted. This Code incorporates those conditions.

Appendix 2: Advertising rules for on-demand services regulated by statute

Principle

The rules in Appendix 2 reflect the legal requirements in the Communications Act 2003 (as amended) with which media service providers must ensure they comply. Failure to ensure that advertising included in a regulated on-demand service complies with these rules may result in the matter being referred to Ofcom. If Ofcom concludes that the media service provider has contravened the relevant requirements of the Act, this may lead to Ofcom considering imposing a statutory sanction against the provider.

Definition

Some video-on-demand services are subject to regulation under the Communications Act 2003 (as amended). ('the Act'). In this section, "regulated on-demand services" refers to those services that are subject to statutory regulation and "media service providers" means providers of regulated on-demand services.

The rules in this section apply only to advertising "included" in a regulated on-demand service, which is advertising that can be viewed by a user of the service as a result of the user selecting a programme to view.

Rules

30.1   Advertising must be readily recognisable as such.

30.2   Advertising must not use techniques which exploit the possibility of conveying a message subliminally or surreptitiously.

30.3   Advertising must not prejudice respect for human dignity.

30.4   Advertising must not contain any material likely to incite hatred based on race, sex, religion or nationality.

30.5   Advertising must not include or promote any discrimination based on sex, racial or ethnic origin, nationality, religion or belief, disability, age or sexual orientation.

30.6   Advertising must not encourage behaviour prejudicial to health or safety.

30.7   Advertising must not encourage behaviour grossly prejudicial to the protection of the environment.

30.8   Advertising of the following products is prohibited:

  30.8.1   cigarettes or other tobacco products

  30.8.2   any prescription-only medicine.

30.9   Advertising for alcoholic drinks is prohibited unless

  30.9.1   it is not aimed at persons under the age of eighteen, and

30.9.2   it does not encourage excessive consumption of such drinks.

30.10   Advertising must not cause physical or moral detriment to persons under the age of eighteen.

30.11   If advertising contains material which might seriously impair the physical, mental or moral development of persons under the age of eighteen, the material must be made available in a manner which secures that such persons will not normally see or hear it.

30.12   Advertising must not directly exhort persons under the age of eighteen to purchase or rent goods or services in a manner which exploits their inexperience or credulity.

30.13   Advertising must not directly encourage persons under the age of eighteen to persuade their parents or others to purchase or rent goods or services.

30.14   Advertising must not exploit the trust of persons under eighteen in parents, teachers or others.

30.15   Advertising must not unreasonably show persons under eighteen in dangerous situations.

Advertisements on regulated on-demand services are also separately subject to the CAP Code. The marketer, not the media service provider, bears the primary responsibility for ensuring compliance with the CAP Code.

CODE OF PRACTICE FOR TRADERS ON PRICE INDICATIONS

Published by, and reproduced here with the permission of, the Department of Trade and Industry.
October 2005

The DTI drives our ambition of 'prosperity for all' by working to create the best environment for business success in the United Kingdom. We help people and companies become more productive by promoting enterprise, innovation and creativity.

We champion UK business at home and abroad. We invest heavily in world-class science and technology. We protect the rights of working people and consumers. And we stand up for fair and open markets in the United Kingdom, Europe and the world.

Contents

Introduction

The Consumer Protection Act

1.   Section 20 of the Consumer Protection Act 1987 makes it a criminal offence for a person in the course of his business to give consumers a misleading price indication about goods, services, accommodation (including the sale of new homes) or facilities. It applies however you give the price indication—for example, in a TV or press advertisement, on a website, by e-mail or text message, in a catalogue or leaflet, on notices, price tickets or shelf-edge marking in stores, or if you give it orally, for example, on the telephone. The term 'price indication' includes price comparisons as well as indications of a single price.

2.   This Code of Practice is approved under s 25 of the Act, which gives the Secretary of State power to approve codes of practice to give practical guidance to traders. It is addressed to traders and sets out what is good practice to follow in giving price indications in a wide range of different circumstances, so as to avoid giving misleading price indications. The Code is not comprehensive. It cannot address every circumstance in which a misleading price may be given, particularly for new and innovative selling practices. It is guidance, rather than mandatory, although it may be taken into account in establishing whether an offence has been committed under the Act. You may, therefore, still give price indications which do not accord with this Code, provided they are not misleading. Equally, compliance with specific aspects of the Code will not, of itself, establish that a price indication is not misleading. Where an offence of giving a misleading price indication is alleged, a Court would have regard to all the relevant circumstances.

3.   'Misleading' is defined in s 21 of the Act. The definition covers indications about any conditions attached to a price, for example, additional charges that may be payable, about what you expect to happen to a price in future and what you say in price comparisons, as well as indications about the actual price the consumer will have to pay, for example, about a price which is additionally subject to VAT. It applies in the same way to any indications you give about the way in which a price will be calculated and to any relevant omissions from an indication which makes a price misleading.

Price comparisons

4. If you want to make price comparisons, you should do so only if you can justify them. You should be able to show that any claims you make are accurate and valid. As a general rule, you should only compare like with like, but comparisons with prices which you can show are being charged for very similar goods, services, accommodation or facilities and have applied for a reasonable period are also unlikely to be misleading. Guidance on these matters is contained in this Code.

Enforcement

5. Enforcement of the Consumer Protection Act 1987 is the responsibility of officers of the local weights and measures authority—usually called *Trading Standards Officers.* Trading Standards Officers operate in accordance with the Home Authority principle (under which a specific Trading Standards Service acts as the Home Authority for a major retailer with multi-store outlets) and with the principles of consultation and co-operation that are set out in the Enforcement Concordat. Further information about the Home Authority principle and the Enforcement Concordat can be obtained from your local Trading Standards Service or your Home Authority. Details of the location of your local Trading Standards Services can be obtained at the main Trading Standards website—http://www.tradingstandards.gov.uk. In Northern Ireland enforcement is the responsibility of the Department of Enterprise, Trade and Investment.

6. If a Trading Standards Officer has reasonable grounds to suspect that you have given a misleading price indication, the Act gives the Officer power to require you to produce any records relating to your business and to seize and detain goods or records which the Officer has reasonable grounds for believing may be required as evidence in court proceedings. Be prepared to cooperate with Trading Standards Officers and respond to reasonable requests for information and assistance. It is in your interest to be able to demonstrate that any claims you have made are accurate and valid. The Act makes it an offence to obstruct a Trading Standards Officer intentionally or to fail (without good cause) to give any assistance or information the Officer may reasonably require to carry out his duties under the Act.

Court proceedings

7. If you are taken to court for giving a misleading price indication, the court can take into account whether or not you have followed this Code. If you have done as the Code advises, that will not be an absolute defence but it will tend to show that you have not committed an offence. Similarly if you have done something the Code advises against doing it may tend to show that the price indication was misleading. If you do something that is not covered by the Code, your price indication will need to be judged only against the terms of the general offence. The Act provides for a defence of due diligence, that is, that you have taken all reasonable steps to avoid committing the offence of giving a misleading price indication, but failure to follow the Code of Practice may make it difficult to show this. The Act also provides for specific defences (eg, if a misleading price indication is given in a book, newspaper or magazine, film or broadcast programme, it is a defence for the publisher to show that the indication was not contained in an advertisement).

Regulations

8. The Act also provides power to make regulations about price indications and you should ensure that your price indications comply with any such regulations. There are specific regulations dealing with indications of exchange rates in Bureaux de Change[1], with price indications where different prices are charged depending on the method of payment (eg, by cash or credit card)[2] and with the resale of tickets for admission to places of entertainment[3]. Your local Trading Standards Service or Home Authority will be able to advise you on these regulations.

Other legislation

9. This Code deals only with the requirements of Pt III of the Consumer Protection Act 1987. In some areas there is other relevant legislation. For example, the way in which prices for goods sold by traders to consumers must be displayed is subject to regulations made under the Prices Act 1974 (eg, the Price Marking Order 2004[4]) and price indications about credit terms must comply with the Consumer Credit Act 1974 and the regulations made

---

[1] The Price Indications (Bureaux de Change) (No 2) Regulations SI 1992/737
[2] The Price Indications (Method of Payment) Regulations SI 1991/199
[3] The Price Indications (Resale of Tickets) Regulations SI 1994/3248
[4] SI 2004/102

under it. Those selling by distance contracts should also be aware of the requirements of the Consumer Protection (Distance Selling) Regulations 2000[5] and where traders make use of advertisements they should have regard to the relevant rules governing misleading advertising (further information on these is available from the Advertising Standards Association—www.asa.org.uk).

10.   Your local Trading Standards Service, or your Home Authority will be pleased to advise you or direct you to sources of information on the regulations that are applicable to your particular business. Some legislation may also be accessed at the website of the Office of Public Sector Information—*http://www.legislation.opsi.gov.uk*

Definitions

Words and expressions used in the Code are explained below. However, the legal effect of terms used in the Consumer Protection Act 1987 and other legislation depends on the definitions in that legislation.

Accommodation	includes hotel and other holiday accommodation and new homes for sale freehold or on a lease of over 21 years but does not include rented homes.
Consumer	means anyone who might want the goods, services, accommodation or facilities, other than for business use.
Distance contract	means any contract concerning products concluded between a trader and a consumer by any means, without the simultaneous physical presence of the trader and the consumer.
Price	means the total amount the consumer will have to pay to get the goods, services, accommodation or facilities or any method which has been or will be used to calculate that amount.
Price comparison	means any indication given to consumers that the price at which something is offered to consumers is less than or equal to some other price.

---

[5] SI 2000/2334

Product	means goods, services, accommodation and facilities (but not credit facilities, except where otherwise specified).
Services and facilities	means any services or facilities whatever (including credit, banking and insurance services, purchase or sale of foreign currency, supply of electricity, and off-street car parking), making arrangements for a person to keep a caravan on land (unless the caravan is the person's main home) but not services provided by an employee to his employer under an employment contract.
Outlet	means any shop, store, stall or other place (including a vehicle or the consumer's home) and any means through which a distance contract may be concluded (including a website) at which goods, services, accommodation or facilities are offered to consumers.
Trader	means anyone (retailer, manufacturer, agent, service provider or other) who is acting in the course of a business.

Part 1: Price comparisons

1.1   Price comparisons generally

1.1.1   Information on different kinds of price comparisons is given in the paragraphs below, although it is the provisions of the Consumer Protection Act 1987 relating to misleading price indications with which you will ultimately need to comply. Generally, you should compare like with like and where a reduced price is claimed then the product should have been offered for sale at the higher price for at least 28 days in the previous six months in the same outlet. If your comparison does not meet those criteria then you should provide an explanation which is unambiguous, easily identifiable and (except where it is impractical, for instance, in distance contracts that are concluded orally) clearly legible to the consumer.

1.1.2   Always make the meaning of price indications clear. Do not leave consumers to guess whether or not a price comparison is being made. If no price comparison is intended, do not use words or phrases which, in their normal, everyday use and in the context in which they are used, are likely to give your customers the impression that a price comparison is being made. Price comparisons should always state the higher price as well as the price you intend to charge for the product (goods, services, accommodation or facilities). Do not make statements like 'sale price £5' or 'reduced to £39' without quoting the higher price to which they refer. If you refer to the previous price for the purpose of claiming there has been a reduction it should be to the cash price. If it is not, then an unambiguous, easily identifiable and clearly legible explanation of what the previous price referred to should be given.

1.1.3 It should be clear what sort of price the higher price is. For example, comparisons with something described by words like 'regular price', 'usual price' or 'normal price' should say whose regular, usual or normal price it is (eg, 'our normal price'). Descriptions like 'reduced from' and crossed out higher prices should be used only if they refer to your own previous price. Words should not be used in price indications other than with their normal everyday meanings.

1.1.4 Do not use initials or abbreviations to describe the higher price in a comparison, except for the initials 'RRP' to describe a recommended retail price or the abbreviation 'man. rec. price' to describe a manufacturer's recommended price (see paragraph 1.6.2).

1.1.5 Follow the part of the Code (ss 1.2 to 1.6 as appropriate) which applies to the type of comparison you intend to make.

1.2   Comparisons with the trader's own previous price

General

1.2.1 In any comparison between your present selling price and the last selling price at which the product was offered, you should state the previous price as well as the new lower price.

1.2.2 In any comparison with your own previous price:

(a)   the previous price should be the last price at which the product was available to consumers in the previous six months unless the situation covered by paragraph 1.2.8 below applies;

(b)   the product should have been available to consumers at that price for at least 28 consecutive days in the previous six months; and

(c)   the previous price should have applied (as above) for that period at the **same** outlet where the reduced price is now being offered.

The 28 days at (b) above may include public holidays, Sundays or other days of religious observance when the outlet was closed (or otherwise unavailable for business); and up to 4 days when, for reasons beyond your control, the product was not available for supply. The product must not have been offered at a different price between that 28-day period and the day when the reduced price is first offered.

1.2.3   If the previous price in a comparison does not meet one or more of the conditions set out in paragraph 1.2.2 above then:

(a)   the comparison should be fair and meaningful;

(b)   give a clear and positive explanation of the period for which and the circumstances in which that higher price applied. The explanation should be unambiguous, easily identifiable and clearly legible to the consumer.

For example, 'these goods were on sale here at the higher price from 1 February to 26 February' or 'these goods were on sale at the higher price in 10 or our 95 stores'. **Display the explanation clearly, and as prominently as the price indication**. You should not use general disclaimers saying for example that the higher prices used in comparison have not necessarily applied for 28 consecutive days.

1.2.4   A previous price used as a basis of a price comparison should be a genuine retail price. It should be a price at which you offered the goods for sale in the reasonable expectation that they could be sold by you at the higher price. In any case where a sale price is compared to a price that is higher than the usual retail price in the particular outlet, that fact should be made clear.

Food, drink and perishable goods

1.2.5   For any food and drink you need not give a positive explanation if the previous price in a comparison has not applied for 28 consecutive days, provided it was the last price at which the goods were on sale in the previous six months and applied in the same outlet where the reduced price is now being offered. This also applies to non-food items, if they have a shelf-life of less than six weeks.

Distance contracts

1.2.6 Where products are sold only through distance contracts, any comparison with a previous price should be with your own last price. If you sell the same products for different prices in different types of outlets (eg, charging a different price in your High Street store compared to a direct sale from your website), the previous price should be the last price at which you offered the product at the outlet in relation to which the claim is made. You should also follow the guidance in paragraphs 1.2.2 (a) and (b). If your price comparison does not meet these conditions, you should follow the guidance in paragraph

Factory outlets

1.2.7 Retailers located in factory outlets sites (ie, sites where it is a condition of tenancy that a substantial majority of the goods must be sold at a discount), who have not sold the same goods at a higher price in the same store, may display an unambiguous, easily identifiable and clearly legible general notice stating that all (or a specified proportion) of goods have been bought in from elsewhere, which may include outlets outside the United Kingdom. Specific comparisons and reductions made for particular items must comply with the other relevant guidance in this Code of Practice and they must be verifiable in the event of a challenge by the local Trading Standards Service or Home Authority.

Making a series of reductions

1.2.8 If you advertise a price reduction and then want to reduce the price further during the same sale or special offer period, the intervening price (or prices) need not have applied for 28 days. In these circumstances unless you use a positive explanation (paragraph 1.2.3):

(a)   the highest price in the series must have applied for 28 consecutive days in the last six months at the same outlet;

(b)   you must show the highest price, the intervening price(s); and

(c)   the current selling price.

1.3   Introductory offers, after-sale or after-promotion prices

1.3.1   Do not call a promotion an introductory offer unless you intend to continue to offer the same product for sale at the same outlet after the offer period is over and to do so at a higher price.

1.3.2   Do not allow an offer to run on so long that it becomes misleading to describe it as an introductory or other special offer. What is a reasonable period will depend on the circumstances (but, depending on the shelf-life of the product, it is likely to be a matter of weeks, not months). An offer is unlikely to be misleading if you state the date the offer will end and keep to it. If you then extend the offer period, make it clear that you have done so.

Quoting a future price

1.3.3   If you indicate an after-sale or after-promotion price, do so only if you are certain that, subject only to circumstances beyond your control, you will continue to offer identical products at that price for at least 28 days in the 3 months after the end of the offer period or after the offer stocks run out.

1.3.4   If you decide to quote a future price, write what you mean in full. Do not use initials to describe it (eg 'ASP', 'APP'). The description should be clearly and prominently displayed, with the price indication.

1.4   Comparisons with prices related to different circumstances

1.4.1   Comparisons should be fair and reasonable. You should only compare like with like or very similar products in terms of quality, composition and description. If there is a difference, then an unambiguous, easily identifiable and clearly legible explanation of the difference(s) should also be provided. This section covers comparisons with prices:

(a)   for different quantities (eg '15p each, 4 for 50p');

(b)   for goods in a different condition (eg 'seconds £20, when perfect £30');

(c)   for a different availability (eg price £50, price when ordered specially £60');

(d)   for goods in a totally different state (eg 'price in kit form £50, price ready-assembled £70'); or

(e)   for special groups of people (eg 'senior citizens' price £2.50, others £5').

General

1.4.2   Do not make comparisons with prices related to different circumstances unless the product is available in the different quantity, conditions etc at the price you quote. Make clear to consumers the different circumstances which apply and show them prominently with the price indication. Do not use initials (eg 'RAP' for 'ready-assembled price') to describe the different circumstances, but write what you mean in full.

'When perfect' comparisons

1.4.3   If you do not have the perfect goods on sale in the same outlet:

(a)   follow s 1.2 if the 'when perfect' price is your own previous price for the goods;

(b)   follow s 1.5 if the 'when perfect' price is another trader's price; or

(c)   follow s 1.6 if the 'when perfect' price is one recommended by the manufacturer or supplier.

Goods in a different state

1.4.4   Only make comparisons with goods in a totally different state if:

(a)   a reasonable proportion (say a third by quantity) of your stock of those goods is readily available for sale to consumers in that different state (eg, ready assembled) at the quoted price and from the outlet where the price comparison is made; or

(b)   another trader is offering those goods in that state at the quoted price and you follow s 1.5.

The price of a collection of items should only be compared with the previous price of the same collection of items, unless any differences are explained in an unambiguous, easily identifiable and clearly legible way. For instance, do not compare the price of a complete fitted kitchen with the price of the items when sold separately, unless this difference is explained in an unambiguous, easily identifiable and clearly legible way.

Prices for special groups of people

1.4.5 If you want to compare different prices which you charge to different groups of people (eg one price for existing customers and another for new customers, or one price for people who are members of a named organisation (other than the trader) and another for those who are not), do not use words like 'our normal' or 'our regular' to describe the higher price, unless it applies to at least half your customers.

1.5   Comparisons with another trader's prices

1.5.1 Comparisons should not be misleading. Only compare your prices with another trader's price if:

(a)   you know that the other trader's price which you quote is accurate and up-to-date—if the comparison becomes misleading it should be removed as soon as is practicable;

(b)   you give the name of the other trader clearly and prominently, with the price comparison;

(c)   you identify the circumstance where the other trader's price applies; and

(d)   the other trader's price which you quote applies to the same product—or to substantially similar product and you state any differences clearly (see paragraph 1.4).

Comparisons should also be with prices of outlets in the same locality, unless it can be shown that it makes no difference because of a national pricing policy.

1.5.2 Do not make statements like 'if you can buy this product elsewhere for less, we will refund the difference' about your 'own brand'products which other traders do not stock, unless your offer will also apply to other traders' equivalent goods. If there are any conditions attached to the offer (eg it only applies to goods on sale in the same town or excluding Internet sales) you should show them clearly and prominently, with the statement.

1.5.3 'Lowest price' claims must be backed up by suitable evidence to show that the trader is offering a lower price than competitors. Offering a 'price promise', for example, to beat a competitors' cheaper price if informed of that price by a customer, does not, of itself, justify a 'lowest price' claim if the latter cannot be supported. You should make clear that the claim is limited to a price matching promise if that is the case.

1.6 Comparisons with 'Recommended Retail Price' or similar

General

1.6.1 This Section covers comparisons with recommended retail prices, manufacturers' recommended prices, suggested retail prices, suppliers' suggested retail prices and similar descriptions. It also covers prices given to co-operative and voluntary group organisations by their wholesalers or headquarters organisations.

1.6.2 Do not use initials or abbreviations to describe the higher price in a comparison unless:

(a) you use the initials 'RRP' to describe a recommended retail price; or

(b) you use the abbreviation 'man. rec. price' to describe a manufacturer's recommended price.

Write all other descriptions out in full and show them clearly and prominently with the price indication.

1.6.3 Do not use a recommended price in a comparison unless:

(a) you can show that it has been recommended to you by the manufacturer or supplier as a price at which the product might be sold to consumers;

(b) you deal with that manufacturer or supplier on normal commercial terms. (This will generally be the case for members of co-operative or voluntary group organisations in relation to their wholesalers or headquarters organisations); and

(c) the price is not significantly higher than prices at which the product is generally sold at the time you make that comparison.

Do not use an 'RRP' or similar for goods that only you supply.

1.7   Pre-printed prices

1.7.1   Make sure you pass on to consumers any reduction stated on the manufacturer's packaging (eg 'flash packs'such as '10p off RRP').

1.7.2   You are making a price comparison if goods have a clearly visible price already printed on the packaging which is higher than the price you will charge for them. Such pre-printed prices are, in effect, recommended prices (except for retailers' own label goods) and you should follow paragraphs 1.6.1 to 1.6.4. You need not state that the price is a recommended price.

1.8   References to value or worth

1.8.1   Do not compare your prices with an amount described only as 'worth' or 'value'.

1.8.2   Do not present general advertising slogans which refer to 'value' or 'worth' in a way which is likely to be seen by consumers as a price comparison.

1.9   Sales or special events

1.9.1   If you have bought in items especially for a sale, and you make this clear, you should not quote a higher price when indicating that they are special purchases. Otherwise, your price indications for individual items in the sale which are reduced should comply with s 1.1 of the Code and whichever of ss 1.2 to 1.6 applies to the type of comparison you are making.

1.9.2   If you just have a general notice saying, for example, that all products are at 'half marked price', the marked price on the individual items should be your own previous price and you should follow s 1.2 of the Code.

1.9.3   Do not use general notices saying, eg 'half price sale' or 'up to 50 per cent off'unless the maximum reduction quoted applies to at least 10per cent of the range of products on offer at the commencement of the sale.

1.10   Free offers

1.10.1   Make clear to consumers, at the time of the offer for sale, exactly what they will have to buy to get the 'free offer'. If any sort of direct payment is required (eg, postal or delivery charges) and is not referred to in the price indication, this may be misleading.

1.10.2   If you give any indication of the monetary value of the 'free offer', and that sum is not your own present price for the product, follow whichever of ss 1.2 to 1.6 covers the type of price it is.

1.10.3   If there are any conditions attached to the 'free offer', give at least the main points of those conditions with the price indication and make clear to consumers where, before they are committed to buy, they can get full details of the conditions.

1.10.4   Do not claim that an offer is free if:

(a)   you have imposed additional charges that you would not normally make;

(b)   you have inflated the price of any product the consumer must buy or the incidental charges (for example, postage or premium rate telephone charges) the consumer must pay to get the 'free offer'; or

(c)   you will reduce the price to consumers who do not take it up.

Part 2: Actual price to consumer

2.1   Indicating two different prices

2.1.1   The Consumer Protection Act 1987 makes it an offence to indicate a price for goods or services which is lower than the one that actually applies. You should not therefore show one price in an advertisement, website, window display, shelf marking or on the item itself, and then charge a higher price at the point of sale or checkout. In addition, specific regulations apply to particular types of sales and ways of selling—for example, retail sales (including the Internet), sales of food and drink which involve service, distance contracts, resale of tickets, package travel, etc. Your local Trading Standards Services or Home Authority will be pleased to advise you on the current regulations that are relevant to your business and of any good practice guidance which is also relevant.

2.2   Incomplete information and non-optional extras

2.2.1   Make clear in your price indication the full price consumers will have to pay for the product. The consumer should always be fully aware of the total cost including (eg, postage, packing, delivery charges, insurance, etc.) before they commit themselves to the purchase. Some examples of how to provide this information in particular circumstances are set out below.

Limited availability of product

2.2.2   Where the price you are quoting for products only applies to a limited number of, say, orders, sizes or colours, you should make this clear in your price indication in an unambiguous, easily identifiable and clearly legible way (eg,'available in other colours or sizes at additional cost').

Prices relating to differing forms of products

2.2.3   If the price you are quoting for particular products does not apply to the products in the form in which they are displayed or advertised, say so clearly in your price indication. For example, advertisements for self-assembly furniture and the like should make it clear that the price refers to a kit of parts.

Postage, packing and delivery charges

2.2.4   If you sell by distance contract, make clear any additional charges for postage, packing or delivery, so that consumers are fully aware of them before they commit themselves to buy. Where you cannot determine these charges in advance, you must indicate clearly how they will be calculated (eg, 'Royal Mail rates apply'), or specify the place where the information is given.

2.2.5   If you sell goods from an outlet and offer a delivery service for certain items, make it clear whether there are any separate delivery charges (eg, for delivery outside a particular area) and what those charges are, before the consumer is committed to buying.

Pricing in different currencies

2.2.6   There are rules about what information must in certain circumstances be provided on exchange rates and commission charges if you accept payment in a foreign currency in addition to sterling, and your local Trading Standards Service can advise you on them. There is a risk that your price indications could be considered misleading if you offer products that are dual priced with sterling and a foreign currency but you will only accept sterling and the sterling price is higher. In these circumstances you should make it clear that you only accept sterling, for instance by displaying a notice to that effect.

Valued Added Tax

(a)   Price indications to consumers

2.2.7   All price indications you give to private consumers, by whatever means, should include VAT.

(b)   Price indications to business customers

2.2.8   Prices may be indicated exclusive of VAT at an outlet or through advertisements from which most of your business is with business customers. If you also conduct business at that outlet or through these advertisements with consumers, however, you should make clear that the prices exclude VAT and you should:

(i)   display VAT inclusive prices with equal prominence, or;

(ii)   display prominent statements that the quoted prices exclude VAT and state the appropriate rate. If should be noted that VAT inclusive prices for all goods offered by traders to consumers are required by the Price Marking Order 2004[6] (further information can be obtained from your local Trading Standards Service).

(c)   Professional fees 2.2.9 Where you indicate a price (including an estimate) for a professional fee, make clear what it covers. The price should generally include VAT. In cases where the fee is based on an as-yet-unknown sum of money (eg, the sale price of a house), either:

(a)   quote a fee which includes VAT; or

(b)   make it clear that in addition to your fee the consumer would have to pay VAT at the current rate (eg, 'fee of 1.5 per cent of purchase price, plus VAT at 17.5 per cent').

Make sure that whichever method you choose is used for both the estimate and final bill.

---

[6]SI 2004/102

(d)   Building work

2.2.10   In estimates for building work, either include VAT in the price indication or indicate with equal prominence the amount or rate of VAT payable in addition to your basic figure. If you give a separate amount for VAT, make it clear that if any provisional sums in estimates vary then the amount of VAT payable would also vary.

Service, cover and minimum charges in hotels, restaurants and similar establishments

2.2.11   Do not include suggested optional sums, whether for service or any other item, in the bill presented to the customer. If your customers in hotels, restaurants or similar places must pay a non-optional extra charge, for example, a 'service charge':

(a)   incorporate the charge within fully inclusive prices wherever practicable; and

(b)   display the fact clearly on any price list or priced menu, whether displayed inside or outside (eg, by using statements like 'all prices include service')

2.2.12   It may not be practical to include some non-optional extra charges in a quoted price; for instance, if you make a flat charge per person or per table in a restaurant (often referred to as a 'cover charge') or a minimum charge. In such cases the charge should be shown as prominently as other prices on any list or menu, whether displayed inside or outside. Your local Trading Standards Service or Home Authority can advise you further on the legislation relevant to price marking in bars, restaurants and similar outlets.

Holiday and travel prices

2.2.13   If you offer a variety of prices to give consumers a choice (eg, paying more or less for a holiday depending on the time of year or the standard of accommodation), make clear in your brochure or website, or in any other price indication what the basic price is and what it covers. Give details of any optional additional charges and what those charges cover, or of the place where this information can be found, clearly and close to the basic price.

2.2.14   Any non-optional extra charges which are for fixed amounts should be included in the basic price and not shown as additions, unless they are only payable by some consumers. In that case you should specify, near to the details of the basic price, either what the amounts are and the circumstances in which they are payable, or where in the brochure etc the information is given.

2.2.15 Details of non-optional extra charges which may vary, or details of where in the brochure etc the information is given, should be made clear to consumers near to the basic price.

2.2.16 If you reserve the right to increase prices after consumers have made their booking, state this clearly with all indications of prices, and include prominently in your brochure full information on the circumstances in which a surcharge is payable and how it is to be calculated. There are specific rules limiting rights to increase package holiday prices in the Package Travel, Package Holidays and Package Tours Regulations 1992[7]

Ticket prices

2.2.17 If you sell tickets, whether for sporting events, cinema, theatre etc and your prices are higher than the regular price that would be charged to the public at the box office, that is, higher than the 'face value', you must make clear in any price indication what the 'face value' of the ticket is as well as the actual price that will be charged. Your local Trading Standards Service or Home Authority can advise you further on the legislation relevant to resale of tickets.

Call-out charges

2.2.18 Free call out claims should be only be made when there will be no charge to the consumer unless remedial work is undertaken with their agreement.

2.2.19 If you make a minimum call-out charge or other flat-rate charge (eg, for plumbing, gas or electrical appliance repairs etc carried out in consumers' homes), ensure that the consumer is made aware of the charge and whether the actual price may be higher (eg, if work takes longer than a specific time) before being committed to using your services.

Credit facilities

2.2.20 Price indications about consumer credit should also comply with the Consumer Credit Act 1974 and the regulations made thereunder governing the form and content of advertisements.

---

[7] SI 1992/3288

Insurance

2.2.21   Where actual premium rates for a particular consumer or the availability of insurance cover depend on an individual assessment, this should be made clear when any indication of the premium or the method of determining it is given to consumers.

Part 3: Price indications which become misleading after they have been given

3.1   General

3.1.1   The Consumer Protection Act 1987 makes it an offence to give a price indication which, although correct at the time, becomes misleading after you have given it, if:

(a)   consumers could reasonably be expected still to be relying on it; and

(b)   you do not take reasonable steps to prevent them doing so.

Clearly it will not be necessary or even possible in many instances to inform all those who may have been given the misleading price indication. However, you should always make sure consumers are given the correct information before they are committed to buying a product and be prepared to cancel any transaction which a consumer has entered into on the basis of a price indication which has become misleading.

3.1.2   The following paragraphs set out what you should do in some particular circumstances

3.2   Newspaper and magazine advertisements

3.2.1   If the advertisement does not say otherwise, the price indication should apply for a reasonable period (as a general guide, at least seven days or until the next issue of the newspaper or magazine in which the advertisement was published, whichever is longer). If the price indication becomes misleading within this period make sure consumers are given the correct information before they are committed to buying the product.

3.3 Mail order advertisements, catalogues, leaflets, websites and similar advertising

3.3.1 Paragraph 3.2.1 above also applies to the time for which these price indications should be made. If a price indication becomes misleading within the period set out in paragraph 3.2.1, make the correct price indication clear to anyone who orders the product to which it relates. Do so before the consumer is committed to buying the product and, wherever practicable, before the goods are sent to the consumer.

3.4 Selling through agents

Holiday brochures and travel agents

3.4.1 Surcharges are covered in paragraph 2.2.16. If a price indication becomes misleading for any other reason, tour operators who sell direct to consumers should follow paragraph 3.3.1 above, and tour operators who sell through travel agents should follow paragraphs 3.4.2 and 3.4.3 below.

3.4.2 If a price indication becomes misleading while your brochure is still current, make this clear to the travel agents to whom you distributed the brochure. Be prepared to cancel any holiday bookings consumers have made on the basis of a misleading price indication.

3.4.3 In the circumstances set out in paragraph 3.4.2, travel agents should ensure that the correct price indication is made clear to consumers before they make a booking.

Insurance and independent intermediaries

3.4.4 Insurers who sell their products through agents or independent intermediaries should take all reasonable steps to ensure that all such agents who are known to hold information on the insurer's premium rates and terms of the cover provided are told clearly of any changes in those rates or terms.

3.4.5 Agents, independent intermediaries and providers of quotation systems should ensure that they act on changes notified to them by an insurer.

3.5   Changes in the rate of value added tax

3.5.1 If your price indications become misleading because of a change in the general rate of VAT, or other taxes paid at point of sale, make the correct price indication clear to any consumers who order products. Do so before the consumer is committed to buying the product and, wherever practicable, before the goods are sent to the consumer. For a period of 14 days from the date a VAT change takes effect, a general notice or notices may be used to indicate the adjustment necessary in prices to take account of the new VAT rate.

Part 4: Sale of new homes

4.1 A 'new home' is any building, or part of a building to be used only as a private dwelling which is either:

(a) a newly-built house or flat, or

(b) a newly-converted existing building which has not previously been used in that form as a private home.

4.2 The Consumer Protection Act 1987 and this Code apply to new homes which are either for sale freehold or on a long lease, ie, with more than 21 years to run. In this context the term 'trader' covers not only a business vendor, such as a developer, but also an estate agent acting on behalf of such a vendor. For provisions applicable to commercial property, or to residential property which is not a new home, you should consult your local Trading Standards Service or Home Authority.

4.3 You should follow the relevant provision of Pt 1 of the Code if:

(a) you want to make a comparison between the price at which you offer new homes for sale and any other price; or

(b) you offer an inclusive price for new homes which also covers such items as furnishings, domestic appliances and insurance and you compare their value with, for example, High Street prices for similar items.

4.4 Part 2 of the Code gives details of the provisions you should follow if:

(a) the new houses you are selling, or any goods or services which apply to them, are only available in limited numbers or ranges;

(b) the sale price you give does not apply to the houses as displayed; or

(c) there are additional non-optional charges payable.

NOTES FOR GUIDANCE ON COUPONS: RECOMMENDED BEST PRACTICE

Produced and published by the Coupon Committee of the Institute of Promotional Marketing. Institute of Promotional Marketing ('IPM'), 70 Margaret Street, London W1W 8SS. Tel: 020 7291 7730. Fax: 020 7291 7731. Website: www.theipm.org.uk. E-mail: enquiries@theipm.org.uk

Notes for guidance on coupons

Introduction

Couponing is a major promotional tool in the UK sales promotion industry and over 6 billion coupons are issued every year. It is clearly necessary in the interests of the efficient processing of coupons that guidelines are regularly updated and observed by all those engaged in the various stages of implementation.

This re-draft of the Best Practice guidelines is the result of extensive consultation throughout the industry and is commended to all users of coupons as essential reading.

First published: January 1994; revised edition published May 1977; re-draft January 2004.

It forms part of a wider project undertaken by the IPM Coupon Committee which includes Guidelines for Coupon Handling Houses, Electronic Coupons, Euro Coupons, Retailer Handling and Compliance (www.theipm.org.uk/coupons).

Overview

When a coupon is issued it is handled by distribution media, the public, retailers and coupon handling houses. Accordingly, it must be made clear to consumers what they're being offered, where the offer can be redeemed and the time duration for the offer; Retailers are relied upon to accept coupons and check that they have been tendered along with the correct product. It is in the interest of all promoters to ensure that their coupons can be processed quickly and efficiently by both retailers and coupon handling houses.

Anyone responsible for the design and/or issue of a coupon that is intended to be redeemed through the retail or wholesale trade should refer to these Notes for Guidance to ensure that all coupons adhere to the basic requirements of good coupon design.

Scope

These Notes for Guidance cover the accepted basic requirements for a coupon which gives 'money off' a nominated product and which is designed to be redeemed through the retail or wholesale trade. They outline its design, size, redemption and handling requirements.

They have been prepared by the IPM Coupon Committee consisting of representatives from leading retailers, coupon issuers, coupon handling houses, the Food and Drink Federation, e.centre and the Newspaper Publishers Association.

They have been endorsed and accepted by the following bodies as standard practice: the Direct Marketing Association, e.centre, the British Retail Consortium, the Federation of Wholesale Distribution, the Food and Drink Federation and the Incorporated Society of British Advertisers.

Special uses of coupons, such as proof of purchase, trade, variable face value and free product coupons, are more difficult to handle and may incur additional handling costs. Your handling house should be consulted before issue. These types of coupon are, however still subject to these Notes for Guidance.

The design of a coupon

Closing dates

- Where an offer closing date is applied, this should be clearly and prominently marked using the words 'Valid until'.

- Promoters should redeem coupons from retailers up to at least six months beyond any stated consumer closing date, but a retailer closing date should not appear on the coupon.

- See also section concerning on-pack coupons.

Value

- The sterling value should appear once as a bold figure on the front face.

- The word 'COUPON' should appear next to or near the stated value.

- The words 'OFF NEXT PURCHASE' should appear in one bold typeface.

Instructions

- Coupons should carry clear instructions to both consumer and trade on usage and redemption. Consumer instructions should be worded along the following lines: 'This coupon can only be used as part payment for (Brand/Product). Only one coupon can be used against each item purchased. Please do not attempt to redeem this coupon against any other product as refusal to accept may cause embarrassment and delay at the checkout.'

- The promoter's name and the redemption address should be clearly stated. The coupon should state that only one coupon can be redeemed per customer and per item purchased.

Coupons incorporated in printed matter

- Where coupons are incorporated in other print matter (e.g. magazines/leaflets), the coupon must be easy to detach.

Bar code

Internal code
(if required)

Product
details

Retailers

Instructions

Closing dates

Value

Size and
shape

1234 56789

VALID UNTIL DD.MM.YY

20P COUPON
OFF NEXT
PURCHASE OF

Bloggo's

BAKED BEANS

240g ONLY
at
STORENAME

9 123442 740203

TO THE CUSTOMER
This coupon can be used in part payment
for (Brand/Product). Only one coupon can
be used against each item purchased.
Please do not attempt to redeem this
coupon against any other product as
refusal to accept may cause
embarrassment and delay at the
checkout.

TO THE RETAILER
Blogg's Ltd will redeem this coupon at its
face value provided ONLY that it has been
taken in part payment for a (Brand/Product).
xxxxxxxxxxxx reserve the right to refuse
payment against misredeemed coupons.
Please submit coupons to (Promotors
handling address, Dept 123, Town, County

- A clear indication around the border of the coupon itself should appear as dotted or 'cut' lines.

- Check that the coupon is not printed on the reverse of another coupon, or on the reverse of any other bar code.

- Care should be taken to ensure that any copy in printed matter that refers to the coupon cannot be construed as being an additional coupon.

Coupon size and shape

- Rectangular

- Minimum size: 4cm × 8cm

- Maximum size: 7cm × 13cm

Internal number

- An internally driven number can be inserted in this space for internal control, for example Manufacturer or handling house code.

Retailers

- Where coupons are only redeemable at specified outlets, the store name should be clearly stated. If the retailers name is not clearly marked the promoter risks the coupon being misredeemed or rejected by retailers or coupon handling houses.

Product details

- The product(s) and, if applicable, size(s) should be stated clearly and conspicuously.

Coupon bar code

- All coupons that are intended for general redemption must carry an EAN-13 bar code (part of the EAN.UCC system for item identification). If you are unable to place a bar code on the coupon, please contact your coupon handling house.

- Each different coupon promotion requires a different bar code symbol to encode its reference number and value. The brand owner should allocate the barcode number except when it is a store specific coupon where the retailer should allocate the barcode number.

- The bar code should be printed wherever possible on white, and depending on the print process, at a size of at least 100% (26.26mm × 37.29mm). This includes the light margins which surround the bar code, and are safeguarded by the leading digit 9 on the left hand side and the light margin chevron on the right hand side. Key lines should not be printed near the bar code as they may cause difficulties when the bar code is scanned. (Preferred print colours for bars are black, dark green, dark blue. For other colour combinations please contact e.centre). (Please note that the magnification range for EAN symbols is from 80% to 200%. The minimum magnification factor that can be used depends on the printing method and substrate. Scannability will be impaired if a magnification factor smaller than print quality can sustain is used.

- The value encoded in the bar code should be the same as the face value of the coupon.

- The bar code, including its surrounding light margins, should be located at least 10mm from the base and right hand edge of the coupon.

- Prior to circulation, artwork or a sample of the coupon should be presented to the coupon handling house to verify its scannability.

- Coupon issuer numbers, which are not the same as company prefix numbers, are supplied by e.centre, 10 Maltravers Street, London WC2R 3BX, telephone 020 7655 9001. Numbers are only issued to e.centre member companies and a charge for issue is made.

Warning

- For a double-sided coupon, the value should only appear once on each face and in such a manner that the coupon could not be divided or tendered in two pieces.

- Coupons with over-redemption insurance must be notified to the coupon handling house in advance as the coupons redeemed will need to be retained. (These might be required for legal/audit purposes).

- The coupon handling house must be notified in advance if additional information needs to be captured or the coupons need to be retained for any other reason.

Coupon usage in non-printed matter

For information and advice on internet and electronic coupons please consult the IPM's website at www.theipm.org.uk/coupons.

Additional bar codes eg. Pin/urn

Additional bar codes can be added to the coupon to provide more information for either the manufacturer, retailer or coupon handling house or all parties. This information is usually encoded in a PIN/URN bar code. For example, these can be printed using a Code 39 or an Interleaved 2 of 5 symbol. Contact your coupon handling house for further information, symbol content and advice. The scanning quality of these symbols should also be checked before circulation. This bar code should be printed where possible horizontal to the main bar code and at least 5mm from the edge of the main bar code (including light margins) so as to avoid mis-scans. If the reverse of the coupon is used, the main bar code should be on the front of the coupon and the PIN/URN code on the reverse. This additional bar code can be placed anywhere on the coupon, ensuring that its placement will not impact the clarity of the coupon, eg. along the top left corner of the coupon. Contact your coupon handling house for guidance. The additional bar code can be used to track the promotion, tie the coupon back to information in a database or to identify specific information such as demographics etc.

Materials

Coupons should be printed on durable material of a weight and texture which is easy to handle without coupons sticking together or ripping. Materials such as polythene or cellophane are feasible although special care will be needed to ensure that the bar code will scan. The use of unusual materials for coupons should be discussed with both trade customers and the coupon handling house prior to production. Unusual or difficult materials, eg. foil, tub lids etc., can cause handling problems at the retailer or coupon handling house.

Additional considerations for on-pack coupons

Care should be taken to ensure that the coupon bar code is not visible at the time of product purchase. This is to avoid potential confusion at the checkout. Promoters should ensure that coupons which are attached to labels or direct to packages are properly secured to prevent loss, yet remain detachable. Coupons should be situated so as not to become soiled or stained by either direct contact with, or use of, the product. Where coupons are embodied as part of a special pack it is particularly important that the words 'off next purchase' must appear in one bold typeface, size and colour. Careful consideration should be given as to the desirability of a closing date, especially where the product carries an extended 'minimum durability' date. In any event, the coupon closing date should always be the subject of specific consideration. When on-pack coupons coincide with any other kind of special on-pack price or money-off marking applied by the promoter, then one should be clearly differentiated from the other.

Trade notification

Promoters should notify their trade customers in advance of their intention to issue on-pack coupons. It is also advisable to notify the trade in advance of major off-pack coupon campaigns.

Outer cases containing coupon packs should be readily identified as such.

During a 'cross-couponing' campaign, promoters should, ensure that both brands are stocked by their trade customers.

Coupon handling costs

Where promotional schemes take the form of coupons redeemable through the trade you will incur the following costs that should be budgeted for when planning a campaign:

- A trade handling allowance for the retail trade (this benchmark figure is agreed between the Food and Drink Federation and the British Consortium).

- Handling house fee.

- Postage reimbursement.

● Any additional charges for handling coupons such as free product coupons or non-barcoded coupons

Allocation of coupon numbers to promotions

The structure of a coupon number is as follows:

Coupon Identifier (allocated by e.centre)	Issuer Number (allocated by e.centre)	Reference Number (sequential number allocated by the company responsible for coding the coupon)	Value (Redemption value in pence, max. £9.98=998)	Check Digit (www. ecentre.org. uk/frameset_ barcodes_ cdc.htm)
9 9	N N N N	N N N	V V V	C

NB. Different coupon reference numbers must be allocated when:

i)   there is any change in the face value;

ii) there is any change in the expiry date;

iii) there is any change in the promotion;

NB. The Issuer number changes when the brand owner changes. All future coupons issued should use the new brand owner's Issuer Numbers. Failure to do so could incur costs on both parties.

For values in excess of £9.98, 999 should be placed as the value in the bar code and the actual value should be printed on the coupon. Please notify your handling house in advance.

The following promotions CAN be encoded using a coupon:

● **Money-off next purchase.** This encodes a specific amount to be deducted from the price of a specified product within a specified retailer. A single coupon can only encode one amount per product to be promoted.

● **Free Product Coupons.** Where there is an intention to provide consumers with a coupon for the entire purchase price of a product, special care is needed. Promoters wishing to issue 'free' product coupons are advised to consult their major trade customers and handling house before issue. The coupon should clearly show a fixed value ie. 'Free up to a maximum retail price of £1.49' or 'Free up to a value of £1.49', which will be the amount redeemable irrespective of the Retail Price charged by the trader. This value can either be encoded in the bar code or '000' can be encoded as the coupon value to identify a free product coupon.

Certain promotions CANNOT be encoded using a coupon such as: Percentage off a product(s) and money off a variable weight item.

Checklist

- Check that the promotion is suitable for the use of a money-off coupon.

- Handling houses must be notified in advance of coupon campaigns.

- Ensure that the coupon wording is legal, unambiguous and clear for the customer to understand.

- Ensure that the coupon identifies the value, the product, promoter and relevant retailers, as detailed in this brochure.

- The coupon handling house must be notified in advance if additional information needs to be captured or the coupons need to be retained.

- Ensure the coupon number is correctly compiled and is encoded within the EAN-13 symbol.

- Check the size of the bar code symbol, both the magnification and the bar height.

- Ensure that there are adequate qlight margins for the bar code symbol.

- Ensure that key lines are not surrounding the bar code on the final coupon.

- Check that the contrast between the bars and the background is adequate and that the colours chosen will scan.

- Ensure that any additional PIN/URN bar codes have been correctly positioned and encode the correct information (see section headed Additional Bar Codes).

- For on-pack coupons, check the position of the coupon on the final product to ensure the coupon bar code cannot be scanned at the point of sale.

- Handling houses must be notified in advance if additional information needs to be retained, particularly if the coupon is subject to over-redemption insurance cover.

- Ensure that no shrink-wrap, tape or other printing will obscure the bar code symbol on the finished product.

If in doubt, seek guidance from your clearing or handling house.

Endorsed by:
Direct Marketing Association
e.centre
The British Retail Consortium
The Federation of Wholesale Distributors
The Food and Drink Federation
The Incorporated Society of British Advertisers.

INSTITUTE OF PROMOTIONAL MARKETING: ELECTRONIC COUPONING AND BRIEFING PACK

Recommended Best Practice for the Distribution of Coupons & Vouchers Online

Published by the IPM with acknowledgement to Couponstar Ltd for their help and guidance (June 2010) and reproduced by kind permission of the IPM.

Table of Contents

1. Executive Summary

This report has been prepared to outline "best practices" for developing and executing marketing campaigns incorporating Internet coupons and to help marketers better understand the challenges of this new medium and navigate quickly through the process to create successful Internet (print-at-home) coupon programs.

While the Internet has become a popular coupon distribution method, there are challenges that need to be considered including replication and copying, coupon attributes manipulation, unintentional distribution, print quality & scannability at Point of Sale, accurate tracking of coupon prints and redemptions and retailer acceptance. These guidelines expand on how to take the following basic steps to mitigate these concerns:

- Employ Coupon Print Software to prevent the coupon from ever being displayed on screen or being stored as a file and unintentionally distributed e.g. as an email attachment.

- Enforce coupon print limitations to control the number of coupons printed per individual, household and/or campaign.

- Use unique barcodes & identifiers to link back to an individual consumer and detect fraud.

- Ensure coupon and barcode print quality for maximum compliance at Point of Sale.

- Employ anti-copying measures for preventing and/or detecting photocopies.

- Set rolling expiration dates to increase response rates and deter fraudulent behaviour.

- Print the consumer's name or other forms of identification on the coupon to deter misuse.

- Take extra precautions when running "Free Product" offers.

A poorly designed Internet coupon may cause problems for retailers and consumers. Therefore, all Internet coupons should follow a standard coupon design with an emphasis on deterring alterations and counterfeits and making it easy for retailers to spot irregularities.

To ensure acceptance of Internet coupons by retailers, the following measures should be taken:

1. Employ an experienced and reputable Internet coupon supplier or software application

2. Notify your sales and accounts team of the coupon promotion and have them notify their contacts i.e. buyers, marketing managers, store managers of the upcoming promotion so that staff at store level are aware of the promotion.

3. Monitor redemption activity with both your Internet coupon supplier and your clearing house.

2. Report Objectives

To develop and publish a comprehensive guide to distributing coupons over the Internet, discussing current trends, benefits, opportunities, and issues associated with Internet distributed coupons as they apply to consumers, manufacturers, retailers and clearing houses.

This report has also been prepared to outline "best practices" for developing and executing marketing campaigns incorporating Internet coupons and to help marketers better understand the challenges of this new medium and navigate quickly through the process to create successful Internet coupon programs.

This re-draft of the Electronic Couponing Guideline and Briefing Pack is the result of extensive consultation throughout the industry and is recommended to all users of Internet coupons including agencies (sales promotion, digital, direct marketing & promotional insurers) as well FMCG marketers and retailers as essential reading.

It forms part of a wider education programme undertaken by the IPM Coupon Committee which includes Notes for Guidance on Coupons, Guidelines for Coupon Handling Houses, Euro Coupons and Retailer Handling and Compliance available from (www.theipm. org.uk/bestpractice). The IPM Coupon Committee will continue to monitor Internet coupons and will inform members of the IPM and of the general marketing community of future changes and factors affecting them.

3. Overview

It has been recognised by the IPM that the Internet has become a very efficient and targeted way of distributing coupons to consumers. The exceptional graphics and dynamic multimedia capabilities of the Internet allow manufacturers and retailers to work together too creatively and intelligently target consumers. Consumers can access manufacturer and retailer websites or third-party coupon distribution sites to find retailer and manufacturer-sponsored coupons. As a result, Internet coupons have become an attractive part of many companies' overall marketing strategies.

The large scale growth in consumers' use of the Internet and the rapid adoption of Broadband in recent years, means that it now offers advertisers both scale and reach on par or in some cases greater than the more common forms of coupon distribution. There are now 38.1m people online representing 75% of the UK Adult population (eMarketer, March 2008). Nine in 10 UK Internet users are on broadband now, and women and the over-50s are also spending far more time online, which makes the Internet a very attractive medium to a broader set of advertisers (IAB UK, 2007).

In 2007, there was an unmistakable shift towards Internet coupons by marketers with an increase of 650% in Internet Coupons printed (Couponstar, 2007). Also, Internet coupons became the 3rd most popular choice for coupon delivery in the UK with 16% of consumers stating that they would most like to receive coupons "over the internet" that they can "download and print at home and then use in-store" (Brain Juicer, 2007).

4. Terms of Reference

The term "Internet coupons" can be defined as anything distributed via the Internet. However, the IPM recognises that there are a number of types of "Internet coupons" and different delivery solutions including, but not limited to:

- **Coupons for Online Redemption (Promotion Codes, Offer Codes, Discount Codes, etc):** A manufacturer or retailer distributes promotional discount codes for consumers to use to receive a discount whilst shopping online.

- **Web to Post Coupons:** A consumer visits website and enters their address, and possibly other information, in order to receive coupon(s) via the post.

- **Internet Print-at-Home Coupons:** Manufacturer sponsored (can be redeemed at any retailer stocking the advertised product) or retailer specific coupons (restricted to a given retailer) which are printed at home by the consumer. They are most commonly offered in a "controlled" web environment, such as the coupon image is not shown on the screen to avoid possible online manipulation, and the number of prints allowed by the consumer are limited.

This report is written in reference to "Internet Print-at-Home Coupons" and can be applied to both manufacturer sponsored and retailer specific coupons. However, many of the best practices and security precautions given here are applicable to any company seeking to maximise the benefits of their online promotions.

5. Benefits of Internet Coupons

Today, Internet coupons provide a variety of benefits for both consumers and marketers:

Benefits to Consumers

As technology evolves, consumers continue to respond to value. Coupons have always provided value in the form of price discounts. Internet print-at-home coupons add further value by giving consumers an innovative, easy and convenient way to save money on a variety of goods and services. The benefits to consumers include:

- **Instant Gratification:** Consumers simply click on the desired coupons and print them straight away.

- **Convenience:** Consumers access Internet print-at-home coupons at their leisure and can elect to receive coupons via e-mail.

- **Relevance and Control:** Marketers can offer coupons and information targeted to individual preferences and consumers can choose the coupons they want to print.

- **Interactivity:** Internet coupon promotions offer interactive and enjoyable presentations for the consumer e.g. watch a video or play a game before printing coupons.

- **Product Research:** Consumers can receive more in-depth information about the brand or product by linking to the brand's site or to other Web pages.

- **Additional Incentives:** Internet promotions (coupons and other) can offer additional incentive value based on further consumer interaction (e.g. enter a competition).

Benefits to Marketers—Both Manufacturers and Retailers

Internet coupon promotions offer various benefits to marketers – both manufacturers and Retailers including:

- **Return on Investment:** Generate measurable in-store sales as a direct result of online marketing and advertising spend.

- **Cost Efficiencies:** The Internet is an easy, cost-effective way to reach a large audience and avoids the unnecessary wastage associated with some traditional forms of couponing.

- **Additional Consumer Insights:** With Internet coupons, marketers can measure activity and success by the standard measurements of coupon distribution and redemption; and their activities such as views or prints, which indicate levels of interest or purchase intent even if the coupons were never redeemed.

- **Access to a New, Desirable Demographic:** Printable coupons reach a younger, potentially more desirable audience. Users spend more heavily and are more likely to try new products.

- **One-to-One Marketing Capabilities:** Internet coupons can be tailored to individual consumer needs. Marketers can learn more about consumer buying habits creating unique one-to-one marketing opportunities.

- **Full Transparency:** Results are measurable from the time a shopper clicks to receive the coupon to when they print it to when they redeem it.

- **Cross Marketing Opportunities:** Marketers can use printable coupons to introduce customers to other brands in the portfolio with incentives to try them out.

- **Extensive Tracking and Measurability:** Marketers can conduct tests in real time and measure the results on an individual promotion and/or consumer level.

- **Flexibility and Speed:** The speed and targeting capabilities of Internet coupons allow marketers to quickly execute promotions, including last-minute programs, and react to changing market conditions or competitor promotions.

6. Challenges of Distributing Coupons Online

FMCG manufacturers, retailers, and others are using the Internet as an effective method for reaching consumers and meeting marketing objectives. While the Internet has become a popular coupon distribution method, there are challenges that need to be considered.

There are six categories of challenges associated with Internet print-at-home coupons:

1. Replication and Copying

The opportunity exists to make multiple copies of Internet print-at-home coupons by photocopying, scanning, or reprinting the original coupon. Consumers can also print multiple copies if the Internet coupon vendor does not have technology in place to limit the number of prints by a consumer.

The primary impact of coupon copying is the potential for unbudgeted redemption liability. In addition, replicated coupons may not have the same print quality as the original offer. Replicated coupons may not move efficiently through the redemption process, resulting in a slow-down at the point-of-sale, reduced checker productivity, and hard-to-handle issues that add costs to the clearing process.

Note: *Replication of coupon offers is not unique to Print-at-Home coupons. Other types of coupons such as direct mail, in-store, magazine, etc. are also susceptible to replication using computer software, colour copiers, printers, etc.*

2. Coupon Attributes Manipulation

Coupon attributes (face values, expiration dates, barcodes, etc.) can be altered. Therefore, it is important for marketers to select Internet partners (Internet coupon providers, vendors, and agencies) who use technology to utilise strict controls. If the technology used by a coupon issuer or vendor does not have appropriate controls in place, an online coupon can be manipulated.

3. Unintentional Distribution

Through e-mail, online forums, and online auction sites all coupons have the potential to reach a wider base than originally planned. As a result, coupons other than those intended by the marketer could be introduced into the marketplace. It's critical to choose the right Internet coupon solution as unintentional distribution and or changes in design could cause:

- Increases in promotion liability

- Inconsistent or incorrect product messaging or targeting

- Deductions resulting from discrepancies between a retailer's expected coupon receivables and a manufacturer's authorised reimbursement

- Decreased productivity at point of sale

4. Print Quality & Scannability at Point of Sale

Print quality can be compromised by the type of printer used by consumers, resulting in coupons that may scan incorrectly at the point-of-sale or the retailer or manufacturer clearing house, resulting in consumer ill-will, slow-down at checkout and hard-to-handle issues that add to the cost or time of the clearing process. It is therefore critical to employ software capable of the proper rendering of coupon barcodes.

5. Tracking Coupon Prints and Redemptions

One of the fundamental advantages of Internet coupons is its ability to be measured. However, if reporting data is not accurate, ambiguous or timely, the marketer is in danger of drawing false conclusions on the success of the campaign. It is important to the successful ongoing management of your internet couponing activity to use applications that can measure the prints taken by consumers and combine this with reliable redemption data.

6. Retailer Acceptance

Understandably, major retailers only want to accept legitimate manufacturer coupons and whilst they are generally supportive of Internet coupons, acceptance of coupons is likely to be much better if these guidelines are adhered to and where possible the software and / or service provider has a reputable track record in this specialist field

7. Industry Initiatives to Manage the Challenges

No technology-driven distribution method is without valid concerns over security, especially one where the consumer is responsible for the printing. However certain basic steps can be taken to mitigate most of these concerns.

- **Employ a Coupon Print Solution**

   The coupon print application software should prevent the coupon from ever being displayed on their computer screen.

   A good coupon print application will allow marketers to maintain control over the coupon printing process and print quality. It will also prevent the coupon from being stored as a file on a consumer's hard drive, making it extremely difficult to manipulate in a graphics application like Photoshop and forward the coupon on as an attachment to unauthorised recipients.

   It should also comply with industry standards for consumer-friendly software downloads and be supported across all the major internet browsers such as Internet Explorer, Firefox and Safari.

- **Detect and Block File Based Printers**

   A consumer trying to print their coupon to a file based printer, image writer or fax application should be detected and denied from proceeding any further through the print process. This prevents the consumer from distributing the coupon uncontrolled online e.g. as an email attachment or manipulating the coupon attributes in a graphics application.

- **Enforce Coupon Print Limitations**

   Marketers should be able to set predetermined limits to at the very least control the total number of coupons printed for a campaign (campaign limits). Further print limitations such as the number of coupons printed by an individual, household or participant should be exercised if required. Once the preset limit is exceeded, the consumer should no longer be able to select and/or print the offer.

- **Use Unique Barcodes & Identifiers**

   Each coupon printed should be marked with a unique barcode and an identifier that ties to the data in a marketer's database.

These unique barcodes and identifiers should enable each coupon to be tracked and linked to a specific consumer or computer. Fraud can then be detected through the reconciliation of redemption data feeds (through cooperation between the Coupon Clearance House and Internet coupon technology vendor) to the marketer's print-activity database. If a duplicate coupon is detected, it can be flagged and the consumer's machine restricted from further printing.

- **Ensure Coupon and Barcode Print Quality**

  Coupon barcodes should be printed clean for maximum compliance at Point of Sale. The software employed should ensure printing of the images, copy and most importantly the barcodes at the highest DPI resolution possible.

- **Employ Anti-Copying Measures**

  Use best efforts to provide methods for preventing and/or detecting duplicates and photocopies.

- **Set Rolling Expiration Dates**

  Limit the amount of time consumers have to copy or manipulate the coupon by setting rolling expiration dates. For example, setting the rolling expiration date to 14 days means the expiration date printed on the coupon will be set to 14 days from the day the coupon is printed unless it encroaches on the final expiration date set which may be sooner.

- **Personalisation – Printing the Consumer's Name on the Coupon**

  Whenever possible, the consumer's name or other forms of identification e.g. their Membership ID should be printed on the face of the coupon to deter consumers from misuse.

- **Include Strong Legal Copy**

  Enhance security messaging and include "It may not be used against any other product as this would constitute a breach of the terms of this offer. Only one coupon may be used against each such retail purchase. Not photocopies accepted. Coupon is not transferrable" in the legal copy, printed on the coupons.

- **Take Extra Precautions for "Free" Coupons**

  Take extra precautions when running "free product" offers. Your coupon partner should advise you of the extra measures to be taken to protect against fraud.

- **Mark Unapproved Coupons "Void"**

  For coupons that are not ready for distribution or still in design mode, mark all coupons and especially their barcodes with the word "void" or a similar marking to avoid the coupon being leaked prior to the live date.

- **Quality Assure Sample Coupons**

  Prior to launching an Internet coupon, validation of the coupon bar code value etc. should be verified to ensure it accurately reflects the intent of the offer. Scanning the coupon barcode is highly recommended to validate the offer, prior to authorising your vendor to release the offer to the public.

8. Redemption Data Analysis

When evaluating Internet coupon vendors, marketers should gain a complete understanding of the control and treatment measures provided by the software employed. The existing coupon EAN barcode and Internet vendor-specific security codes provide marketers the ability to capture additional data components for analysis.

If a coupon carries specific consumer demographic information, the information can be obtained through the clearing house as part of the redemption process if the vendor is integrated with the clearing house or are sent the coupon information afterwards. This information can be utilised to determine if fraudulent activity has occurred at the consumer or retail level. Currently, this type of fraud analysis takes place after the coupon has been redeemed by the consumer and processed for payment by the manufacturer.

It is important that the client and Internet coupon supplier agree as to how success is measured. The clearing house will provide redemption activity based on the number of physical coupons submitted by the retailer(s). In order to provide the client with additional redemption analysis the Internet coupon supplier can provide the client with the exact number of "printed" coupons. The client can measure redemption activity based on the number of coupons actually "printed" and redeemed not the number of times the offer was "viewed" or "clicked". Also, statistics of online to in-store consumer behaviour at the individual level can be provided to the client where the solution is part of the campaign management.

9. Internet Coupon Speed of Redemption

On average, three to four weeks elapse from the time a coupon is printed by the consumer until it arrives at the clearing house for processing. During this time, the coupons may be collected by stores and shipped to a retail chain's headquarters before they are shipped to a clearing house.

It then takes approximately one to two weeks for the clearing house to scan both the EAN-13 barcode and the unique identifier barcode.

All in all, clients should not expect to see their detailed Internet coupon redemption statistics until four to six weeks from the day the coupon was printed.

10. Recommendations for Internet Coupon Design and Layout

A poorly designed Internet coupon may cause problems for retailers and consumers. The result: coupon rejected in store, confused consumers, unhappy retail customers and wasted budgets.

Therefore, all Internet coupons should follow a standard coupon design with an emphasis on deterring alterations and counterfeits and making it easy for retailers to spot irregularities.

Coupon Not To Scale

Using the Internet coupon example above for reference please find the following recommended guidelines for developing a secure and retailer friendly internet coupon:

A. Size & Shape: The coupon should be rectangular in shape and have minimum dimensions of 5cm × 12cm and maximum of 7cm × 16cm. The coupon should also include a dotted line around the perimetre to indicate the need to cut out the coupon before use.

B. Logo or Product Shot: A colour image of the brand logo or product shot should always be displayed on the coupon to provide a strong visual cue for cashiers to check the product is included within the consumers shop.

C. Coupon Header: The words "Manufacturer's Coupon" should be printed in bold type within a box at the top of the coupon to distinguish its origin

D. Expiration Date: The words "Valid Until" with the actual date "dd/mm/yyyy" should be printed clearly on every coupon. To limit your promotion liability use rolling expiration dates.

E. Personalisation: Whenever possible, the consumer's name or other forms of identification e.g. their Membership ID should be printed on the face of the coupon to deter consumers from misuse.

F. Face Value: The face value should appear once as a bold figure on the coupon. The coupon should offer specific savings amount i.e. pence or pounds to be discounted versus a "percentage discount". Whenever possible, use nonstandard fonts to discourage alteration.

G. Offer Description: The description of the of the offer should be clearly stated and shown directly under or next to the "Face Value" and the words "your next purchase" should appear in bold type face. Also, the product name, purchase requirement, quantity and if applicable, size should be stated clearly and conspicuously. Clients should avoid complicated offers; consumers and retailers prefer simplicity.

H. Consumer Instructions (Legal Copy): Consumer instructions should be worded along the following lines: "This coupon can only be used as part payment for (Brand/Product). Only one coupon can be used against each item purchased. Please do not attempt to redeem this coupon against any other product as the refusal to accept may cause embarrassment and delay at the checkout. Void if reproduced, altered or expired. Coupons cannot be sold, transferred or auctioned. Photocopies will not be accepted. This coupon is valid until the date specified at the top of this coupon."

I.   Retailer Instructions (Legal Copy): Retail instructions should be worded along the following lines: "To the retailer, (the promoter) will reimburse you the full face value plus an agreed handling charge provided this coupon has been accepted against (the product). (The promoter) reserves the right to require proof of purchase, or to refuse redemption of defaced or damaged coupons or those that have not been correctly redeemed as instructed. Send the coupon to (name and address of the clearing house).

J.   Internet Coupon Provider Marks: If your Internet coupon provider is well respected and known in the industry, printing their name or logo on the face of the coupon will increase the integrity, security and chance of retailer acceptance.

K.   EAN-13 Barcode: Each different coupon requires a different EAN-13 barcode to encode its reference number and value. The EAN-13 must be printed in black on a white background and should be at 100 percent magnification and have sufficient 'quiet zones' on both sides of the bar code to avoid miss scans. When issuing a retailer specific coupon, please use the retailer's bar code and clearly state the retailer's name on the coupon.

L.   Unique Identifier Barcode: As with the EAN-13 barcode, the unique identifier barcode should be printed in black on a white background and should be at 100 percent magnification and have sufficient 'quiet zones' on both sides of the bar code to avoid miss scans. The identifier number should also be printed below or near the barcode in case of poor print quality for improved data capture and authentication.

IMPORTANT NOTE: Avoid distracting background textures and colours. Don't try to fill in the entire coupon; white space is okay. Even though many Internet coupons are printed in black and white, UCC scan guidelines for colour should be adhered to as colour impacts scannability.

11. Avoiding Retailer Refusal of Internet Coupons

With every Internet coupon promotion, there will always be a few customers who have problems redeeming their vouchers in-store, but on the whole, the numbers are insignificant. The most common reasons for retailer refusal are:

- Poor print quality making the barcodes unscanable.

- Cashier perception that they need special handling.

- The consumer did not cut the coupon out from the A4 page.

- Cashiers not recognising the coupon promotion or the brand in question.

- The coupon looking blurry, enlarged or reduced, altered or a clear photocopy.

To avoid consumers experiencing retailer refusal of Internet coupons, the following measures should be taken:

1. Employ an experienced and reputable Internet coupon supplier or software application that:

    - uses a standard, professional-looking coupon format.

    - has a process in place that notifies both the clearing house and the retailers of the upcoming coupon promotions.

    - is transparent about what measures they take to avoid retailer refusal and what their process is for dealing with coupon rejection in-store.

2. Notify your sales and accounts team of the coupon promotion and have them notify their contacts i.e. buyers, marketing managers, store managers of the upcoming promotion so that staff at store level are aware of the promotion.

3. Monitor redemption activity with both your Internet coupon supplier and your clearing house.

12. Acknowledgements

- Couponstar, for being the lead contributor to these guidelines. Couponstar are one of the leading UK Internet Coupon technology vendors and are an active member of the IPM Coupon Committee (www.couponstar.co.uk)

- Valassis Ltd UK (www.valssis.co.uk)

- Multi Resource Marketing – MRM (www.mrm.co.uk)

- Association of USA Coupon Professionals (www.couponpros.org)

- CMS, Inc. (www.couponinfonow.com)

- Coupons Inc. (www.couponsinc.com)

INSTITUTE OF PROMOTIONAL MARKETING: GUIDELINES FOR BRIEFING FULFILMENT HOUSES

Reproduced here with permission of the Institute of Promotional Marketing, 70 Margaret Street, London W1W 8SS

1. Promoter or agency brief

The following Checklist is information the Promoter/Agency needs to give the Handling House for briefing purposes.

NB

1. If all the details are not known then give clear assumptions on which the Fulfilment House can base costs, and remember that if these assumptions change, costs may also change.

2. There are potential benefits in involving a Fulfilment House as early as possible in the planning of a promotion. The House may be able to add value in terms of design or presentation from their experience.

(a) Title and brief description of the promotion:

- Start and close dates.

- Quantities involved (including contingency plans).

- Promotional media—on pack, direct mail, leaflet, sample site, door to door, Internet.

- Response rates—anticipated volume and pattern.

- Is the promotion insured? If so, what specific spec has been required by the insurer?

- Territories—is it UK only, ROI etc.

(b) Applications:

- Application form or plain paper? Send sample. Phone/Internet applications?

- Special instructions eg, one per household.

- Tolerance levels eg, POP's, cash contributions, 'one per household'.

- Payment: cash, cheque, credit card. Await cheque clearance before despatch?

- Proof of purchase tolerance levels.

- Storage of POP's: with application? In-bulk? Destroy?

    - If destroying—burn or recycle. Security issues?

- Data-capture: what?

    - Name, address, date of birth, e-mail address, tick boxes?

    - De-dupe by name? Address?

    - Separate opt-out database.

    - PIN number usage and recognition.

    - Is the data to be used for analysis or to add to an existing database?

- Rejection of Application—see (g) Consumer Queries.

(c) Postage/Carriage:

- Delivery speed eg, 1st or 2nd Class, Mailsort; Proof of Delivery required; Insurance required.

(d) Packing:

- Samples of ALL components for size/weight.

- Packing requirements.

- Packaging samples: who supplies?

- Additional Inserts eg, compliment slip.

(e) *Banking:*

- Paid into Promoters bank (supply details) or client account?

- If client account, how and when repaid?

- Postal Float; invoiced or deducted?

- Bounced cheques.

- Confirm whether banking charges to include cheque clearance.

(f) *Stock:*

- List of all stock required by the Fulfilment House eg, premiums, packaging, stationery. Send samples.

- Will these be sourced by the Promoter/Agency or by the Fulfilment House?

- Delivery Schedules; Supplier contact details; pallet or handball delivery?

- Reports on stock levels needed weekly/monthly?

- Will quality checks be required?

- Storage requirements eg, temperature control, sell-by dates, rotation.

- Plans for re-ordering and/or disposal at end of promotion.

- Insurance requirements.

(g) *Consumer queries:*

- Phone: is a dedicated line required?

  – Local, freephone, premium or standard rate.

- Written: stock letters? Promoter or Handling House letterheads?

- E-mail queries?

- Is the Promotion affected by the 'distance selling' regulations? If so are specific arrangements required?

(h) Account management:

- Reports, daily/weekly/monthly etc:

  - Format: fax, post, e-mail.

  - Information required: redemptions, volume, stock, customer services, banking.

- List authorised contacts at the Promoter and Agency (if applicable).

- Detail any requirements for regular meetings.

- See attached notes on relationship management.

(i) Promotion data:

- Will a data file of respondents be required? If so when?

- Format required.

- Manipulation, eg, de-duping, adding mail-sort codes.

Note:

(1)   Seek advice on a suitable Fulfilment House. You need to assure yourself of their ability to handle your requirements and of their financial probity. Ask for a client's list and check credentials. Better still obtain a good recommendation.

(2)   Involve the Fulfilment House at the earliest possible stage. You should visit any house you seriously contemplate using to see the site, meet the people, look at storage facilities etc.

(3)   Many Promoters maintain an on-going relationship with one or two Houses with whom they have a contract that covers key

working practices. This enables a new brief to concentrate on the specific variables.

Once you have your responses:

When comparing two or more competitive quotations extreme care needs to be taken to compare like with like. The clarity of your brief will help to ensure that the responses will be broken down in a way that enables comparisons to be made accurately. You may specifically ask for the response to be set out in a user-friendly of pre-specified way.

- Watch particularly for costs that are not specified, eg, monthly minimum cost, and ask for confirmation that there are none.

- Make sure that storage costs and stock handling costs are transparent and explained.

- Ensure that banking charges include cheque clearance charges.

Above all, if you are not sure, ask for clarification before you proceed—accept responsibility and do not make assumptions.

Handling house response

In addition to checking that all the points in your brief have been addressed and priced, the following checklist includes all the elements that could be relevant to the cost of a promotion:

Handling costs

Receipt of applications, opening and removing contents
Checking P.O.Ps, remittance etc
Different rates for plain paper entries
Packing charges:
Removing from stock
Collating and packing
Sealing and preparation for dispatch
Cost of packaging if sourced by fulfilment house

Data capture costs

To include separate costs for data storage, analysis, manipulation.

Supplying and printing address labels/envelopes

Storage archiving and disposal of applications

Banking and cheque clearance charges and costs for any lost in post outbound cheques for money back's etc that have to be stopped.

Set-up and/or monthly minimum charges (sometimes shown as management fees)

Sortation charge to be included.

Report costs:

Redemptions and stock movements.

Storage costs:

Receipt including pallet charges
Storage costs during promotion and post promotion
Cost of disposal

Consumer services:

Turn-backs (due to non-compliance with terms and conditions)
Queries (written, phone and email)
Out of stock
Return to stock
Promoter stock requests
Replacements
Promotion closed

Terms and conditions

Relationship management

The management of the relationship between promoter, agency and handling house is crucial to the smooth running of the activity and is one of the areas where problems most often occur unnecessarily.

Remember—you are all on the same side. An appreciation of what each party does should lead to understanding and mutual respect and the seamless execution of each project. Promoters and agencies should visit the handling house and vice versa in order to understand the nature of each other's businesses. Whilst day to day contact on both sides may be at a relatively junior level, senior level contact should be made too.

Handling houses and agencies are 'invisible' to the end consumer/ recipient - they are usually involved in what they believe to be a direct relationship with the promoter and that is how it should appear.

Whether an agency is involved or not, there are a number of key areas that need to be addressed in relationship terms:

Who is the contract with—i.e. who is the client? There can be only one and that party must accept total responsibility for the project.

Who are the contacts (agency and/or promoter) that need to receive information?

Who is authorised to give instructions or alter the brief?

Who is ultimately responsible at the agency/promoter and handling house in the event of problems?

Who pays the invoices and when? (Schedule?)

What happens in the event of a delay in receipt of payment?

What happens in the event of a delay in receipt of stock?

If all of these issues have been discussed and agreed in advance of the project commencing, both parties will have gone a long way to develop a sensible and open relationship based on an understanding that potential problems can be solved and the process by which they are dealt with.

Accredited Response Management Scheme (ARM)

The IPM, DMA and ISBA have collaborated in the formation of an accreditation scheme for response handling operations—the Accredited Response Management Scheme (ARM). This is an industry standard which is rigorous and transparent, with the aim of raising standards and confidence within the Response Management industry thus achieving customer and consumer satisfaction.

This accreditation scheme, which is already recognized by promoters, ensures that buyers gain access to proven, high quality Response Management companies.

For more information go to www.arm-uk.org.uk.

USEFUL CONTACTS

Advertising Standards Authority
Mid-City Place, 71 High Holborn, London, WC1V 7QT
Tel: 020 7492 2222
Fax: 020 7242 3696
Website: www.asa.org.uk

Advertising Standards Board of Finance Ltd
5th Floor, 21 Berners Street, London, W1T 3LP
Tel: 020 7580 7071
Fax: 020 7580 7057
Website: www.asbof.co.uk

Broadcast Advertising Standards Board of Finance Ltd
5th Floor, 21 Berners Street, London, W1T 3LP
Tel: 020 7580 7071
Fax: 020 7580 7057
Website: www.basbof.co.uk

Chartered Institute of Purchasing and Supply
Easton House, Easton on the Hill, Stamford, Lincs PE9 3NZ
Tel: 01780 756777
e-mail: info@cips.org.uk
Website: www.cips.org

Clearcast
2nd Floor, 4 Roger Street, London, WC1N 2JX
Tel: 0207 339 4700
e-mail: enquiries@clearcast.co.uk
Website: www.bacc.org.uk

Committee of Advertising Practice (CAP)
Mid-City Place, 71 High Holborn, London, WC1V 6QT
Tel: 020 7492 2222
Fax: 020 7404 3696
e-mail: enquiries@cap.org.uk
Website: www.cap.org.uk

Direct Marketing Association
DMA House, 70 Margaret Street, London, W1W 8SS
Tel: 020 7291 3300
e-mail: info@dma.org.uk
Website: www.dma.org.uk

European Advertising Standards Alliance
10a Rue de la Pépinière, B-1000 Brussels, Belgium
Tel: +32 (0)2 513 7806
Fax: +32 (0)2 513 2861
Website: www.easa-alliance.org

Independent Reviewer of ASA Adjudications
5th Floor, 21 Berners Street, London, W1T 3LP
e-mail: indrev@asbof.co.uk

Information Commissioner's Office
Wycliffe House, Water Lane, Wilmslow, Cheshire, SK9 5AF
Information Line: 0303 123 1113
e-mail: internalcompliancedepartment@ico.gsi.gov.uk
Website: www.ico.gov.uk

Institute of Promotional Marketing
70 Margaret Street, London, W1W 8SS
Tel: 020 291 7730
Website: www.theipm.org.uk

OFCOM
Independent Regulator and Competition Authority for the UK Communications Industries
Riverside House, 2a Southwark Bridge Road, London, SE1 9HA
Tel: 0300 123 3333
e-mail: contact@ofcom.org.uk

Office of Fair Trading
Fleetbank House, 2–6 Salisbury Square, London, EC4Y 8JX
Tel: 020 7211 8000
e-mail: enquiries@oft.gsi.gov.uk
Website: www.oft.gov.uk

PhonePayPlus (PPP)
Clove Building, 4 Maguire Street, London, SE1 2NQ
Tel: 0800 500 212
e-mail: webmaster@phonepayplus.org.uk
Website: www.phonepayplus.org.uk

Preference Services
DMA House, 70 Margaret Street, London, W1W 8SS

Baby Mailing Preference Service
DMA House, 70 Margaret Street, London, W1W 8SS

E-mail Preference Service
UK Address: Deltey House, Thornbridge Road, Iver Heath, Bucks, SL0 0PU
Tel: 01895 850 181
Website: www.e-mps.org./en/

Fax Preference Service
Tel: 020 7291 3330
e-mail: fps@dma.org.uk
Website: www.fpsonline.org.uk

Mailing Preference Service
Tel: 020 7291 3310
e-mail: mps@dma.org.uk
Website: www.mpsonline.org.uk

Telephone Preference Service
Tel: 020 7291 3320
e-mail: tps@dma.org.uk
Website: www.tpsonline.org.uk

Radio Advertising Clearance Centre
77 Shaftesbury Avenue, London W1D 5DU
Tel: 020 7306 2620
e-mail: adclear@racc.co.uk
Website: www.racc.co.uk

The Safe Home Ordering Protection Scheme (SHOPS)
18a King Street, Maidenhead, SL6 1EF
Tel: 01628 641930
e-mail: enquiries@shops-uk.org.uk

INDEX